BETWEEN THE ANDES AND THE AMAZON

ANNA M. BABEL

BETWEEN THE ANDES AND THE AMAZON

Language and Social Meaning in Bolivia

THE UNIVERSITY OF
ARIZONA PRESS
TUCSON

The University of Arizona Press
www.uapress.arizona.edu

First paperback edition 2021

ISBN-13: 978-0-8165-3726-6 (cloth)
ISBN-13: 978-0-8165-4340-3 (paper)

Cover design by Carrie House, HOUSEdesign, LLC
Cover photo by Anna Babel

Library of Congress Cataloging-in-Publication Data
Names: Babel, Anna, author.
Title: Between the Andes and the Amazon : language and social meaning in Bolivia / Anna M. Babel.
Description: Tucson : The University of Arizona Press, 2018. | Includes bibliographical references and index.
Identifiers: LCCN 2017042856 | ISBN 9780816537266 (cloth : alk. paper)
Subjects: LCSH: Sociolinguistics—Bolivia—Saipina (Santa Cruz) | Anthropological linguistics—Bolivia—Saipina (Santa Cruz) | Speech and social status—Bolivia—Saipina (Santa Cruz)
Classification: LCC P40.45.B5 B33 2018 | DDC 306.44/0984—dc23 LC record available at https://lccn.loc.gov/2017042856

Printed in the United States of America
♾ This paper meets the requirements of ANSI/NISO Z39.48-1992 (Permanence of Paper).

Este libro es para mi suegra, por lo mucho que ha luchado, por todo lo que ha sufrido y disfrutado en la vida, por tanto que ha cuidado a sus hijos y a los demás, y por todo lo que ha hecho por mí. Con mucho cariño y respeto le dedico este libro.

CONTENTS

ILLUSTRATIONS

ACKNOWLEDGMENTS

En primer lugar, quiero agradecer de corazón a mi familia en Bolivia. A mi suegra, a quien admiro más allá de las palabras; a sus hermanos, cuyas historias también cuento en este libro; a "los abuelos," con mucho respeto y aprecio; a mis muy queridos cuñaditos y sobrinitos, que me han hecho reír y me han acompañado tanto a través de los años. Agradezco también a mis amigos y amigas en Saipina. A la finada doña Fermina Blanco y su familia; doña Fermina me dio mi primer hogar en Saipina y me enseñó muchísimo de su vida compartiendo conmigo en la casa y en los potreros. Agradezco a las personas que me han tratado como una amiga—en especial a doña Miriam Cabello, doña Beneranda Cabello, doña Angela Soliz, doña Julia Choque, doña Anastasia Arce, doña Sofía Navia y su familia, mi comadre doña Catalina Navia y su familia, la Lic. Maribel Covarrubias, la Dra. Silvana Carvallo, y a todas las señoras que eran del CIAL en aquellos años.

Thanks also to my family in the United States: Raomir Avila, por todos los años que compartió conmigo; my children, Salomé and Emil, who make all of this worthwhile; and my parents, Deb and Ed Babel, who taught me to love writing and learning and exploring the world from a very early age.

I am incredibly fortunate to have an extensive and supportive academic family. From my years at the University of Michigan, thanks to Sarah Thomason, Bruce Mannheim, and Robin Queen, who have remained mentors and become friends over the years, and to Judy Irvine, who deeply influenced my intellectual development. Thanks to my old friend Kevin McGowan for many productive conversations, and to Lauren Squires, who has walked a parallel path to mine for many years. At the Ohio State University I have been lucky to be taken under the collective wing of the Linguist Ladies, an informal mentoring network at OSU—special thanks to Judith Tonhauser, Cynthia Clopper, Leslie Moore, Laura Wagner, Kiwako Ito, and Monique Mills. Thanks to Kathryn Campbell-Kibler and the students in the SoMean discussion group for providing a stimulating intellectual space that I look forward to every week. And thanks to Kendra McSweeney and Marissa Kaloga, momfriends and scholars extraordinaire. I am grateful for the international community of Español de los Andes scholars: Stefan Pfänder, Juan Carlos Godenzzi, Azucena Palacios, Angelita Martínez, Philipp Dankel, Mario Soto, and Víctor Fernández Mallat, among others. And of course, my deepest appreciation goes to my colleagues in the Department of Spanish and Portuguese at OSU, particularly Paloma Martínez-Cruz, Ana Puga, Eugenia Romero, Elena Foulis, and Rebeka Campos-Astorkiza. Your company keeps me sane in a crazy world. I'm also grateful to Glenn Martínez for his material and symbolic support. My graduate students in the Department of Spanish & Portuguese at OSU are another reason why this job is fun—you all make me better at what I do. In particular, thanks to my first "batch" of advisees—Devin Grammon, Ashlee Dauphinais, and Justin Pinta. Finally, my wholehearted thanks to my writing partners at the National Center for Faculty Development & Diversity, Jenny Lobasz and Janet Decker. This book would never have been written without their moral support. And to the various online groups for mothers who are also academics and vice versa—thanks for your stories and empathy.

I deeply appreciate positive feedback on this manuscript at important junctures from Norma Mendoza-Denton, Galey Modan, Rusty Barrett, and Tony Webster. Thank you for believing in this project. I also greatly appreciate comments from Kate Graber, Nick Emlen, Karl Swinehart, and a plethora of anonymous reviewers who read my book proposal and/or manuscript draft.

The research that led to this book was supported by a National Science Foundation Graduate Research Fellowship, the University of Michigan Rackham Graduate School, and the Ohio State University College of Arts and Sciences. I gratefully acknowledge permission to reprint my essay "On Being a Near-Native Speaker" from *Anthropology* News and permission from the *Boletín de Filología* to reprint an article that formed the basis for chapter 2.

BETWEEN THE ANDES AND THE AMAZON

INTRODUCTION

Why Can't a Quechua Speaker Wear Pants?

IN 2008, while doing my dissertation fieldwork, I was chatting with an acquaintance, Plácida, in the open patio at the center of her house in the town of Saipina, Bolivia. Plácida complained to me about her neighbor, who had built a large store abutting her house. She was resentful of her neighbor for a number of reasons. As she complained about her neighbor, she added that the neighbor had recently switched her style of dress from the *pollera*, a gathered skirt, to pants. Plácida criticized her appearance, saying she didn't look good in pants, and added, "Everyone knows she's a Quechua speaker, one of those people from [the political party] MAS."

Why shouldn't a Quechua speaker wear pants? In the context of the social system that I describe in this book, this comment seems completely natural, indeed, self-explanatory. Through many different channels and in many different ways, people align groups of categories that "match up" with each other. In this comment, Plácida aligned a linguistic identification (being a Quechua speaker) with a political one (supporting the Movimiento al Socialismo, or Movement for Socialism [MAS], political party) and with a gendered stylistic practice (the use of the pollera). Implied in her comment is the assumption that these categories *should* match up: if you are a Quechua speaker and a supporter of the MAS political party, then you should wear a pollera. The comment included an implicit contrast with Plácida herself, who wore pants, spoke Spanish, and was not a supporter of MAS.

A few months later, I attended a meeting of a group of about seventy people who were requesting government funding to construct a housing project on the edge of town. Everyone was weary at the end of the long meeting, but the group could not reach consensus over whether they would travel together to a neighboring town to see the president speak and to make their request in person. A wiry man stood up in the back of the audience and wisecracked, "Todos los indios van a ir y los autonomistas no" (All the indians will go, and the autonomists won't). The room broke up in laughter. The first indigenous president of Bolivia, Evo Morales of the MAS political party, had positioned himself firmly as a representative of highland indigenous groups, while the lowland elites were carrying out a furious campaign for economic autonomy. In my field site, at the border of the highlands and lowlands, about half the population supported Evo, and the other half supported the *autonomistas*. While everyone in the room wanted the government to build them a house, not everyone was a political supporter of the current government. Those who did not support the government did not want to take the day off from work to ride for three hours in the back of a truck to attend a rally for the president. These lines were not only political but often interpreted in racial terms—thus the speaker's joking use of the racial slur *indio*. The speaker's contrast of the racial category *indio* and the political category *autonomista* cut to the heart of the matter, effortlessly cross-referencing race and politics.

If a Quechua speaker can't wear pants, will an autonomista travel to see the first indigenous president of Bolivia? These incidents encapsulate the heart of the social system that I describe in this book. Language, styles of dress, race and ethnicity, and political orientation are categories that in this context are aligned with each other and treated as equivalent through a linked series of situated practices and discourses. Just as important as the equivalence of sets of categories to each other is their opposition to a matched set of opposing categories. If people equated the use of the pollera, indigenous ethnicity, MAS supporters, and the use of Quechua, these also stood in opposition to other categories: MAS supporters were not autonomistas, people who wore polleras did not wear pants. Both the relationships between categories and the oppositions between them were essential to creating the social context that made these comments interpretable to their audiences.

In this book, I use detailed exploration of the social dynamics of Saipina, a town located at a midpoint between eastern and western, highland and lowland Bolivia, to examine social categorization through a set of overlapping, mutually interrelated binary oppositions. Each chapter of the book focuses on a particular binary opposition. There is a focus on language and linguistic practice that runs throughout the book, reflecting my training as a sociolinguist and linguistic anthropologist.

MEANING AS A SYSTEM

This book is about a system of social meaning: the way that people generate meaning through systematic alignments and oppositions between apparently disparate categories, such as language, ethnicity, political affiliation, and styles of dress. Social meaning often seems natural or commonsensical when we live and work "inside" a system. However, stepping outside the social system—as an ethnographer does—reveals practices and assumptions that work to hold together a coherent or "commonsense" system of ideas and rules that organize daily life and social relations.

The relationship between these structures and the way that people live in them has been described as a dialectic between "structure" and "practice" (Bourdieu 1972, 1991; Sahlins 1976, 1985). Structure—an idealized system of written and unwritten rules, assumptions, and "commonsense" notions—is reproduced, borne out, and reinscribed through "practice," the many apparently insignificant actions that people engage in from day to day (Giddens 1984; Mahmood 2005; Ortner 1984, 1996, 2006). Scholars working in this field, generally labeled as "practice theory," have tussled over the relationship between practice and structure, the role of consciousness and intentionality, and the degree of consensus or agreement that people share in developing practice and structure. However, at its heart, practice theory is an attempt to bridge the ways that societal structures—some might say "culture"—are produced through everyday actions (for critiques of the "culture concept," see Abu-Lughod 1996; Clifford 1983, 1986; Geertz 1973). In Sherry Ortner's words, these structures are

> the little routines people enact, again and again, in working, eating, sleeping, and relaxing, as well as the little scenarios of etiquette they play out again and again in social interaction. All of these routines and scenarios are predicated upon, and embody within themselves, the fundamental notions of temporal, spatial, and social ordering that underlie and organize the system as a whole. In enacting these routines, actors not only continue to be shaped by the underlying organizational

> principles involved, but continually re-endorse those principles in the world of public observation and discourse. (1984:154)

Practice theory exists in conversation with the earlier intellectual tradition of structuralism (Lévi-Strauss 1962, 1966). Structuralism's key insight is that signs take on meaning through participation in systems of contrast. Yet these oppositions are always made, not found. When people make comments like "Quechua speakers can't wear pants" and "All the indios will go, and all the autonomistas will stay," they create discourses that reinforce the naturalized distinction between binary oppositions, which in turn are linked to and aligned with other sets of oppositions. These oppositions form the raw material of the social system that people accept as "normal" or "the way things are."

We can tell that these are idealizations rather than descriptions of reality because social categorization is not only complex but also malleable, subject to change. Plácida's neighbor might be criticized for wearing pants, but she in fact made the choice to change away from the pollera, a choice that she maintained in the following years. The autonomistas in Saipina might not support the president, but they were ultimately successful in their request for a government-supported housing development. Within a few years, many of the same autonomy supporters who resisted traveling to see the president speak had moved into houses built by the federally funded project. Some of them, years later, identified as MAS supporters due to changing political currents and regional identifications. While people may produce and refer to a simple and balanced system of social categories, there is a wealth of complexity from which to draw and interpret the raw material of the system of signs.

Sometimes the opposition seem clear: MAS stands in opposition to the autonomy movement, the pollera is opposed to wearing pants. But others are not so clear: there is no neat equivalent for the word *indio* beyond the somewhat clumsy "nonindigenous." While terms like *mestizo*, *ladino*, and *criollo* are historically relevant and are used in other parts of contemporary Latin America (Canessa 2012; de la Cadena 2000), they are not particularly salient markers of identity categories in my field site. Even the categories that seem to present a clear opposition are ultimately simplifications of a more complex social landscape. While MAS is often opposed to the "Greens" of the autonomy movement, these are only two of more than a dozen active political parties in Bolivia, each one of which has a history and a particular political stance and flavor of politicking (on Bolivian politics, see Albro 2010; Fabricant 2012; Fabricant and Gustafson 2011; Gustafson 2009a;

Klein 2003; Postero 2007). There are many different styles of polleras, all of which have different meanings; likewise, a woman who does not wear the pollera might wear pants, but she might also wear jeans or a miniskirt or a tailored straight skirt that indexes a Santa Cruz valley identity (on gendered styles of dress in Bolivia, see Haynes 2013; Stephenson 1997, 1999).

This wealth of signs, many of them changing or open to varied interpretations, provides the raw material from which people organize consistent ways of understanding social positioning. The great intellectual shift in anthropology and cultural studies from structuralism to poststructuralism and postmodernism in the mid-20th century emphasized the constructed, fractured, contested nature of apparently "clean" underlying binary oppositions and challenged the primacy of "scientific" or "objective" approaches to language and culture (Crapanzano 1996; Derrida 1978; Giddens 1984; Spivak 1988). People *do* create social structures, but they do it messily, creatively, and in ways that create not solid underlying oppositions but dynamic relationships that are constantly negotiated and transformed. These alignments bring together disparate ideas into coherent structures of meaning, or, as Stuart Hall calls them, "articulations" (1986, 1996; see also Grossberg 1986). The idea of articulation is a play on a double meaning between the sense of *articulation* as production of speech in the form of discourse and the idea of *articulation* as connections that people make between apparently disparate ideas by forging relationships that may be based on likeness or difference, identity or rupture (see Hall 1990:223; Gegeo and Watson Gegeo 1999:24). Language exists within a semiotic system that generates meaning in the context of a particular set of concepts that are linked through the alignment of binary categories. Thinking about the relationships between social categories in terms of alignment and contrast helps to link language across different scales and types of reference (Abbott 1995; Gal and Irvine 1995; Irvine 2001). This point of view is well described by the concept of *articulation*—an examination of how apparently disparate categories are related to each other through alignment and differentiation (Clifford 2001; Hall 1996; Laclau 2006; Slack 1996).

In many cases, "meaning making" happens through language use and language play. As I show in this book, Spanish and Quechua are not just two "languages," nor are they simply linguistic resources or tool kits that speakers open up when they have need for one or the other. Rather, the practice of using Spanish or using Quechua is a claim to an identity or a social position. The fact that people from Saipina often use a mixture of Spanish and Quechua is a way of staking out a place "between" two extremes or binary oppositions. This "in-between" positioning runs through many different types of social meaning, cutting across disparate categories of practice.

LINGUISTIC ANTHROPOLOGY AND MEANING MAKING

Social and linguistic structures are real; however, they are produced, modified, and contested through interaction and in discourse. Language is one element in a group of social systems that participate in meaning making in ways that are tightly related and mutually influential. This work draws on semiotic approaches to linguistic anthropology and sociolinguistics, in particular, indexicality and iconization (Irvine and Gal 2000; Peirce 1955) and indexical fields (Eckert 2008). According to Peircean semiotics, indices (or indexes) are sign relationships that are generated because of a relationship between one sign and another—for example, a cause-and-effect kind of relationship. The classic example of an indexical relationship is the idea that "where there is smoke, there is fire"—smoke is an *index* of fire. Relationships between linguistic features and social categories are commonly described as indices because they exemplify this type of relationship: there is no inherent resemblance between most words and the ideas that they denote, but they are linked through associative cognitive processes.[1] Icons, on the other hand, are sign relationships that rely on the perception of some kind of resemblance or likeness. Judith Irvine and Susan Gal's use of the verb *iconization* underlines the active nature of the process through which links between language and different types of social categorization are presented as if they were natural and inherent. When categories such as "pollera wearer" and "Quechua speaker" are so closely linked that they seem to share a natural resemblance, the indexical relationship between them is transformed into an iconic one. The crucial ingredient of this transformation is the role of the *interpretant*—the entity that connects signs and their objects. For most linguistic anthropologists, the interpretants are embodied by people—people whose perceptions of likeness and difference can transform the sign relationship.

Through the process of *iconization*, one type of sign comes to stand for another because it is understood to have an essential connection to it, to resemble it in some way. Irvine and Gal characterize iconization in the following words:

> *Iconization* involves a transformation of the sign relationship between linguistic features (or varieties) and the social images with which they are linked. Linguistic

1. This view has been challenged by, for example, Nuckolls (1996) and Dingemanse (2012).

> features that index social groups or activities appear to be iconic representations of them, as if a linguistic feature somehow depicted or displayed a social group's inherent nature or essence. This process entails the attribution of cause and immediate necessity to a connection (between linguistic features and social groups) that may be only historical, contingent, or conventional. The iconicity of the ideological representation reinforces the implication of necessity. By picking out qualities supposedly shared by the social image and the linguistic image, the ideological representation—itself a sign—binds them together in a linkage that appears to be inherent. (2000:37)

Through their use of Peircean semiotics, Irvine and Gal draw attention to the social processes by which language becomes a sign and to the importance of the actors who interpret these signs. While these links may appear natural, they are created through social processes, in social contexts, and by particular people with particular perspectives. The process of iconization is not limited to language; as Irvine and Gal point out, iconic relationships can be drawn between categories like nationality, race, color, and religion.

The process of iconization creates relationships between signs (like "Quechua speaker" and "pollera wearer") that appear natural to the people who use them. In this book, I draw attention to the way that systems of iconic linkages work together in a logical, structured way. The resulting pattern of meaning becomes a system that structures many different types of reference. This pattern of meaning is larger than a single iconic relationship, even one that is embedded in a larger cultural system.

The particular configuration of meaning attached to signs and sign relationships can shift based on social context. One way to approach the role of context in interpreting linguistic and other types of signs is through the concept of *indexical fields* (Eckert 2008). Penelope Eckert explains the indexical field as a "constellation of meanings [related to a linguistic variable] that are ideologically linked" (464). As has been shown repeatedly in work in sociolinguistics and linguistic anthropology, the meaning of linguistic features is embedded in systems of social signification. Eckert shows that the context in which a given sociolinguistic variable is used can pick out a particular association with that form from a "field" of related meanings, some of which may be contradictory, and all of which are constantly shifting and open to (re)interpretation. Sociolinguistic variables do not have a single meaning but are associated with varying meanings based on the larger social context.

As Eckert indicates, meaning is not rooted in a single definition entry but is tied to a web of related concepts. The meaning of a linguistic sign shifts depending on the circumstances of its utterance; while some aspects of the indexical field are related to fleeting attitudes or stances, others are understood to be more permanent personality types or characteristics. Eckert's (2008:466) examples are quite explicitly presented as involving binary oppositions between variants that are linked to opposing qualities.

Linguistic forms are processed through a detailed analysis of a system of meaning that is enmeshed in a particular community and used by particular speakers as members of social groups. We know, for example, that listeners' expectations about speakers influence the way listeners evaluate speakers' dialect (Campbell-Kibler 2008; Carmichael 2016; Hay and Drager 2010; Hay et al. 2006; McGowan 2015). Yet when we observe that social meaning shifts depending on context—that signs are interpreted in relation to other signs—this does not mean that they are uninterpretable or unpredictable. Eckert's model begs us to look more broadly at how the larger social field is configured and how linguistic signs are linked to each other and to social personae (Agha 2005; Babel 2011; Johnstone et al. 2006; Remlinger 2009). No single linguistic feature stands alone; rather, its apparent multitude of meanings is related to the patterns of linguistic features in which each one participates and to the social personae that use these patterns. As I describe in chapter 2, a bilingual Quechua speaker from Cochabamba can use the same enregistered contact feature as a Spanish speaker from Saipina, but she will be interpreted differently by her audience because of the different ways that the two speakers are understood to fit into social categories.

Indexical fields participate in larger social structures that guide the interpretation of the meaning of particular linguistic features within a larger, comprehensive social system. Placing the concept of the indexical fields within this context reveals the processes that structure the indexical field, such as the production and alignment of binary contrasts, and provides the raw material that speakers use to position themselves and to interpret others when they use language to make claims to membership in social categories.

SEMIOTIC ALIGNMENT, CLUSTERS, AND THE SEMIOTIC FIELD

I introduce three related theoretical concepts in order to understand the social structure that I analyze and describe through my ethnographic examples. First, I suggest that there is a *semiotic field* that encompasses many different kinds of signs—language, ethnicity, political orientation—into a coherently structured system of signs that constitutes "commonsensical" points of reference for people within a given community.

The semiotic field provides the opportunity to construct similarity and difference, giving rise to contrast, an essential element of the production of meaning. When people act in a way that is congruent with the semiotic field—when they do what they are expected to do—their behavior is classified as "normal" or unremarkable. When they act differently, their actions may be framed as being deviant or surprising. One way of visualizing these differences is as a mosaic in which white chips on a black background stand out more than white chips on a white background. Language, like other signs, is constantly compared to the social and linguistic context in which it appears and to the history of use of a particular speaker. This "history of use" can be extended to moment-to-moment stances or to the social group or groups that a speaker is understood to represent at a particular moment. Because patterns of language use are built on a constant comparison to existing models and frames of reference, even small deviations from the norm may stand out. This is why a very skilled public speaker may occasionally use Quechua contact features in Spanish in a way that highlights his oratorical ability, while the same features when used by a Quechua-dominant woman who wears a pollera may be a mark of her rurality or backwardness (see chapter 2). It is also why a person who changes her style of dress—from pollera to pants—may be subject to discourses that attempt to control her by framing her as a person for whom the new style is categorically inappropriate.

The second idea that I introduce is *semiotic alignment*. I use this term to describe the process by which individual iconic relationships are organized into a larger cluster of ideas. This process of alignment draws multiple iconic relationships into binary clusters of signs. In the example at the beginning of this chapter, membership in the MAS political party is aligned with the category *indio* through such an iconic relationship. Likewise, MAS affiliation and speaking Quechua are treated as icons of each other by Doña Plácida. She suggests that the use of pants is contrary to the relationship between these categories; her neighbor has violated a sign relationship.

If we take the two examples together, we can begin to develop a sketch of the social system that these two comments reference:

Pollera = Quechua speaker = MAS = indio
Pants = Spanish speaker = autonomista = nonindigenous

Wearing a pollera, speaking Quechua, and belonging to the MAS political party are treated as natural equivalents by Doña Plácida—to the extent that she finds her neighbor's behavior outrageous. Given personal tensions between the two women and larger-scale tensions between long-term residents and migrants in the community, we might be tempted to dismiss this incident as simply a case of hard feelings between neighbors and Plácida's attempt to censure a person for whom she feels antipathy for reasons that go beyond her style of dress. However, what we want to attend to here is the "commonsense" structures that Doña Plácida appeals to in her critique of her neighbor—the assumption that these categories not only should but do belong to a single natural group.

Once groups of ideas have been aligned into binary pairs, each term within a group of categories acts as an icon of the others. There is no single category that guides or determines the alignment of the rest of the ideas; rather, they are all treated as mutually equivalent. This process allows us to account for a larger system of meaning that reaches beyond particular binary oppositions to form a social framework in which language is embedded as one of a group of signs.

I describe this grouping using the term *cluster* to describe the way that the process of iconization relates bundles of different categories to each other. Through the process of semiotic alignment, multiple binary oppositions are drawn together into clusters of related categories. Within these clusters, each category is conceived of as being equivalent to, interchangeable with, the other categories that form part of the cluster. Likewise, each category within a cluster stands in opposition to any category in the opposite cluster. These relationships of alignment and opposition create a strong binary structure that serves as a frame of reference through which systems of meaning and reference are created. Often, one side or one cluster of the opposition is marked, while the other can be read as unmarked or "normal."

WHY LANGUAGE IS IMPORTANT

Language is an especially complex piece of this puzzle. In the Santa Cruz valleys of Bolivia, where this research takes place, many people are bilingual in Spanish and Quechua. Both languages have influenced each other deeply at multiple levels of language structure so that the Spanish of the valleys is mixed with Quechua and the Quechua of the valleys is mixed with Spanish. Often, language is interpreted through the context of surrounding social categories.

Given two equally fluent bilinguals, one who wears the pollera and supports MAS and another who wears pants and supports the autonomy movement, the MAS supporter is more likely to be considered a *quechuista*, or "Quechua-dominant speaker."

Language takes a number of different forms in the analysis that I present. At the most abstract level, I discuss Spanish and Quechua as they are understood as distinct languages. The labels *castellanista*, or "Spanish speaker," and quechuista are not purely linguistic distinctions but social categories like those related to ethnicity, gender, and race. I also examine how particular words and labels become politicized and racialized through their role in a broader social and political system. At the most specific level, throughout the book I use people's words to give illustrative examples of how my friends and consultants framed the information that they gave me. In a few cases, I present word-for-word transcriptions of recordings. In these cases, I discuss word and language choice in order to illuminate the way that language reveals attitudes and social positioning. There are multiple levels at which "language" acts as a symbol and multiple ways in which it participates in the social system that I describe in this book.

The meaning of language and linguistic features is rooted in social context. This work joins other recent work in linguistic anthropology that focuses on the organization of language as part of a system of signs. Much recent work on this topic has focused on the materiality of language and its embodied qualities (Bucholtz and Hall 2016; Goodwin 2000; Hall et al. 2016; Mondada 2016). For example, Nicholas Harkness, writing about Korean singers, writes that "a voice, the emotions it expresses, the person in whom it is embodied, and the social relations that it mediates can be relatively more old-fashioned or modern, more marginal or central, more holy or less, relatively clean or unclean on the basis of phonosonic practice that is apperceived in terms of a Christian aesthetic of progress" (2014:226). The way that the qualities of the voice are embedded into systems of tradition and modernity, marginality and centrality, cleanliness and uncleanliness, or, as Harkness writes in other work, qualities of "lightness" and "darkness" echo the sets of binaries that we can observe in Quechua- and Spanish-language practices in the eastern Andean slopes of Bolivia. While particular instances can be placed on a scale between binary poles, the binary itself governs the way that these positions are interpreted and linked to bodily practice.

This way of structuring social meaning is not limited to the place and time that I describe; it works in many different contexts. For example, gang-affiliated girls in

Los Angeles place the use of particular linguistic features within a social landscape of color symbolism (red/blue for *norteño/sureño*), makeup, taste in music, and styles of dress (Mendoza-Denton 2008). As in the data I have presented in this book, these divisions are ideological formations that are rooted in practice, systems of interpretation that organize lived experiences that are often messy, dynamic, contested, or "in-between." To take another example, Lal Zimman observes that trans people and trans voices are often perceived and performed within scales of more or less normative masculinity and femininity. This work also points to the way that an "in-between" persona or category can be constructed (Zimman 2016; Zimman et al. 2014). In the complex discursive construction of voice, gender, and sexuality, the opposing poles of "masculine" and "feminine" are produced, reified, questioned, and manipulated to suit the aims of actors.

Language use is a sign that can be both explicit, as in metalinguistic and metapragmatic commentary about language use and standards, and implicit, in the use of extremely subtle linguistic signals as a way of positioning oneself with respect to social categories. Language is also commonly embedded in other systems of meaning in ways that are often taken to be natural or inevitable (Eckert 2000). As such, language is a privileged window to the construction of social categories.

ANDES-AMAZONIA

There is a long-standing dichotomy between the Andes and the Amazon that assumes strong cultural distinctions between highlands and lowlands (Barbieri et al. 2014; Emlen 2015; Santos-Granero 2002). In this book, I explore the transition zone between the Andean highlands and the lowlands of the Amazon and the southern Bolivian Chaco. This area has been the site of rich cultural contact, change, and diversity as long as there is evidence of human habitation (Rivera 2015). Along with these scholars, I question the division between highland and lowland by examining how this opposition is produced in the very region in which these boundaries are least clear.

The transition between the Bolivian Andes and the lowlands is a "contact zone" in the fullest sense of the term: "social spaces where cultures meet, clash, and grapple with each other, often in contexts of highly asymmetrical relations of power, such as colonialism, slavery, or their aftermaths as they are lived out in many parts of the world today" (Pratt 1991:34). The links between highland

and lowland zones reach to precolonial, indeed to pre-Inca times (Murra 1985). However, the particular currents that I describe in this book are rooted in the more recent flow of migrants from the Andean highlands toward the lowlands of Santa Cruz, a pattern that has been driven by pressures toward wage labor and the increasing difficulty of sustainable small-scale farming. The first explosion of highland migrants to the city of Santa Cruz occurred in the 1960s and 1970s (Stearman 1987). The migration of Quechua speakers from the rural highlands to lowland cities has been a major shaping force of Bolivian regional demographics over the past fifty years, and it is this West-to-East migration that forms the constant linguistic and cultural contact zone that characterizes Saipina.

In Bolivia there is a strong and coherent linguistic and cultural ecology at the border of highland and lowland zones. However, this region—the *valles cruceños*, or Santa Cruz valleys—has received scant attention in the scholarly literature. While anthropologists have written about the Bolivian highlands (Canessa 2005; Van Vleet 2009), the Cochabamba valleys (Albro 2010; Goldstein 2004, 2012), and lowland Santa Cruz (Gustafson 2009b; Postero 2007), the transition zones between highland and lowland, the very place where the process of distinguishing the two is most fraught, have been little explored. Nicole Fabricant (2012) demonstrates the extent to which highland and lowland identities are mutually constituted and a constant site of negotiation as she traces the links between highland and lowland through discussions of struggles over land and indigenous political identity. Fabricant's work focuses primarily on a discussion of the Movimiento sin Tierra, a loosely affiliated group of highland indigenous settlers who have claimed large sections of lowland territory in northern Bolivia. In the Santa Cruz valleys of central Bolivia, however, the lines between local and migrant, insider and outsider are much less clear, even as they reflect broader national discourses about divisions between highland and lowland (see chapter 3). Working at the border of highland and lowland Bolivia, I examine how the two sides of this dichotomy are produced through discourse and practice yet also rejected through claims to an "in-between" identity.

WHAT YOU CAN EXPECT TO FIND IN THIS BOOK

This book is divided into chapters, with ethnographic interludes between them. Following the introduction, in chapter 1, I discuss the geographical location of

Saipina in the Santa Cruz valleys of Bolivia and the *camba* versus *colla* categories that structure much of Bolivian discourse regarding regional identity. In chapter 2 I discuss the role that social categorization plays in the interpretation of linguistic material. In chapter 3 I discuss Spanish and Quechua in the context of the Santa Cruz valleys, with a particular focus on the relationship between the two languages and the production of "Spanish speaker" and "Quechua speaker" as identity categories. In chapter 4 I discuss the intersection of language, race, and legitimacy through a discussion of the locally salient categories *conocido* (acquaintance, member of polite society) and *desconocido* (stranger, unknown person). In chapter 5 I discuss national politics as they are experienced on a local scale, particularly through the racialization of public discourse. In chapter 6 I discuss the production of a "traditional" local identity, which stands in contrast to "modernity," "development," and "progress." In chapter 7 I make a detailed study of *cholitas*, women who wear the pollera, a category that stands in opposition to *señoritas*, women who wear straight skirts. In chapter 8 I discuss migration from Saipina to the urban center of Santa Cruz, then link this to popular perceptions of sexuality and migration using a set of popular songs. Finally, in the conclusion, I review the evidence that I have presented and summarize the theoretical framework that I propose to understand these data.

Between each chapter I include an ethnographic vignette based on the work that I have done in Saipina over the past fifteen years. These vignettes focus on the lived personal experience of particular individuals who have informed (and transformed) my understanding of the social life of this area. Many of the vignettes focus on Don Francisco and Doña Antonia and their family, key consultants who have been my hosts, friends, and family for many years in Saipina. I use the half-chapters as another way of embodying the "betweenness" that this book examines—they are more personal and less analytical than the full chapters that they divide, and I use them to remind the reader of the way that the abstract theoretical structures that I discuss in the book shape the lives of real people dealing with real challenges and joys in their lives. I want the reader to keep sight of the fact that this book is written by a person whose interactions and experiences with other people resulted in the material that provides the basis for the analysis that I present in this book. To this end, the half-chapters represent not only ethnography but also some pieces of autoethnography, stories about who I am and how I came to be a participant in the community that I describe.

Given this point of view, I feel I should provide some background on my own biography and place in the community. I was born in the United States and moved frequently during my early childhood. I first visited Bolivia as a tourist in 1999, then returned for two and a half years as a Peace Corps volunteer in 2002–4. Since then I have returned for long periods of time on an almost annual basis, including a full year of fieldwork in 2008, and I keep in touch with my consultants via phone calls and social media when I am away. Though I am not a "native" of my field site, I am connected to my consultants by kin ties due to my marriage to a local man, placing me within a family structure in which I can be understood as a daughter-in-law, sister-in-law, cousin-in-law (if a somewhat exotic one). This connection placed me within a social universe and opened many doors during my fieldwork. Nevertheless, I write from a particular, often privileged, viewpoint as a highly educated, highly mobile white woman from the United States who was raised as a monolingual English speaker.

As I describe further in the ethnographic interlude following chapter 3, my variety of Spanish is closely aligned with local speech. This nonstandard variety incorporates extensive Quechua influence at all levels, that is, in terms of accent/phonology, grammar/syntax, and vocabulary/lexicon. My Spanish is near enough to that of native speakers that it is often difficult for strangers to determine whether I am a native speaker or not. I learned to speak this variety of Spanish from my friends and family—women, older people, small landholders, and skilled laborers—and I sound like them when I speak. Though I speak Spanish very well and have used it on a daily basis for almost half my life, I am not a native Spanish speaker, and though I hold Bolivian citizenship due to marriage, I am not a native-born Bolivian, nor yet a U.S.-born Latina—though my children, who often accompany me during my fieldwork, belong to the latter category.

In dress, too, I conformed to local standards during fieldwork by wearing black tire sandals, a black fedora, a button-down shirt or T-shirt, and slacks—all of which I found practical and comfortable in the dry desert heat and cactus-prickered dust of Saipina. Because I liked plain tire sandals and pants rather than flip-flops, strappy sandals, and knee-length skirts, my style of dress was similar to that of the women I worked with but somewhat less feminine, and perhaps more conservative, than that of my younger or more urban-oriented consultants.

I try to strike a balance between recognizing the personal nature of my relationships with my consultants and protecting the privacy of my friends and relatives. In a departure from my privacy practices up to the date of this book, I use the real name of the town where I work, Saipina. I made this decision because I cite and use sources that I must recognize as the intellectual property of people who live in Saipina, and these sources reference the town of Saipina explicitly. However, with the exception of the authors of such intellectual property and public figures like Evo Morales, the president of Bolivia, I continue to use pseudonyms for the personal names of other participants in my research.

Because some of my material is drawn from field notes, while other material is drawn from recordings, I differentiate in the text between word-for-word quotes transcribed from recordings and approximate glosses from my field notes. Word-for-word quotes in Spanish are enclosed in quotation marks, with the English translation enclosed in parentheses, or they are presented in table format with the Spanish original on the left and the English gloss on the right. Approximate glosses are enclosed in double quotation marks.

CONCLUSION

Language is a system, but it is not only a linguistic system. It is embedded in structures of power and privilege, in relationships of familiarity and distance. In this book I give a detailed analysis of a system of meaning that is enmeshed in a particular community and used by particular individuals. Throughout this work I situate language within a semiotic system as produced in a particular cultural context, as well as in the histories and stances of individual speakers. The meaning of language in use is produced through systems of contrast and is rooted in particular communities, speakers, and utterances. Therefore, the production of meaning must be located in a physical act of speaking or signifying, in the history of participants or audiences within an event, and within a particular cultural system.

I describe a community located in central Bolivia in which speakers use Quechua and Spanish to situate themselves with relation to dialectics of tradition and modernity, East and West, highland and lowland, styles of dress, gender and sexuality, and positioning as certain types of speakers and ultimately as certain types of people. Language use and language identification must be understood as one part of the construction of meaning in this community, which participates in a much broader system of signs.

The distribution of sociolinguistic indices—different ways of speaking—over social contexts is determined by the way they fit into meaningful patterns that are associated with ideas about language and social structure. These patterns go beyond language, but language provides a unique potential for replication, reflection, and transformation of these structures. I argue that language becomes meaningful only in context and through contrast with models of use that are developed by speakers and linked to the larger semiotic field.

This project is strongly influenced by structuralism and by practice theory. The relationship between structure and practice is fundamental to all production of meaning. The particular form or shape that it takes in this context is only one manifestation of the many possible ways that it could develop, and indeed the symbolic material of social systems has assuredly developed differently even in communities that are otherwise very similar to the one that I describe here. Binary structures are powerful vehicles for meaning production. However, in the end, conceptual binaries are only reference points; they are produced, contested, complicated, and modified through practice and in interaction.

INTERLUDE

My Arrival Story

THE FIRST time I came to Saipina, as a newly minted Peace Corps volunteer, I took the 4:00 p.m. bus from the city of Santa Cruz. I was with Martín, an agronomist who would be my local counterpart, the person responsible for supporting me both socially and professionally in a town I had never seen. We had just spent several hours being lectured by Peace Corps staff about the responsibilities of volunteer and counterpart. This included severe warnings to Martín and the other male counterparts about the dire consequences of sexually harassing a female volunteer. It must have made an impression, because Martín not only didn't harass me, he seemed afraid to look at me. He stretched out in the window seat and pretended to fall asleep. I knew he wasn't asleep because there were a solid six inches of empty space between us, and on the cramped minibus we were riding, maintaining that space required focused muscle control.

Back then, in early 2002, the minibuses were only fifteen to twenty rows long, four seats across, with a narrow aisle in the middle. They were painted blue or yellow, with bright stripes and the company's name, TransSaipina, blazoned across the windshield in enormous letters. They bore legends like "Viajar como en avion pero por tierra" (Traveling as if in an airplane but on land), and they boasted tiny icons depicting television, air conditioning, meal service, bathrooms, reclining seats—things they in fact lacked but perhaps either had at one time or aspired to have in the future. The crew always consisted of a driver and one or two ayudantes (helpers) who collected tickets, loaded the bus, and generally dealt with passengers. The buses departed two or three times a day from the city, from an office on a gritty, industrial, four-lane highway heading out of the city of Santa Cruz. The buses would pull up to the office, parking on the side of the road, about half an hour before they were scheduled to leave. Then there was a flurry of activity as the passengers climbed aboard and the ayudantes dragged their packages up to the top of the bus. These often included large items of furniture, rebar and other construction materials, 100-kilo sacks of foodstuffs, live animals in crates, and innumerable smaller items, and they were all loaded by brute force.

These teenage boys and young men who worked as ayudantes, nicknamed ayucos, were muscled like Olympic athletes. They spent half their time running alongside the bus, loading or unloading packages and people from the side of the road. If the bus was too crowded, they rode on top, wedged amid the baggage. If they were sleepy, they rode in the luggage bins underneath, with the door cracked so they wouldn't suffocate. In the case of a mechanical failure, the ayuco and his boss, the driver, would rush to unload the tools, then grunt and sweat as they worked at the engine or, more likely, the tire. When there were blockades, accidents, or impassable roads due to flooding, the ayuco went ahead on reconnaissance. I can't count the number of times I have seen an ayuco, shivering with the cold and in the dead of night, roll his pants up to the thigh and wade into a river in flood so that the driver could judge whether the bus would pass. It was also the ayucos' job to clean up the bus after the trip, which could be as short as six and a half hours or as long as two or three days, depending on road conditions and blockades.

That afternoon, though, all I saw was Martín's profile and the view out the window. We made good time through the suffocating lowlands surrounding the city, where the road was long and wide and straight, and the packed-in urbanization of the city slowly gave way to strings of houses, tiny stores, and farms. At each toll stop the bus was surrounded by flocks of women holding up plastic bags and bottles, reaching toward the passengers: "Soda, soda, soda!" "Tangerines, tangerines, only five pesos a bag!" Humintas, charque, sonso, peanuts, wrapped candy—everything divided into tiny portions and held out like a particularly insistent offering. Then, abruptly, the mountains tightened in on the road, and there were few houses. Instead, there were vertical cliffs on one side rising up to mountain peaks, vertical cliffs on the other side stretching down to the river, and between them a narrow, crumbling road. All of it seemed to be ready to slide off into the river at any moment. As I later learned, this impression was not an illusion. The cliffs were constantly crawling with rockslides. In some spots, the driver paused, head cocked, watched the rocks tumbling down from far above, and waited for a gap, timing the speed of his vehicle to make it through without major damage. In other parts, the road looked as if a bite had been taken out of it, and there was only just enough space for a single vehicle, hugging the cliff, to pass. Sometimes large trucks passed with their outside wheels spinning in the air. The bus crunched over loose gravel and slid through mud slicks. Drivers sped to the maximum of their ability, passing slower trucks on curves and in the face of oncoming traffic.

In Samaipata the terrain became more moderate, the road widened, and the tension eased. It was not even dusk when we reached the lush hills of this easternmost Inca fort. Now largely supported by weekend tourists from the city, populated by European and American expatriates, and located on the border of one of the beautiful national parks in Bolivia, Samaipata was a haven. I loved the area on first sight; it reminded me of my home in the Smoky Mountains of the southeastern United States. I hoped Saipina would be similar.

The bus stopped for dinner and a pit stop just down the road in Mairana. Mairana was a valley of wide fields, cows and corn, mountains in the middle distance. The town itself was like a truck stop anywhere in the world, smelling of urine and litter and populated by stray dogs. Martín and I each ate a hamburger and hurried back onto the bus so as not to be left behind. We passed through a handful of little towns, then we left the main road. It was pitch-black out. The lights of Palizadas and San Rafael flashed by, and we were nearly in Saipina. My heart sank as I saw the outlines of cactus flashing against the night sky and low, ugly houses silhouetted in the night. This place was not lush and green. I would not be renting an adorable cottage. It is not, it seemed, a place where one could get a decent pizza or a plate of spaetzle. Martín stretched, yawned, and hopped off the bus. Here we are, he said. Welcome to Saipina. Then he disappeared into the night.

CHAPTER 1

WESTERN HIGHLANDS VERSUS EASTERN LOWLANDS

Cambas and Collas

LIKE MANY people from Saipina, Rogelio migrated from Saipina to the eastern Bolivian lowlands as a young man. First he traveled to the large urban area surrounding the city of Santa Cruz; subsequently, he relocated to Mineros, a city located just an hour north of Santa Cruz and in an area with a rich industrial economy. The population of Mineros exploded over the latter decades of the 20th century due to economic opportunities, with the growth driven primarily by immigration from the western highlands of Bolivia. When I met him in Saipina, Rogelio told me the following joke:

> Two collas are standing on the banks of the river Piraí (a famous river that runs through the city of Santa Cruz). They are told that in order to become cambas they must swim to the other side of the river. The first colla jumps in and swims across. When he reaches the other bank, he becomes a camba. The second colla jumps in. When he nears the other bank, the first guy is waiting for him. Kicking and swearing, he prevents the second guy from getting out of the water, yelling, "Damn you, colla, go back where you came from!"

This joke encapsulates much about the rivalry between collas and cambas in Bolivia. The country is often understood to be organized around a tension between collas, Quechua- or Aymara-speaking highlanders from western

Bolivia, and cambas, monolingual Spanish-speaking lowlanders from eastern Bolivia (see, e.g., Bergholdt 1999; Fabricant and Postero 2013; Hasbún 2003; Hurtado 2005; Postero 2007; Stearman 1987). Collas come from the western highlands, particularly the departments of La Paz, Potosí, Oruro, Chuquisaca, and Cochabamba, while cambas come from the lowland departments, particularly Santa Cruz, but also the sparsely populated northern provinces of Beni and Pando. Tarija, in the south, is often grouped with the lowland departments, though others claim the region stands outside the highland/lowland dichotomy (Humphreys et al., 2010). Because the lowland regions lie along a semicircle east of the Andes, this region is referred to as the *medialuna* (half-moon or crescent shape), embracing the western highlands (Assies 2006; Fabricant 2009; Gustafson 2006, 2010; Molina 2008).

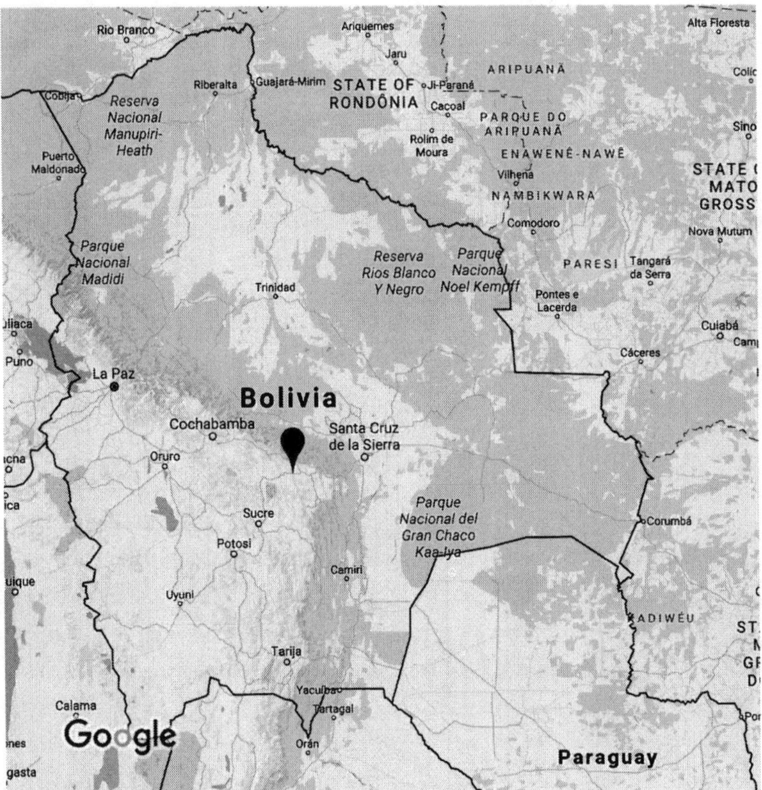

FIGURE 1. A map of Bolivia showing Saipina's location at the border of eastern and western, highland and lowland Bolivia (Google maps).

FIGURE 2. A map of the medialuna, or crescent moon, shape of the lowland departments of Bolivia. *Source*: https://commons.wikimedia.org/w/index.php?curid=4795537.

The town of Saipina stands almost exactly halfway between the western highland city of Cochabamba and the eastern lowland city of Santa Cruz. Each city is the capital of the department of the same name, and the town is located on the border of the Cochabamba and Santa Cruz departments (a department is the equivalent of a U.S. state or a Canadian province). The river Mizque—the name means "sweet" in Quechua—marks the border between the two departments. In the town of Saipina, people who are born on one side of the river come from Cochabamba, while people born on the other side of the river come from Santa Cruz. Until about fifty years ago, the town was located on the Cochabamba side of the river in an area known as Saipina Alta (High Saipina). Then the river shifted, and people began to settle on the other bank, which fell in Santa Cruz. Saipineños—people from Saipina—often said that they were "ni camba ni colla" (neither camba nor colla).

Camba identity was most firmly entrenched in the city of Santa Cruz, where Nación Camba (Camba Nation) bumper stickers were ubiquitous during my fieldwork. However, much of lowland Bolivia underwent massive immigration from the western highlands over the latter decades of the 20th century. In the fertile tropical valleys of the Chapare, which lies between Santa Cruz and Cochabamba, lowland indigenous groups were entirely replaced by highlanders who worked in coca production and processing. Likewise, in northern Bolivia, highland "colonists" settled the fragile Amazonian lowlands and cleared them for farming (Fabricant 2012; Fabricant and Gustafson 2011; Fabricant and Postero 2013).

This migration pattern meant that a large proportion of the population of the lowlands had highland roots and histories of migration. Echoing Rogelio's joke, a taxi driver in Santa Cruz told me that he had been accused of being racist because he was a native-born camba. "We're not the racist ones," he told me. "It's those people who come from elsewhere, these children of highlanders, our plurinational brothers.[2] I think you must have some kind of resentment in order to feel that way." This comment echoed the perception that highlanders who moved to Santa Cruz rapidly adapted to the lowland positioning. When I asked a young woman from Saipina whether people changed the way they talked after moving to the city, she joked, "Some of them are in the city for a week, and they sound more like cambas than the people who are from there!"

These comments also highlighted the tensions between East and West, lowland and highland, camba and colla. Highland migrants were resented in lowland Santa Cruz, and the political struggle between highland elites and President Evo Morales's Movimiento al Socialismo (Movement for Socialism, known by the acronym MAS) in the 2000s exacerbated and took advantage of these divisions (Chumacero et al. 2010; Eaton 2011; Gustafson 2009b; Regalsky and Quisbert 2008; Tapia 2009; Tockman and Cameron 2014). Verbal barbs and insults morphed into violence in the streets and gang-like "social clubs" in Santa Cruz, particularly around 2008 (Fabricant 2009; Gustafson 2006; see also chapter 5). These groups took positions that were often explicitly racist; one image I found online showed young men in a jeep sporting the Nación Camba symbols alongside a Nazi swastika. Racist commentaries were also expressed in more subtle economic and social terms. A contact in the city complained to me

2. The phrase "nuestros hermanos plurinacionales" refers to Bolivian president Evo Morales's "plurinational" state, which has been closely associated with the interests of highland indigenous groups. The speaker uses this phrase ironically.

that Santa Cruz was a "productive" department and that its wealth supported the poverty-stricken highland departments. This image of a wealthy, developed Santa Cruz keeping the rest of the country afloat was often repeated in comments that I heard in the city.[3]

These images made Bolivia seem polarized, East pitted against West, highland against lowland. Indeed, the East/West tensions were consistently present over the years of my fieldwork, structuring the social and political scene of the country into a clear binary opposition that was not only explicitly named but also reproduced through many forms of practice. Yet at the same time, the East/West, lowland/highland dichotomy also illustrated the mobility and dynamism of the social scene in the country. Many, perhaps even most, residents of the eastern lowlands were themselves highland migrants or the children or grandchildren of migrants (Fabricant 2009; Fabricant and Postero 2013; Stearman 1987). In-between areas like Saipina and peripheral zones like the southern province of Tarija fell somewhere between the extremes of East and West. Mobility, migration, economic ties, and shifts in political positioning all complicated the camba/colla divide without making it any less pervasive or any less central to the way that social and linguistic categories were organized through the semiotic field. Indeed, the contrast between cambas and collas was in many ways a central axis that organized other kinds of social practice—from language use, to styles of dress, to migration patterns—that were encapsulated in the labels "camba" and "colla." Thus, calling someone a colla not only was a statement about their regional origins but also entailed a comment on their ethnic orientation, their language practices, their political affiliation, and even their modes of interaction.

BIG PICTURE: HISTORY AND GEOGRAPHY

The Andes mountain range stretches along the length of western South America through the modern-day countries of Chile, Bolivia, Peru, and Ecuador and parts of Argentina, Colombia, and Venezuela. All of these countries have different geographical characteristics—one notable difference between Bolivia and the other Andean nations is its lack of coastline—but they all share some part

3. See, for example, "Santa Cruz el motor económico de Bolivia y la proyección de las autoridades," EABolivia.com, accessed May 2, 2017, http://www.eabolivia.com/bolivia/9327-santa-cruz-el-motor-economico-de-bolivia-y-la-proyeccion-de-las-autoridades.html..

of the Andes mountain chain. For political, historical, and economic reasons, Bolivia, Peru, and Ecuador are often thought of as the core Andean nations (Archibald 2011; Coronel-Molina and Grabner-Coronel 2005). Unlike Peru and Ecuador, where coastal cities like Lima and Guayaquil are important economic and cultural centers, Bolivia's wealth and political power have historically been concentrated in the highlands. The dominance of highland Bolivia is so strong that people often seem to forget that more than half the country is lowlands, much of it part of the Amazon basin. The lowlands were thinly populated, and until the end of the 20th century, they held little political power. However, beginning in the 1980s, the lowland regions and in particular the city of Santa Cruz grew in influence due to industry, gas and oil deposits, and large-scale agricultural production (see, e.g., Stearman 1987).

This highland/lowland cultural divide has a long history (a good general overview of Bolivian history is Klein 2003). The Inca Empire, the most powerful and extensive precolonial empire in South America, expanded in all directions from its center near Cuzco in modern-day southern Peru. Incan trade networks reached from the Pacific coast to the Andean highlands to the Amazonian lowlands (Browman 1978; Lathrap 1973). However, while the Inca Empire reached far beyond today's national boundaries, it came to an abrupt halt at the transition to the lowlands (Covey 2006; Kuznar 1999).

Despite the long-standing highland/lowland divide, there have always been communication, trade, and personal ties between highland and lowland groups (Murra 1985). Goods and food have been traded between highlands and lowlands for as long as the archaeological record can account for. Indeed, the highlands and lowlands depend on each other, though the ways in which they interface have changed with changing political realities (Rivera 2015).

Even today, people regularly engage in cyclical migration from the valleys to the highlands and back in order to engage in agriculture and pastoral pursuits. It is not at all unusual for valley dwellers to own agricultural fields or ranch land (*estancias*) high in the mountains. Farmers from Saipina trade for potato seed in highland markets, maintaining relationships with particular seed traders that can go back decades, even generations. When they are ready to sell, they look mainly to Santa Cruz, where prices have tended to be higher than in the highlands in recent years. Families who travel regularly to the lowland capital for economic reasons often maintain a house there, which they use on trips to the city. Conversely, Saipina depends on the western highlands for agricultural labor. In the dry season, highland farmers whose land depends on rainfall travel to Saipina to work as day laborers (*peones*) and sharecroppers (*partidarios*). Over the years, many of these western migrants have settled in Saipina, established families, and bought land.

LOCAL HISTORICAL ACCOUNTS

Local versions of the area's history emphasize cultural encounters, ethnic blending, and the position of Saipina in the middle of the highland/lowland divide. A book produced by local historian Leocadio Rojas (1998) begins with two paragraphs about the precolonial history of the area. Rojas describes encounters between the local Chané, a group characterized by a mixture of highland and lowland influences; the "bellicose" Guaraní from the east, who took the lowland areas of the valleys; and the Quechua-speaking Inca from the West, who held the highland *pukara* (forts). The rest of the first chapter describes the colonial history of the area, quoting from colonial documents that characterize the region as fertile and pleasant for human habitation. Under the subhead "Ethnographic Data," Rojas includes the following information:

> During the time of the colony, Spanish and Creoles were "graced with concessions of lands 'in the Valle Grande' by bequests and in return for services to the Crown" [Sanabria Fernandez 1965:7]. . . . These were added, therefore, to the population of the valleys. On the other hand, the Quechua settlers were quickly subdued and annexed to the colonies, although not so the Guaraní, who contested inch by inch the possession of the land. Only around the end of the 17th century did some factions begin to coexist with the whites. And as the Spanish had few women, they took indigenous wives, resulting in a Hispano-Quechua mestizaje and another that was Hispano-Guaraní. In time, these would mix with each other to produce a unique physiognomy. Blacks and mulattos who arrived as slaves or during the war of independence also had a part in this mestizaje. (1998:23, my translation)

At first glance, this passage reads like a textbook account of *mestizaje* in Latin America (de la Cadena 2000), emphasizing the mixture of the ethnic European groups (Spanish and Creoles, people of European descent born in the Americas) with highland and lowland indigenous groups (here identified as Quechua and Guaraní). However, the author contrasts "Hispano-Quechua" mestizaje with "Hispano-Guaraní" mestizaje, constructing not just Guaraní and Quechua indigenous groups but highland and lowland mestizos as separate populations from the very early colonial period. These different mestizo populations then mixed "to produce a unique physiognomy": the ethnic mixture that now characterizes the "in-between" people of the Santa Cruz valleys. This passage describes an internally differentiated mestizo population that reflects ideologies regarding highland and lowland indigenous peoples. While the Guaraní are characterized as savage and indomitable, the Quechua are portrayed as more civilized but also easily "subdued" in this passage, setting up additional dimensions of contrast between highland and lowland peoples.

Through passages like this one, binaries of West and East, highland and lowland, Quechua and Guaraní, civilized and savage are aligned. These binaries are treated not as individual oppositions but as clusters of ideas that contrast across different categories—lowland Guaraní people are aligned with resistance to European expansion and opposed to Quechua groups, which in turn are characterized as less savage and more easily subdued. The semiotic field is composed of multiple clusters of ideas with an internal alignment (lowland, eastern, Guaraní, savage versus highland, western, Quechua, civilized) that stand in opposition to each other. It is important to note here that the central axis of differentiation is not European versus indigenous but highland mestizo versus lowland mestizo, two populations that later "coalesced" to form a unique valley identity. The act of characterizing the valley identity as between two poles has the effect of reifying the poles themselves.

An official analysis of the socioeconomic status of the municipality produced by the municipal government in 2004 also placed racial mixture and in particular the highland/lowland divide at the center of local identity:

> The municipality of Saipina . . . consists of a population that is largely immigrant, that is, that comes from different communities from neighboring departments (Cochabamba, Chuquisaca, Potosí, etc.), due to its agricultural potential.
>
> This pattern has existed since the foundation of Saipina, which has generated a population with distinctive characteristics that extends over the Santa Cruz valleys. Therefore, the population that resides in the municipality of Saipina corresponds to the mixture of three migrations: eastern, western, and foreign (Spanish and Arab).
>
> The population of the municipality of Saipina is a conglomerate or mixture of the races that come from the East (Yuracarés) and the West (Incas). After the conquest and especially after the foundation [of the town] (in 1616), Spaniards inserted themselves along with the Arabs, which resulted in a population that is

> integrated among the three races (eastern, western, and from the Old World). Nevertheless, the current population has more pronounced characteristics that are closer to the western population, at least where it concerns language, since more than 1,400 people speak or have as their first language Quechua, a fact that demonstrates the influence or the migration of the population that speaks the languages of the West. (FORTEMU 2004:2–3, my translation)

As in the historical account quoted above, Saipina is framed as a place in which highland and lowland indigenous groups meet European settlers. These are referred to as "three races": eastern indigenous people, western indigenous people, and foreign colonists from the "Old World." Arabs and people of African descent play a less prominent part in this mixture. Immediately following this passage, the racial mixture of the distant past is layered with a description of current migration from the western provinces (identified as Potosí, Chuquisaca, and Cochabamba) by Quechua speakers. Indeed, in the last sentence, the category "Quechua speaker" is presented as an equivalent for "immigrants from the West."

Though they did not explicitly reference the terms *camba* and *colla*, these sources followed local practices that frame the distinction between eastern and western, lowland and highland Bolivians as ethnic categories. These historical accounts contrast the lowland groups characterized as Yuracaré and Guaraní to the highland Inca or Quechua. They characterize modern Quechua-speaking migrants from the western highlands as part of a continuous pattern of settlement and cultural contact that goes back to precolonial times. Through this juxtaposition, historical contact between highland and lowland indigenous groups is laminated onto modern-day immigration processes. Saipina's positioning as a borderland where highland meets lowland is linked to a history of contact that reaches into prehistorical times.

In these sources, eastern and western indigenous people are placed in contrast to each other, with the central opposition described as a contrast between highland and lowland indigenous groups. After colonial contact with foreign colonists, highland and lowland are "integrated" into the in-between valley identity. These contrasts contribute to the construction of a semiotic field in which the contrast between highland and lowland is historicized, ethnicized, and connected to larger narratives of race, migration, and colonization in Latin America. The semiotic field as interpreted through these sources centers first and foremost on a highland/lowland distinction that contrasts two clusters of ideas: western, highland, Quechua, Inca versus eastern, lowland, Yuracaré, Guaraní. It also includes commentary on the social characteristics of these groups, past and present.

LAZY CAMBAS AND DUMB COLLAS: STEREOTYPES OF HIGHLANDERS AND LOWLANDERS

"¡Camba flojo!" (Lazy camba!)
"¡Colla burro!" (Colla donkey!)

People often quoted the above exchange of insults to me when I asked about the difference between cambas and collas. This exchange exemplified both the animosity between cambas and collas and their most salient stereotypical qualities. Cambas were said to be nice people but lazy and unreliable. Collas, on the other hand, were hardworking but stubborn and rather dumb—qualities that people associated with burros, the small donkeys that were used to transport goods in rural areas before the network of roads became widespread.

When I spoke with Marina, a local politician and a friend, she characterized cambas as lazy and carefree, in contrast to hardworking collas who desired to accumulate wealth.

Transcript 1: M (Marina), A (Anna)

1. M: Porque los cambas tienen cabalito para el día, tienen que tener.	1. M: Because the cambas have exactly what they need for that day, that's what they need.
2. A: Mhm.	2. A: Mm-hmm.
3. M: Mientras los collas en cambio, es, pues, a ellos les gusta trabajar, y ahorrarse y tener algo pues, no ve? Trabajar, pues. Y los cambas—en cuanto no tengan *nada*. Están siguen felices.	3. M: But collas, on the other hand, it's, well, they like to work and save and have something, right? To work. And the cambas, even when they don't have *anything*, they're still happy.

	Spanish	English
4.	A: Cuando estabamos por alla, nos decíannn, tal vez no acabamos nuestros platos, nos decían, "Acabátelo, porque tal vez mañana no va a haber," nos decían.	A: When we were there, they told usss, maybe we didn't finish our plates, they said, "Finish it up, because tomorrow there might not be any," they said.
5.	M: ¿Ves? Y los collas no tienen esa mentalidad ellos. Trabajan y quieren tener, y. Porque en, hasta en la ciudad de Santa Cruz se ve, ¿los que son grandes comerciantes y todo?	M: You see? And collas don't have that mentality. They work and they want to have something, and. Because in, even in the city of Santa Cruz, you see, the people who are big businessmen and everything?
6.	A: Hm.	A: Mm-hmm.
7.	M: ¡Son de allá! Son los collas.	M: They're from over there! They're collas.
8.	A: Hm.	A: Mm-hmm.
9.	M: No son los cambas.	M: They're not cambas.

Marina's comments emphasized the role of collas as businessmen, even in the modern economic context of lowland Santa Cruz. As she expressed, people saw cambas as living only for the day, while collas "work and want to have something." Later in the interview, she told me that virtually everyone in Saipina came from the West and had western roots. While many people expressed hostility toward collas, Marina, who proudly recounted her own western highland roots, saw their hardworking qualities in a positive light.

People naturalized these stereotypes through links to history, geography, and climate. I was told that in the tropical lowlands, food literally grew on trees; traditional lowland cultures relied on hunting and gathering for subsistence, and many modern settlements did essentially the same. Excesses of food were difficult to preserve because of the hot, moist climate. In the highlands, on the other hand, many areas produced only one crop a year during the short growing season. Food had to be processed and preserved for survival. Rather than hunting, many highlanders relied on herding and breeding animals for their basic needs.

Political materials that were distributed during the 2008 autonomy debate also drew on these naturalized distinctions. One proautonomy (i.e., prolowland) flyer that I obtained described precolonial highland cultures as hierarchical and autocratic, while lowland groups were characterized as egalitarian and peaceful. The flier criticized Bolivian president Evo Morales for his *centralista* (centralist) government. The implication was that the peaceful, egalitarian lowlanders were ill served by the autocratic central government based on the social principles of highland indigenous groups.

Morales and the MAS political party aligned themselves strongly with highland indigenous culture. Morales was not only the president of Bolivia but also the leader of the transnational Aymara nation, and he appeared each winter solstice in a highly publicized ceremony at the pre-Incan site of Tiwanaku, welcoming the return of the sun. Political leaders of highland origins often quoted the "Ama qhella / Ama llulla / Ama sua" moral code of the Inca, a Quechua phrase that exhorts people not to lie, steal, or be lazy.

The links between lowland indigenous groups and modern-day residents of the lowlands, regardless of their descent, were also explicitly embraced in the construction of a camba identity. In Santa Cruz, the restaurant La Casa del Camba (The house of the camba) promoted itself as the quintessential Santa Cruz experience. Waiters served food dressed in white button-down shirts and straw hats, and bands played music in lowland styles under a roof of palm fronds. When the restaurant expanded to the fast-food market, it excerpted a lowland indigenous identity in its branding materials. A kid's meal that I

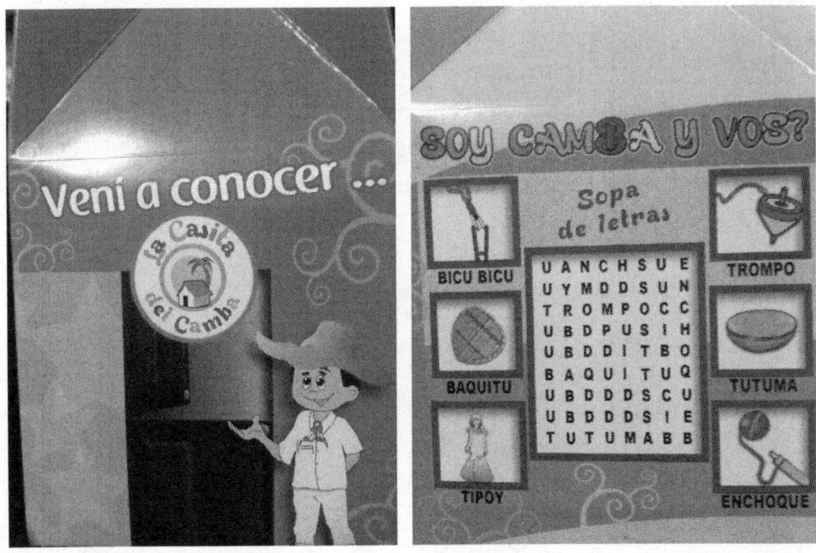

FIGURE 3. Kid's meal box from the restaurant La Casa del Camba in Santa Cruz, Bolivia. The image shows a "camba" dressed in lowland indigenous style in the Santa Cruz department's colors of white and green and wearing a straw hat. The word-search game features Guaraní and Chiquitano loanwords.

bought for my daughter featured the words ¿Soy camba y vos? (I'm a camba, and you?) along with a cartoon figure wearing a straw hat, button-down shirt, white pants, and green-checkered necktie.[4] A word-search game for children featured artifacts linked to a lowland indigenous identity along with Hispanicized versions of the loanwords—*bicu-bicu*, a kind of slingshot; *baquitu*, a woven fan; the *tipoi*, a long, loose dress worn by women; and *tutuma*, a dried gourd used for serving liquids. Politicians also embraced these symbols, appearing in white button-down shirts and using the green-and-white colors of the Santa Cruz flag as their election colors.[5]

Through the use of these symbols, modern-day cambas and collas were constructed as part of the historically continuous tradition of opposition between highlanders and lowlanders. The personal qualities associated with these groups—easygoing but lazy versus hardworking but stubborn and unpleasant—were associated with naturalized links to geography, climate, and food production that were used to justify and explain the differences between the two groups. The personality characteristics that I describe in this section were linked to the racial, ethnic, and linguistic binaries of highland and lowland, West and East, colla and camba. The links were drawn in multiple ways and through multiple modalities—from the visual elements of the design of the kid's meal referenced above, to political acts like Morales's performance at the Puerta del Sol (Tiwanaku) on the Aymara New Year, to discussions like Marina's in which she explained differences between cambas and collas. All of these sources point to a coherent picture organized around two binary oppositions: being a camba stands as a metonym for being from the eastern lowlands, having lowland indigenous roots, and being irresponsible and lazy, while being a colla means being from the western highlands, having highland indigenous roots, and being hardworking but mean.

RESENTMENT TOWARD COLLAS

Not all Saipineños were as well disposed toward collas as Marina was in her open-minded statement, transcribed above. The negative animus toward collas

4. The second-person singular pronoun *vos* has a complicated valence in Bolivia. While it is often used as an icon of Quechua-influenced speech, the use of the pronoun with *s* aspiration and *voseo* verb forms, as in the phrase *vení a conocer* below, acts as an index of lowland identity.
5. See Gustafson (2006) for an incisive analysis of Santa Cruz identity symbolism.

was dramatically illustrated in 2015 when a local taxi driver was stabbed in the back by a teenaged couple who wanted to steal his car. Rumors and gossip flew in Saipina. People said that this kind of crime was unprecedented in Saipina, although it was all too common in urban Santa Cruz. Details emerged slowly. The young people had a tiny baby. They came from a town a few kilometers to the west, on the Cochabamba side of the river. They had lived in Saipina and then disappeared for a time. They were working with a gang led by another young man who already had a criminal record.

For many people, the young couple's western origins were sufficient to explain their antisocial behavior. "They worked with Doña Carla," Reynalda told me, naming a prominent merchant in town. "I don't know who they were. She works with all kinds of collas." She looked at me sharply. "People one doesn't know." Later in the day, her son Iván commented, "The town has grown so much. There are big new neighborhoods, and all sorts of people live there." He paused. "Mostly collas," he added with a knowing smile.

The violent nature of the crime may have prompted an especially strong response. Many of the people I knew in Saipina had been born on the other side of the river, even in the small town where the young couple was from, and they were generally accepted as locals and as Saipineños. The young couple's violent act placed them beyond the pale, however, and despite the fact that they came from only a few kilometers away and had lived in Saipina, they were consistently described as collas and outsiders. Status as a colla was tied not only to place of residence but also to moral character.

Not all incidents were as dramatic and sensational as the stabbing of the taxi driver, but the complaints I heard during that episode were not isolated. Complaining about her new neighbor, who bickered over the property line and let her aggressive dogs roam around the neighborhood, Doña Juana told me, "It's that she's a colla." "There are all kinds of collas," protested her son. "Good people and bad people, just like us." Doña Juana nodded reluctantly. But whether or not she agreed at an abstract level, she and others whom I spoke with consistently characterized collas as antisocial, untrustworthy, and downright mean.

Sometimes it seemed that whenever something bad happened, it was the collas who were at fault. The words "Colla es, pues" (It's that s/he's a colla) explained all kinds of ills, from shopkeepers who overcharged their clients, to inconsiderate neighbors, to violent crime. People told me that I was lucky that my mother-in-law wasn't a colla, because a colla mother-in-law would be critical, mean, and even violent toward a daughter-in-law.

In contrast, attitudes about cambas were less virulently negative. A crew of road workers was brought in from Santa Cruz to complete a project, and people laughed when they told about how lazy they were. "They'd do better to hire people from around here," I was told. "They'll never get it done otherwise." But these cambas were transient and did not settle in town. Given the overwhelming west-to-east migration pattern, the new neighbors that people in Saipina had to live with were mostly collas.

The strongest negative comments that I heard aimed at cambas portrayed them as arrogant. "The cambas are more shameless than the collas," Marina told me. "They don't care, whatever they do, whatever they say, they're the cambas, and that's all there is to it. While the collas are more reserved, and they don't say the things that other people say."

NEITHER COLLA NOR CAMBA: LOCAL POSITIONING BETWEEN THE BINARY

Given their positioning on the border of Santa Cruz and Cochabamba, people from Saipina had experience with outsiders who were clearly identifiable as cambas and collas. However, when it came to characterizing themselves, they were quick to point out that they fell somewhere between the two. When I asked her how people from Saipina talked, Blanca answered, "Ni cambas ni collas nosotros hablamos" (We speak not-camba-not-colla). Likewise, Patricia told me that people from Saipina were characterized by "una mezcla entre camba y colla" (a mix between camba and colla). However, Patricia added that most of the people in Saipina were from the other side of the border, in Cochabamba. "I was born there," she told me. She told me that the people who came from Sucre and the Chuquisaca area were viewed more negatively than those from Cochabamba, adding that people from the former region were called *kharapanzas*, a Quechua/Spanish hybrid insult meaning "naked belly." Blanca also told me that "there are more people who are collas than those from Saipina in town these days. They come from Omereque and Mizque [towns to the west], from all around there."

The question of how far the colla/camba boundaries extended and who was included in each category was subject to negotiation. While people who had lived for a generation or more in Saipina framed immigrants from the West as outsiders, this was not necessarily how recent immigrants saw themselves.

Glover, a young man whom I interviewed as he was finishing a university degree, had moved to Saipina as a ten-year-old. Though he came from a Quechua-dominant family, he quickly shifted to Spanish after the move. When I asked him whether he considered himself a Saipineño, a native of Saipina, he answered strongly in the affirmative.

In 2008 I spoke to Don Gilberto, an older man who was originally from Cochabamba but had lived in Saipina for more than forty years. Don Gilberto was proud of his Quechua-language abilities. He was one of the few bilinguals who would regularly greet me in Quechua and converse with me in Quechua just for fun. When he spoke to me, he discussed the cambas he had met during his military service in Santa Cruz, contrasting them with collas.

Transcript 2: G (Gilberto), A (Anna)

1.	G: Pero era puro cambas digamos, castellanistos. Castellano *cerrados* eran.	1.	G: But it was all cambas, that is, Spanish speakers. *Closed* [monolingual] Spanish speakers.
2.	A: Ah ha ah ha.	2.	A: Uh-huh, uh-huh.
3.	G: Tampoco no hablaban. Eso nomás también hablan. No entienden otra cosa. Así que, no son como esos originales del altiplano, esos hablan de los tres, Aymara, Quechua, y castellano hablan.	3.	G: They didn't speak either. That's all they speak. They don't understand anything else. So they're not like these natives of the altiplano, those ones speak all three, Aymara, Quechua, and Spanish.
4.	A: Ah, los tres.	4.	A: Oh, all three.
5.	G: Esos Mamanis Tatanis Hayt'anis Sajmanis son.	5.	G: They're those Mamanis Tatanis Hayt'anis Sajmanis.
6.	A: [laughs]	6.	A: [laughs]

Don Gilberto linked cambas with monolingualism, using the negatively loaded term *cerrado* 'closed', a term much more often applied to monolingual Quechua speakers by Spanish speakers. In contrast, he linked multilingualism with the western highlands and with indigenousness, referring to highlanders as "natives of the altiplano."[6] Don Gilberto, a native of the Cochabamba valleys, placed himself outside both groups, using the pronoun "they" to describe both

6. The altiplano is a geographical formation in western Bolivia, a high plain between the eastern and western Andean cordilleras. It is well known for its harsh climate and living conditions, as well as its vibrant indigenous culture.

cambas and collas. Finally, he made a little joke, using the stereotypical altiplano surname Mamani, then continuing with Tatanis Hayt'anis Sajmanis. "Hayt'ani saqmani" means "I kick, I punch" and provides an indexical link to the stereotype of highland people as violent and aggressive.[7] Gilberto marked this linguistically with the use of a loud ejective on Hayt'ani.

Don Gilberto, while apparently criticizing cambas for being culturally incompetent monolingual Spanish speakers, also added a subtext that linked Quechua contact features to indigeneity and to violence. In doing so, he implicitly positioned himself somewhere between these two undesirable extremes. According to many people in Saipina, as a Quechua-Spanish bilingual from the Cochabamba valleys, he fell unambiguously within the colla category. However, he presented "natives of the altiplano" as being *more* colla than he himself was, placing himself in an in-between position much as other Saipineños did by emphasizing their distinctness from collas from the West and cambas from the East. While these comments shifted the exact social and geographic boundaries of the terms *camba* and *colla* and in some cases the positive/negative valence attached to the characteristics of the two groups, the terms themselves and their associations within the semiotic field remained consistent.

The negotiation of identity categories through migration history, language use, and a sense of in-betweenness blurred the clear lines between cambas and collas that were drawn in the larger national discourses. "When we go to Cochabamba, people say we're cambas. When we go to Santa Cruz, they say we're collas. You see, we live right here on the border," Ana María, a high school student, told me. This comment was repeated by several other interviewees.

LANGUAGE: EMPHASIZING *PUES* AND MAKING THE *S* WHISTLE

One of the principal ways in which people established their positioning as neither camba nor colla was through linguistic markers. When I asked her about the local dialect, Blanca said, "We don't emphasize *pues*, nor do we make the *s* whistle." These two features were among the most salient markers of regional identity for people in Saipina. Lowlanders, I was told, "eat their *s*'s," a reference

7. This may be a bit of a cliché; there is a line from a colonial manuscript dedicated to the Virgin of Copacabana that goes "Hayt'ani, saqmani, hinari . . ." (I kick, I punch, thus . . .).

to the elision or weakening of syllable-final *s*. This dialect feature is common to much of lowland South America and indeed has been extensively studied by linguists (Brown and Cacoullos 2003; File-Muriel and Brown 2011; Poplack 1980). In contrast, people said that highlanders "make the *s* whistle." Pronouncing all one's *s*'s made a person sound like a highlander; they added that I sounded a bit like a colla because of my habit of pronouncing the *s* at the ends of words (Babel 2014a).

The pronunciation of *s* was particularly connected to the discourse marker *pues*. Pues was used in both highlands and lowlands, but lowlanders used a sentence-final version, often with a drawn-out diphthong and rising prosody. Maribel told me, "The only thing that I got [linguistically] from the time I spent in Santa Cruz is *pueh*. You know, if someone says something that I don't believe, instead of calling them out I just say *pu-e-e-e-h*." In contrast, Juana told me that highlanders spoke "medio ps-ps" (kind of ps-ps). Maintaining the *s* and deleting the vowels in *pues* was seen as a prototypical highland feature.

These features were so prominent that one summer, when I asked people to listen to recorded words and describe the person who spoke, people who perceived the speaker as a highlander reported hearing *s* even when there were no *s*'s in the recording. To be a highlander was to speak with *s*; to be a lowlander was to speak with *pu-e-e-e-h*.

In characterizing local speech, people often mentioned the use of Quechua loanwords. "We speak mixed," people told me. Several people gave me the example of "Andá khará la khucha" (Go feed the sow), a prototypical mixed phrase.

TABLE 1

SENTENCE:	ANDÁ	KHARÁ	LA	KHUCHA
Gloss:	Go	feed	the	sow
Language:	Spanish	Quechua + Spanish	Spanish	Quechua + Spanish
Root:	*andar* 'to walk'	*qaray* 'to feed'	*la* 'the'	*khuchi* 'sow'
Inflection:	*á* second-person singular	*á vos* second-person singular	feminine definite article	*-a* feminine

(adapted from Babel 2011)

This sentence was not just a fossilized expression; people used both the verb *kharar* 'to feed' and the noun *khuchi* 'pig' independently. Though I heard these words unselfconsciously in natural speech, it was also a phrase that people frequently called on to describe the complex mixture of Spanish and Quechua in the area. The first word, *andá*, was Spanish, but consultants identified the *vos* conjugation, *andá*, as Quechua influence.[8] The verb *kharar*, with an aspirated k^h, comes from Quechua *qaray*. However, the Quechua verbal ending *-y* is removed, and the verb root is conjugated as a Spanish verb (in imperative *vos* form). Finally, the noun *khucha* (with Spanish feminine definite article *la*) is an example of double borrowing: the colonial Spanish *cochino* was borrowed into Quechua as *khuchi*, then reinserted into Spanish as *khuchi*. This word can be modified for grammatical gender to designate a sow, *khuch-a*. In Quechua, the unmarked sex for domestic animals is female (i.e., you would be more likely to say "a male pig" than to have to specify that the pig is female), but most Spanish speakers understand *khuchi* to fit the Spanish markedness system, in which the unmarked form is male (therefore, *khuchi* needs to be modified in order to specify that the pig is, in fact, a sow).

As examples of mixed language go, this is a beautiful one. People used it not only to demonstrate the extent to which their language was mixed but also to index an identity that was midway between the bilingual highlands and the monolingual lowlands. People from Saipina were Spanish speakers, but they used Quechua loanwords. Indeed, people described speaking Quechua as being a mark of an outsider. "The people from here, who are *really* from here, they don't speak Quechua at all," Mónica told me.

Through these discourses, the use of Spanish and Quechua was presented as another binary that was integrated with the camba/colla dichotomy within the semiotic field. While collas were fluent Quechua speakers and cambas were monolingual Spanish speakers, people from Saipina positioned themselves as between these two poles by their use of Spanish mixed with Quechua. Phonetic markers of camba Spanish, such as aspiration of the sentence-final *s* in *vos* 'you', singular, and the discourse marker *pueh* indexed the entire cluster of markers surrounding camba identity. "Making the *s* whistle," on the other hand, was a marker of colla identity. These subtle linguistic features were linked to individual language practices (Spanish, Quechua, and language mixing) and to large-scale

8. In Bolivia, as in most of Latin America, the use of *vos* indicates extreme familiarity and/or contempt. I'm not sure why people think this is Quechua related, although in parts of Latin America (e.g., Guatemala) the *vos* person form was used as recently as the 1980s as an insulting form of address for indigenous people. Confusingly, it can also be used (with final *s* aspiration) as a sign of lowland identity.

distinctions between West and East, highland and lowland, colla and camba. The act of speaking Spanish mixed with Quechua positioned people from the valleys in the center of a binary opposition that aligned with colla/camba categories.

BETWEEN HIGHLAND AND LOWLAND: THE VALLES CRUCEÑOS

When Saipineños characterized themselves as "in between," they drew not only on their own positioning on the border of Cochabamba and Santa Cruz but on a broader regional identity—as residents of a group of towns that were jointly characterized as the *valles cruceños*, the Santa Cruz valleys. The central town representing valley identity in this area was Vallegrande, which had been an important colonial settlement and remained a cultural icon and administrative center throughout the region. Although it was located about a forty-five-minute drive off the main highway, a solid three- to four-hour trip from Saipina, people from Saipina and the other towns in the valles cruceños often traveled to Vallegrande for business reasons, local government meetings, access to slightly better medical care, technical-level education, and *tramites*, or "paperwork." Vallegrande was also part of the international tourist trail through Bolivia, particularly for Argentine backpackers, due to the fact that Che Guevara was killed in one of the smaller towns in the municipality and buried under the small military airfield in Vallegrande.

Vallegrande was known for its corn, pork, and dairy products and for its seasonal fruits, such as plums and apples. However, it did not have reliable irrigation, and the scale of production was relatively small. Many Vallegrandinos—people from Vallegrande—immigrated to the city of Santa Cruz to make a living. After decades of out-migration, there were many times more Vallegrandinos living in Santa Cruz than in the town of Vallegrande. Given that it was relatively close to the city—three or four hours by car—people often traveled back and forth to visit relatives and for important festivals.

The massive Vallegrandino presence in Santa Cruz led to an economy of nostalgia for the valleys in general and for Vallegrande in particular in the urban center. Cultural products such as music and music videos, windshield banners and bumper stickers, and social organizations such as neighborhood football teams, Carnaval fraternities, and cultural festivals enshrined and propagated the idea of a "valley" identity and presented images of a typical valley person, typical valley dress, typical valley music, typical valley food. These images were broadcast from the city back to the valleys, where residents of Vallegrande and the broader Santa Cruz valley region held to the *valluno* (valley) identity in contrast to the camba/colla dichotomy.

Vallegrande's importance to the Santa Cruz valley region was partially due to its *emisora* (radio station), the most powerful and best received in the Santa Cruz valleys. In Saipina I found that people of all walks of life listened to the radio constantly. It formed the background to farmers working in the fields, women cooking and washing clothes in the house, laborers and carpenters working on new construction, and people just hanging out or snacking in the plaza. At almost any time of day, I could walk from one end of Saipina to the other and back again without missing a word of the broadcast because it was playing in every single home on every single block.

The radio station played music, but it also broadcast the news, advertisements, notices, invitations, and public service announcements. In particular, it carried a series of radio skits and advertisements that were produced by a group from Vallegrande called Los Cumpas. The group took its name from the shortened version of *compadre*, the term for a ritual kin relationship between adults who share responsibility for each other's children through a parent/godparent relationship. While this is a serious relationship, not taken lightly, the radio commercials produced by Los Cumpas used this form of address as a sign of local culture in a parodic, humorous vein.[9] The group's best-known advertisement was for a commercial pesticide known by the English name Success. In the commercial, two *cumpas* are chatting about their crops. One cumpa tries to convince his interlocutor to switch to the Success brand, but his clueless friend misunderstands the confusing English word Success ([súk se] or [sú se]) as the woman's name Suzy ([sú si] or [sú se]). He indignantly threatens to reveal the relationship to his *comadre*, the first man's wife. The same skit also contains a rapturous description of tomatoes (or perhaps that Suzy woman?) that prominently features the Quechua loanword *llusk'ita* 'smooth'. The use of the terms *cumpa* and *comadre* as forms of address, the references to an agricultural lifestyle, the extended double entendre, and the use of Quechua loanwords all work together to produce the figure of an ignorant but slyly picaresque farmer of the Santa Cruz valleys (on personae, see Agha 2007a). The clueless cumpa may not know English, but he knows trouble when he sees (or hears) it.

9. See Los Cumpas, accessed December 3, 2017, http://loscumpasbolivia.blogspot.com/2008/06/los-cumpas.html.

There is no question what style of dress these cumpas might have adopted. In music videos and in other materials that circulated in the region, valley people were depicted as wearing a black fedora, black tire sandals called abarcas, button-down shirts, and dark pants or straight skirts for women. During my time as a volunteer, I adopted the local style of a black fedora and abarcas, which I found comfortable and practical in the dry desert heat and strong sun of Saipina. This choice of headgear and footwear was interpreted as an identity stance by people in Saipina; one morning, an older man commented to me that he liked the fact that I always wore the *sombrero valluno* (valley hat) and that I had the local pride of a real valley person. This comment or words to similar effect were repeated several times by other contacts and acquaintances. One university student I spoke with referred approvingly to a young man in her class who always wore the sombrero valluno, remarking that it showed that he took pride in his roots, unlike many of her other classmates. This style of dress was also associated with figures like the stereotypical cumpa of the radio advertisement.

This reliable yet distinctly humorous figure of the valluno cumpa gradually became solidified into a recognizable figure that was excerpted for many types of messages. In 2015 I picked up a flyer from the local credit union that urged members to open a savings account. The flyer was also reproduced as a large poster on the wall. On it, a cartoonish man wearing a black fedora, a white collared shirt, a braided leather lasso, and an *alforja* (a set of two hand-woven bags, one of which hangs over the chest and the other over the back) extended a friendly hand next to the printed words "Ahorre Cumpa la vida no es chiste" (Save, cumpa, life is no joke). Each of these details indexed a rural lifestyle typical of the Santa Cruz valleys: the tire sandals, the braided lasso for catching cattle, the woven bag thrown over the shoulders to hold a midday meal and perhaps some supplies. Through wide circulation, these signs solidified into the figure of the cumpa, iconic of a traditional, authentic valley identity.

People from Saipina told me that their style of speech was distinct from that of Vallegrande, and indeed the particular loanwords that I heard used in Saipina were often different from those that I heard in Vallegrande. Yet when they moved to the city, my consultants were assimilated to a larger identity associated with the Santa Cruz valleys. "People tell me, 'You're Vallegrandina, you're from the valleys somewhere,'" Diana told me in an interview. "I just say I'm from the valleys, because nobody really knows where Saipina is," another college student reported.

FIGURE 4. Flyer from the local credit union. The text reads, "Save, cumpa, life is no joke." The man's dress represents the Santa Cruz valley persona, with a black fedora, a white button-down shirt, a hand-woven alforja bag, a hand-braided lasso, and tire sandals.

The existence of Vallegrande as a recognizable nexus of culture for the Santa Cruz valleys gave a form and a shape—and a voice—to a "traditional" identity for the broader geographical region in which Saipina was located. The fact that many people in urban Santa Cruz were familiar with the image of the Vallegrandino as a figure distinct from camba or colla identity provided a public conceptual space for the in-between identity that Saipineños claimed.

CONCLUSION

The camba/colla divide is a powerful discourse in the Bolivian national context. Ultimately, however, it is important to remember that the highland/lowland divide is an ideological one, not the result of a natural geographical or historical fact. Nor is it totalizing—the highland/lowland dichotomy is pervasive in the region, but it blurs or erases the transitions, interrelations, and ambiguous zones that are neither clearly highland nor lowland. Politically, geographically, linguistically, and culturally, the Santa Cruz valleys are a "swing" region, an intermediate point between the highlands and lowlands.

People from Saipina saw themselves as treading a line between highland and lowland identity—neither colla nor camba. They used language as an index of the divide: while highlanders "made the *s* whistle," lowlanders "ate their *s*'s." People from Saipina used Quechua loanwords in their speech, but they were not Quechua speakers. Even the local concept of mestizaje included reference to highland and lowland groups; it referred not only to European and indigenous racial mixture but to a mixture of, and a contrast between, highland and lowland indigenous people. The distinction between highland and lowland also encompassed moral claims and the policing of polite society, insiders and outsiders, social and antisocial types of people.

The claim to an in-between identity is one that is easily contested or erased by dominant national discourses. Even in the act of questioning the camba/colla binary by claiming a unique identity associated with the Santa Cruz valleys, people framed their uniqueness in terms of the binary: neither eastern/highlander nor western/lowlander. People from Saipina were most comfortable identifying themselves as residents of the fertile agricultural valleys—a geographical feature that is quite literally between highland and lowland. This positioning did not in any way erase the camba/colla binary; rather, it was dependent on it in order to construct an in-between identity within the colla/camba poles of the broader semiotic field. Positioning oneself as "neither colla nor camba" acknowledged and reified the reality of this system of contrast.

The colla/camba opposition is only one of a coherent set of binary contrasts I continue to describe in the later chapters of this book. Colla and camba worked together as axes of distinction that provided a central framework for other types of oppositions, such as language, politics, and styles of dress. Together, the respective poles of these binaries clustered together into two opposing groups of ideas that organized the semiotic field, which in turn acted as a framework for the production of social meaning.

INTERLUDE

Living in Saipina

THE ROUTE that I traversed from the lowlands to the Andean intermontane valleys was a significant one. While in some sense the journey was continuous, crawling by kilometer after kilometer, hour after hour, it was also one that I quickly learned to divide into stretches of travel between towns: here is Bermejo, this is Vallegrande territory, now we are winding up the hill toward La Abra del Quiñe. And just as the mountains quickly closed in on the road at La Angostura—literally, "The Narrows"—people perceived the lowland plains surrounding Santa Cruz as being qualitatively different from the small towns nestled into mountainsides and valleys in the Andean foothills. The division between the lowlands and the highlands is both physical and ideological. The relationship between continuity and contrasts—different ways that people understand and divide up space and social categorization—is at the heart of this book.

I lived in Saipina from 2002 to 2004 as a Peace Corps volunteer. My main job was facilitating a women's group. The twenty or so women in the group worked with me to design and implement projects falling under the general category of agriculture. Together we planted no-spray kitchen gardens and were awarded a grant to expand the project through the United Nations Food and Agriculture Organization; we made trips to nearby nurseries, dairies, and apiaries and participated in grant-writing workshops and integrated pest management seminars. I also worked with local farmers testing saline-resistant crops for the highly alkaline soil, and I cultivated a flourishing worm garden, which I tried unsuccessfully to duplicate in other households. I was nominally affiliated with the town hall and an agricultural nongovernmental organization. However, the town hall was closed down under allegations of corruption shortly after I arrived, and I found many of the agronomists I worked with obnoxious. They came and went from the city, sometimes leaving the community for weeks at a time; some of them were condescending and crude, whistling at women in the fields and engaging in unpleasant sexual innuendo in conversation. In turn, they found me unprofessional: like local farmers, I took my dog with me everywhere I went, I became deeply embroiled in the politics of the women's organization, and I fell in love with and moved in with a young man from the community.

I married this young man at the end of my service, and we moved back to the United States while I attended graduate school in Michigan. However, we made a point of returning each year for several months at a time during the long Northern Hemisphere summer break. In 2008 we returned with our daughter for a year of dissertation fieldwork and built a house in town. Building a house and having a child cemented us as community members in good standing, if often absent ones. We were understood to follow the pattern of community members who emigrated for years or decades but maintained social and economic ties in the expectation of an eventual return.

Between 2000 and 2008 six Peace Corps volunteers were stationed in Saipina, and I am also a member of that group, the link that connects them all to each other and to the community. Two volunteers preceded me, one was in site during virtually the same period as I was, and two more succeeded me in Saipina. I often assisted these volunteers with their projects, and we shared gossip, rare treats from home, and contacts in the community. In 2008, in the wake of the expulsion of the U.S. ambassador, the Peace Corps abruptly left the country and was not expected to return.

My first introduction to the country was through the Peace Corps, and my experience is often framed in these terms. People still sometimes call me by the name of the volunteer who preceded me fifteen years ago, showing that we never fully outgrow our history and first impressions. Still, my relationship with Bolivia and with Saipina has changed considerably since the early 2000s. I now travel to Bolivia as a head of household, a married woman with children, and as a member of an extended family. My husband and I have strong friendships that we have built over the years and ritual kin relationships in town, comadres and compadres of our children and godchildren. We make an effort to return every year to visit family, renew friendships, care for the small house that we own, and conduct research.

Because I now travel to Saipina as a researcher, people have grown accustomed to my digital recorder and my questions about language. My Peace Corps relationships grew into friendships, kin and ritual kin relationships that are now the center of my research. At the same time, I never "grew out" of my social position in town—though I now hold a doctorate and am a professor at a major U.S. university, my contacts in Saipina call me "la Anita" or "Doña Ana," local terms of respect and affection, rather than using a more formal title (licenciada or doctora) that references my level of education. I have ready access to many ordinary households in town and on the peripheries, but it's hard for me to get an appointment with the mayor or busy local politicians. For this reason, my perspective comes largely from the group of people I worked with as a volunteer: women of all social classes, small farmers, and skilled laborers. Increasingly, I have been fortunate to develop adult friendships with young adults whom I first met as preschoolers or school-age children, and they are part of a new generation of consultants and participants in my research.

CHAPTER 2

MEANING IN CONTEXT

THIS CHAPTER focuses on the use of contact features as social indices in the variety of Spanish spoken in Saipina. Context of use is important in producing social meaning, and indeed context can redefine the indexical relationship between any particular sociolinguistic variable and its social referent or referents (Eckert 2008; Silverstein 2003). Spanish-Quechua contact features act as part of a system of linguistic features that are linked to the semiotic field. The meaning of these features is built through contrast to or congruence with the expected forms of speech for a speaker or group (Agha 2007a; Babel 2011). These expected forms of speech are related to a listener's personal experience with the speaker over time and with their conceptions of the types of speech that members of certain groups engage in. Group membership is determined by the way that particular people "fit into" the binaries articulated through the semiotic field. Because the semiotic field is complex and dynamic, the interpretations of these patterns are highly context dependent and produced through particular individual interactions. Through these types of social negotiations, we can observe a system that produces meaning at a variety of scales and over a variety of dimensions, as part of a constantly shifting mosaic of linguistic performance.

It has been well established that contact features respond to social context of use (Bakker and Mous 1994; Thomason 2001; Thomason and Kaufman 1988;

Winford 2005). That is, the extent and type of contact between speakers define the ways that linguistic features move between languages. As I show in this chapter, the ways that particular people use language features are also subject to interpretation; contact features are more recognizable in the mouths of some language users than others. This points to the fundamental importance of both social categorization and patterns of linguistic usage in the interpretation of contact features and of sociolinguistic indices more generally.

Language users' interpretation of linguistic features in interpersonal interactions is built through contrast to and congruence with large-scale semiotic systems of interpretation. The interpretation of particular features always takes place against the backdrop of an understanding of typical patterns of interaction not only at the community level but also for social groups and even individuals. In this chapter, I describe the construction of social meaning through the interaction of social categorization and linguistic features. The same contact features used by individuals identified with different groups result in differing social interpretations and characterizations of the speaker. These ways that people interpret language are tightly tied to the ways that they understand the larger semiotic field in which language participates.

Linguistic features—of which contact features are a subcategory—are not only part of a language system but also signs that link to systems of social interpretation and positioning. Highly skilled speakers use contact features in novel and unexpected ways, and listeners take these tendencies into account when evaluating their interlocutors. Because of the social knowledge that people hold about surrounding patterns of speech, less proficient speakers' use of contact features may be categorized as "mistakes," while in the speech of more fluent language users the same features may be evaluated as "strategies." Listeners evaluate language use based on their expectations of co-occurrence patterns for particular speakers in particular situations. In this chapter, I compare language use and social evaluation of Spanish-dominant speakers from the local Santa Cruz valleys (vallunos) and Quechua-dominant migrants from the western Bolivian highlands (collas). Quechua-dominant speakers were evaluated as less able speakers, undesirable neighbors, and unknowledgeable about the relevant context of speech. Spanish-dominant speakers, even when they used the same contact features, were framed as knowledgeable and deserving participants in the interactions that I observed. Finally, I examine the strategic use of contact features by two local politicians and discuss when and how such strategic uses "work."

Meaning is produced in relationship with context, both social and linguistic. Sociolinguistic meaning is a creative practice, and linguistic features are part of an interrelated web or pattern of meaning. This pattern encompasses both a variety of sociolinguistic indices and other ways of producing social meaning, such as dress, migration history, and identification as a language speaker, which I discuss throughout the rest of the book. I use Quechua contact features in Spanish to gain a foothold, a point of entry, into this complex relationship.

THE SEMIOTIC SYSTEM

Quechua and Spanish have been in contact for nearly five hundred years, and in the local valleys that include Saipina, they have been in contact since the early 17th century (discussed in more detail in chapter 3). Due to this long-term contact and the persistence of large groups of Quechua speakers, especially in Bolivia, Quechua contact effects on Spanish have been demonstrated at every level of linguistic structure (Calvo Pérez 2000; de Granda 2001; Escobar 2000). However, Andean Spanish varies along social and geographical axes (Escobar 1988, 1994; Klee 1996), including the speaker's language-learning history and identification as a language speaker (Howard 2007).

The contact features I discuss in this chapter are among the most recognizable and least common features used in the Spanish of my field site (Babel 2011). Speakers tend to be very conscious of them and to use them in parodies and jokes, as well as in natural discourse. They also carry a strong stigma (cf. Lipski 2004:132). Nevertheless, they are employed under certain social conditions across social and linguistic groups.

The semiotic field is a complex geography of social signification that encompasses not just language but also styles of dress, political stances, gender expression, migration and residence patterns, and even emotions and affective stances. The semiotic field is an "exoskeleton" of meaning that enfolds but also structures the relationships of different kinds of social signs to each other. The things that my consultants do or say, and the ways that they do or say them, can be linked to different poles within the broader semiotic field. Contact features, in general, are associated with a cluster of features that is linked to older people, women, and people from the countryside. However, this general association does not always hold in the same way for all people or, indeed, for all contact features. It is the context of use, and people's expectations of language users from particular social groups, that picks out a set of meanings based on language use in any particular discourse setting. This set of meanings depends greatly on experience with language and social groups and may not be identical for all listeners, though it is similar enough that we can observe large-scale patterns and areas of consensus.

The contact features that I describe here participate in a semiotic field linking them to a complex of features that includes traditional styles of dress (such as use of the pollera, a gathered skirt) and to Quechua-dominant speakers, the rural countryside, indigenous heritage, and individuals with little formal education. Under certain conditions, they may also be linked to hospitality, respect, and expressions of affect (anger, sorrow, empathy, humor, mocking; see, e.g., Nuckolls 1996; Nuckolls et al. 2016). Contact features, then, are often linked to the speech of those most likely to have contact influence, such as older women, people from the rural countryside, and immigrants from the western highlands. These features tend to be used most often in informal, relaxed conversational contexts among family and friends. While many of Saipina's residents recognize and use contact features as markers of a distinct local identity, constant waves of migration produce a long-term language contact situation. Members of different social groups not only have different language abilities and histories but also are understood to orient differently toward features associated with Quechua and speakers with significant contact influence. Thus, Quechua-dominant immigrants with little experience with local Spanish are understood to use contact features because of interference from a first-language base. In contrast, Spanish-dominant speakers from the local area use many of the same features, but these are interpreted as markers of rurality or a traditional identity.

CONTACT FEATURES

Quechua has a very regular penultimate stress pattern. The default stress pattern in Spanish is also penultimate stress, but there are more exceptions in Spanish than are found in Quechua (Escobar 1976). Often, words without penultimate stress in normative Spanish are used with penultimate stress in the contact variety of Spanish spoken in Saipina as a way of evoking a local identity. For example, the proper name Ángela is pronounced as Angéla, or *plátano* 'banana' becomes *platáno*.

One of the most salient, most iconic markers of Quechua speakers in Spanish is the influence of the Quechua three-vowel system, *a*, *i*, *u*, with backed allophones in the context of uvular *q* and glottalized consonants, on the Spanish five-vowel system *a*, *e*, *i*, *o*, *u*. Speakers tend to use vowel raising of *e* and *o* to *i* and *u*, and they also hypercorrect, using vowel lowering of *i* and *u* to *e* and *o*. This phenomenon affects both Spanish-dominant speakers and Quechua-dominant speakers.

Both Spanish and Quechua tend to have CV (consonant-vowel) syllable structure, but Quechua is much more regular; often, both Spanish-dominant and Quechua-dominant speakers create CV syllable structure in Spanish diphthongs. For example, they insert a glide in the verb *traer* 'to bring', making it *trayer*, or they change *ie* diphthongs to *e*, changing *bien* 'well' to *ben*.

Leveling irregularity in verb paradigms, such as the diphthongization in verbs like *tiene* 'he has' (from *tener*, becoming *tene*) and *entiende* 'he understands' (from *entender*, becoming *entende*), is a common phenomenon. Because Quechua does not have a distinction between /e/ and /i/ in these contexts, these features are probably also related to phonological influence from the Quechua three-vowel system (Calvo Pérez 2008; Mendoza 2008).

Consonants also bear traces of Quechua contact. Because Quechua does not have contrastive voicing, /β/ (orthographic b or v) is often realized as [w] by speakers with contact influence. In addition, speakers commonly use a nonstandard realization of /f/ as a bilabial voiceless fricative [φ], or more accurately, [$φ^w$], with lip rounding. This version of the labiodental /f/ also appears in rural and archaic varieties of peninsular Spanish. While Quechua does not have a labiodental fricative, /f/ is usually borrowed into Quechua as /ph/. It is possible that some degree of variation in /f/ comes from Quechua speakers, but it is at least as probable that it has a historical Spanish source. This feature is strongly associated with orientation to a traditional, rural lifestyle and with Quechua-dominant speakers in contemporary Bolivia.

At the morphological level, nonstandard gender and number agreement is common in Andean varieties of Spanish (Sánchez 1996). Variable number and gender agreement, including variation in the interpretation of collective nouns, is often associated with speakers who have Quechua contact influence (Martínez 2009). An abundance of diminutives is typical of Andean Spanish, as it is of contact varieties of Spanish throughout Latin America (Escobar 1994). Prosodic influence from Quechua is also common (Muntendam 2011), and women with Quechua influence tend to speak in a higher phonetic register. Under certain circumstances, falsetto voice is utilized by both women and men (Albó 1979; Babel 2011).

At a lexical level, loanwords from Quechua, especially in toponyms, plants, animals, agriculture, cooking practices, child-rearing, weaving, swear words, and nicknames, are also commonly used by individuals, both bilinguals and monolinguals, who have contact influence (see Adelaar and Muysken 2004:590–591; see also chapter 3).

COLLAS: LORENZA

Lorenza, a Quechua-dominant speaker, learned Spanish as an adult after moving with her husband and young children to Saipina. She could be identified as a colla, a bilingual western highlander, by a number of social indices: she came from the western highlands, wore a pollera, spoke primarily Quechua, and worked with her husband in agriculture. Her husband was a fluent bilingual who used primarily Quechua in the home.

Lorenza consistently used phonetic variants that marked her as a first-language (L1) Quechua speaker, in particular, the use of [w] for /β/, the [φ^{w}] variant of /f/, stress shift on the lexical item *vibóra* 'snake' (normatively *víbora*), and variable vowel height. She had frequent influence from the Quechua three-vowel system and sometimes hypercorrected. Lorenza leveled verb paradigms, using the forms *entendo*, *entenden* instead of *entiendo*, *entienden*, and *vienendo* for *viniendo*. Lorenza's speech also showed extensive morphological interference in Spanish, especially in the following areas: (1) grammatical and natural gender categories; (2) number, pronouns, and address forms; and (3) verb conjugation.

Lorenza and I were friends, and we often stopped on the street to chat with each other or visit each other's houses. On this occasion, Lorenza and I spoke in her house. She had offered to give me a Quechua lesson, and after speaking for a while in Quechua, we returned to Spanish to continue chatting. In the transcript below, Lorenza explained the differences between Quechua speakers from different regions of Bolivia to me, focusing on the negative characteristics of people from the Cochabamba valleys (she was from another region of Bolivia).

Transcript 3: L (Lorenza), A (Anna)

1. L: Más habladoras son. Libre **habla todos**, están, más **feos** está hablan. Esos vallunos.	1. L: They've got bigger mouths. They **all talk** excessively, they're, they talk **uglier**. Those people from the [Cochabamba] valleys.
2. A: Aaah, ¿más feos?	2. A: Aaah, uglier?

3. L: Más feos se está hablan.	3. L: They talk uglier.
4. A: Mmm.	4. A: Mmm.
5. L: ¡Huuu! ¡Tratan, después, mmm! Unas **vibóras** son.	5. L: Whuuu! They scold you, then, mmm! They're **snakes**.
6. A: [laughs]	6. A: [laughs]
7. L: El Omereques no es.	7. L: The person from Omereque isn't like that.
8. A: Ah ya ya.	8. A: Yeah, yeah, yeah.
9. L: No es así.	9. L: They're not like that.
10. A: Más calladito?	10. A: They're quieter [less gossipy].
11. L: Más calladito es. El valluno es, huuucha, graves son.	11. L: They're quieter. The valley person is, whuuu, they're awful.
12. A: Hm.	12. A: Hm.
13. L: Hm. Malas algunas. Si no sabía, enton, después de, **vos está**, no entendía nada, no ve, el Quechua, no ve, ¿nadita no **entende**?	13. L: Hm. Some of them are mean. If you don't know, then, after, **you're**, didn't understand anything, right, Quechua, right, you don't **understand** even a little?
14. A: Ah ha, ah ha.	14. A: Uh-huh, uh-huh.
15. L: Enton pa Ud. nomás está, con Quechua.	15. L: Then they [talk] about you, in Quechua.
16. A: Ah ha.	16. A: Uh-huh.
17. L: ¡**Feo** tratan!	17. L: They scold **ugly**!
18. A: Hmmmm!	18. A: Hmmmm!
19. L: ¡**Feo** tratan!	19. L: They scold **ugly**!
20. A: Al que no entiende?	20. A: To someone who doesn't understand?
21. L: No **entende**.	21. L: Doesn't **understand**.

In this passage, multiple nonstandard features appear, such as nonstandard agreement (turns 1, 13) and nonstandard verb conjugation (turns 13, 21). These features, as well as nonstandard /f/ and stress shift, are in boldface in this transcript. Lorenza uses nonstandard /f/ on the lexical item *feo* in turns 1, 17, and 19. In turn 5, she uses penultimate stress marking for the lexical item *vibóra* 'snake, malicious person'.

Despite the fact that virtually all Spanish speakers use all of these features occasionally, Lorenza was seen as an unskilled speaker because she used these features frequently, indeed, pervasively, and with no particular sociolinguistic or contextual pattern. Other consultants characterized Lorenza as a poor speaker of Spanish, and their imitations of her speech included her lack of gender and number agreement, verb conjugations, and vowel height, all of which are stereotypical characteristics of second-language Spanish speakers. No one single feature marked her as a Quechua speaker. Rather, it was the overall patterns of her speech that did so.

COLLAS: BEATRÍZ

Beatríz was a merchant. She ran a store on the main road alongside many similar stores, several of which were also run by highly educated, relatively wealthy bi- or multilingual schoolteachers. She spoke good Spanish, but it seemed to be laborious for her, and she had the telltale high pitch of a Quechua-dominant woman. For me, the most notable second-language feature of Beatríz's Spanish was her vowel quality; although she consistently distinguished between high and low vowels, her low vowels were higher than the usual Spanish targets. In addition, as can be seen in transcript 4, her grammatical constructions were fairly simple. She omitted an article before *papel* 'paper' and *interés* 'interest', and she used penultimate stress on the word *ultímo*, as opposed to normative antepenultimate *último*. The repetition of "cuatro cuatro cuatro cuatro" (four [by] four [by] four [by] four) would also sound more natural in Quechua than in Spanish.

Transcript 4: B (Beatríz), F (Froilán)

1. B: La palabra, de esa parte yo le he preguntado aquí más al **ultímo** ahorita, la, all, a Doña Mariela le he preguntado ¿no ve? Si no vamos a presentar papel cuánto va a ser **interés**? Un punto más va a ser más interés, nos dijo, sí o no, ¿a ver? Y están escuchando Uds. Yo he preguntado. Y además en Santa Rosa, no están sacando con **papel**. Entre ellos se han garantizando, **cuatro cuatro cuatro cuatro**.	1. B: May I have the floor? On this front, I **recently** asked, um, Doña Mariela, I asked her, right? If we're not going to present paper, how much will [the] **interest** be? It will be one point more, she said, yes or no, right? And you are hearing me now. I have asked. And besides in Santa Rosa, they're not getting [loans] with **papers**. They're guaranteeing among themselves, **four four four four**.

2. F: Pero señora, si vamos a presentar el plano—	2. F: But ma'am, if we're going to present the design—
3. B: Sí, por eso.	3. B: Right, exactly.
4. F: Ya está aprobado por el consejo, la directiva nos va a balar—	4. F: It's already approved by the council, the officers will [?]—
5. B: Claro.	5. B: Of course.

Beatríz spoke up in a meeting after her husband, the president of the group that requested government funding for housing, came under heavy fire from audience members regarding the difficulties in the plan for the members of the group to get loans for the construction of their houses. In Saipina as in much of the Andes, community offices were often ostensibly held by men, but it was tacitly understood that the job involved the combined efforts of a married couple (see Allen 1998, 2011 on the topic of *warmiqhari*). Beatríz spoke using proper meeting etiquette, but her sentence construction was choppy, and she phrased her first several sentences as questions. An audience member responded, somewhat patronizingly, calling her *señora* (ma'am) and patiently reviewing aspects of the deal with her. Beatríz responded defensively in turns 3 and 5, saying "Right, exactly," and "Of course" in response to the implication that she did not adequately understand what was going on. As the wife of the leader of this group, it was unlikely that she was unaware of the subtleties of the matter under discussion.

It was unusual for Quechua-dominant bilingual women to speak up in meetings. Beatríz was motivated to do so by a series of highly charged attacks on her husband. In transcript 4, others framed her contributions as ill informed and irrelevant, that is, as inappropriate to the meeting setting, at least in part because of her lack of skill in Spanish oratory, as manifested through the contact features in her speech.

COLLAS: EMILIA

Emilia came from the rural western highlands. In her sixties at the time of this recording, she had lived in Saipina for most of her life, ever since she was married as a young woman. Her husband was a Spanish-speaking farmer; they used Spanish in the home, and their grown children were all monolingual Spanish speakers. Emilia commented to me that she grew up speaking Quechua. Her stories showed that her father was a Quechua-dominant bilingual and a person of importance in the community, a landowner with plenty of cattle and an abundance of kin and ritual kin relationships.

While Emilia's Spanish was fluent and easily understandable, she consistently used enregistered contact features such as the [φ^{w}] realization of /f/. Her realization of vowels was inconsistent; sometimes she raised *o* and *e*, and sometimes she hypercorrected, lowering *i* and *u*. These changes were occasional in her speech, occurring in only five sentences over the ten minutes of transcribed conversation. Once or twice, she used nonstandard gender marking, referring to "esas borrachos" (those [fem.] drunks [masc.]) and "una nomás se ha casado" (only one [fem.] has married), using the feminine form of "one" to refer to her son.

Transcript 5 shows Emilia employing a high density of contact features. She describes how her father, as ritual godparent to a young married couple, resolved disputes between his *ahijados* 'godchildren'. Vowel raising or lowering in turns 1 and 2 is underlined and marked with boldface.

Emilia spoke to me in her home during an interview that I carried out with her and her husband. Emilia's husband was a distant relative of my husband, and he knew me well from projects I worked on with him during my Peace Corps service. I knew Emilia a little less well, but she was still comfortable speaking with me and seemed eager to be interviewed. In this interview, we talked mainly about their children and their family history. The three of us sat in their patio chatting, occasionally interrupted by people who came to buy small items from the store Emilia and her husband ran out of their home.

Transcript 5: E (Emilia), A (Anna), N (Emilia's husband)

1. E: Nosotros sabíamos, como **wawas** éramos, una pelea se hacía para ahijados carajo. V**e**nieron a q**ue**jarse. Como este, este, padrinos, ese es. Yaaa, y le daban con un chicote ellos. A quien que tenía culpa leee **wasqueaban** ahi. **Hacían** arrodillar—"¡Arr**o**dillense ahi! ¡Perdónese de su mujer! ¡Tiene que **perdonar** de su mujer, porque **ha pegado**!" Y así que le perdonaban; ya, ¡pr**i**merito tienen que darlo **wasca** [laughs]! **Wasca** le daban, y después ya	1. E: We used to, since we were just **children**, there was a fight between godchildren, by golly. They came to complain. How this, this, the godparents, that's it. Yaaa, and they hit him with a whip. Whoever was at fault they **whipped** him there. They **made** them kneel—"Kneel here! Beg forgiveness of your wife! You must **ask forgiveness** of your wife, because [**you**] **hit** [**her**]!" And so they forgave each other; yes, but first they had to be **whipped**

hacía perdonar, le hacía abuenar ahi, mi papá, de ahí tiene que haber, lo que sea, aunque sea **mote** con queso, como a nosotros no nos faltabámos nada, nos faltaba, la este, vacas allá—	[laughs]! They **whipped** them, and then they were **made** to forgive each other, they made up to each other there, my father, then there had to be, whatever, even if just **corn** with cheese, since we never lacked for anything, we lacked, this, cows out there—
2. A: Ah-ha.	2. A: Uh-huh.
3. E: Y queso cada uno, una bola ponía sobre el mote, de ahí tiene que **hacer** comer el uno al otro, al otro así. Eso era.	3. E: And cheese, he put a ball of cheese over the corn, and they had to **feed** each other, like that. That was the way it was done.
4. N: Eso era seguro una forma de—	4. N: That must have been a form of—
5. E: Abuenarse, claro!	5. E: Making up, of course!
6. N: Reconciliación! [chuckles]	6. N: Reconciliation! [chuckles]

In transcript 5 Emilia both narrates and quotes her father dealing with the errant godchildren. She uses loanwords from Quechua such as *waska* 'whip, rope' (turns 1, 2), *mote* 'boiled corn' (Quechua *mut'i*, in turn 3) and *wawa* 'child, baby' (turn 1). She also uses grammatical constructions that are unusual for Spanish-dominant speakers. For example, while she begins with the reflexive *se* in "Perdónese de su mujer" (Beg forgiveness of your wife), the reflexive disappears in the next sentence, "Tiene que perdonar de su mujer" (You must ask forgiveness of your wife), and she omits a clitic where one would ordinarily have occurred, "porque ha pegado!" (because you hit [her]!) (turn 2). All of these occur when she animates the voice of her father, a Quechua-dominant speaker. She uses the verb *hacer* 'to do, to make' as a causative extensively in this excerpt (turns 1, 3, 5), each time with a different agent. Likewise, her vowel height (underlined and in boldface) is inconsistent throughout the reported dialogue, part of which is reproduced here; at first she raises vowels, then she lowers them. This feature is gradient, and I marked only those instances that were clearly higher or lower than normal Spanish targets. Because this feature is so sociolinguistically salient and such a strong index of Quechua speakers, even a few occurrences are highly significant, and language users pick up on them quickly.

Turns 7 and 8 are also interesting with respect to the use of contact features. Emilia uses the word *abuenarse* 'to make up, to make good', from the Spanish root *bon-* 'good'. This word is fairly common in Latin American Spanish but is not recognized by the *Diccionario de la Real Academia Española* (Real Academia Española 2009). There is a cluster of Quechua words for "reconciliation": *allitupanakuy*, *allipanakuy*, *allinyanakapuy*, *allinyay*. All of these use the root *alli-* 'good', usually translated into Spanish as *bueno* 'good', and many involve the reflexive verb construction *-ku*, which parallels the Spanish *-se* in *abuenarse*. Emilia's husband (N) jumps in to explain that this was a form of *reconciliación* 'reconciliation', a relatively high-flown vocabulary term. In doing so, he constructs himself as a more educated, elegant speaker than his wife.

Emilia was consistently identified as a colla, a Quechua speaker, and a migrant from the West by her neighbors in Saipina. This evaluation was certainly related to the way she talked; however, it was also a way of expressing antipathy related to petty rivalries with her neighbors. Emilia owned a business selling chicken, keeping the poultry in pens in her backyard. In a separate conversation with a neighbor of Emilia's, the neighbor complained that Emilia's business selling chickens attracted vermin to the area around the house. The neighbor gossiped that she had complained directly to Emilia, and Emilia had responded by saying, "If you're so envious of me, then you can support me." After describing the interaction, the neighbor commented to me dismissively, "Colla es pues" (It's that she's a colla). Through this comment, Emilia's (allegedly) rude and unneighborly behavior was linked to her status as a bilingual from the highlands of Cochabamba.

COLLAS: SUMMARY

People who are identified as collas were expected to have Quechua interference, despite their different histories, circles of interaction, and Spanish-language abilities. The three collas I have discussed here met these local expectations. Lorenza spoke primarily Quechua and had persistent Quechua contact features in her speech despite her friendships with Spanish speakers. Beatríz was a merchant who interacted with her customers in both languages and supported her husband's political role. Finally, Emilia was a highly fluent Spanish speaker who manipulated the use of contact features to voice different characters in her narrative.

There is a close relationship between classification as a language speaker and evaluation of a person's social worth or appropriate sphere of influence. In comments about these speakers' language abilities, others characterized them not just as poor Spanish speakers but also as inconsiderate neighbors and as people who were ignorant of important aspects of political discussions.

However, contact features in themselves were not sufficient to show that a speaker was Quechua dominant or any of the associated personal characteristics that this entailed. In the following sections, many of the same features that I identify in the speech of people who were labeled collas appear in the speech of vallunos, Spanish-dominant speakers from the local valleys.

VALLUNOS: PRIMA

Prima was a Spanish-dominant speaker in her sixties. She wore a straight skirt, not a pollera, and she lived in the center of town. Like many women of her age, she was raised in the local rural highlands and moved to Saipina as an adult; her husband was a successful farmer who owned valuable farmland near town. Other informants identified Prima as a local, that is, a person from the valleys, and I never heard her characterized as a poor or inept speaker.

Prima frequently used contact features in her speech, and I was surprised to learn that she knew no Quechua at all, because her older sister wore the gathered pollera skirt and was a fluent bilingual. Prima used the $[\varphi^{w}]$ variant of /f/ and stress shift quite regularly in relaxed speech, along with loanwords and prosodic features, such as a high pitch, that are linked to contact. On separate occasions, she expressed discomfort with speaking in formal situations and reluctance to be recorded. This linguistic self-consciousness is clear in the contrast between the two excerpts I present below.

I interviewed Prima on a couple of different occasions during my fieldwork. While I wouldn't describe the relationship as particularly close, we spoke on a daily basis because I rented a room in her house and she was a family friend of my husband's. In transcript 6, taken from an interview about language ideologies that I carried out in her kitchen with her husband present, she was on her best linguistic behavior, talking about her hope that her children would study English.

Transcript 6: P (Prima), A (Anna), N (Nicolás, Prima's husband)

1. P: <u>En cambio</u> yo harto **he** deseado que mi hija antes entre a estudiar inglés.	1. P: <u>On the other hand</u>, I **have** always wished that my daughter would study English.
2. A: Mhm.	2. A: Mm-hmm.

3. P: También, Nelly, Nestor, y así como que, allá. ¿Si hay, no ve, para llevar, puro inglés, no ve?	3. P: Also, Nelly, Nestor, and so on, over there. There is, isn't there, to study, just English, right?
4. A: Hay.	4. A: There is.
5. P: Hay, pues, pa salir y, de, profesora de inglés están, ¿no ve?	5. P: There is, to graduate and, be an English teacher they're there, right?
6. A: Sí, sí, sí. Hay eso.	6. A: Yes, yes, yes. There is that.
7. P: Y, ellos, no han tenido interés. Igual el Henry. Ha hecho dos, tres meses, parece, inglés—	7. P: And they, weren't interested. Henry was the same. He did two, three months, I think, of English—
8. A: Mhm.	8. A: Mm-hmm.
9. P: Y de ahí lo ha dejado también. Porque ya también, no podía alcanzar, si—	9. P: And then he stopped too. Because at that point, too, he couldn't [afford], and—
10. A: Mm,sí.	10. A: Mm, yes.
11. N: Mm.	11. N: Mm.
12. P: Yy, lo ha dejado así. Y, es bien es saber [el in—]. De los dos.	12. P: And, so he just stopped. And, it's good to know [En—]. Both.
13. A: A ha.	13. A: Uh-huh.
14. P: Entender.	14. P: To understand.

In transcript 6, Prima uses formal-sounding phrases such as "en cambio" (on the other hand) and "así como que" (on the other hand) (turns 1 and 3, underlined). She also uses *también* twice in turn 9; también is used and overused when speakers are trying to establish a formal register (Babel 2011). These aspects of her speech suggest that Prima is monitoring her speech. She is fairly dysfluent; she corrects herself in turn 12, and she phrases her statements as questions in turns 3 and 5. In the first line, Prima's e vowel is slightly raised (boldface), but there are no other phonological or morphological contact features in this segment. Later in the conversation she asks me, "Usted va a pasar clases alll, a su idioma de Usted, o no?" (Will you [formal] be teaching classes innn, in your [formal] language, or not?). The use of the formal pronoun *Usted*, which she rarely used with me in more casual settings, is one more sign of a formal style of speech, and she draws attention to this by using the explicit pronoun twice in this short sentence. She certainly did not need to use the formal pronoun with me, a much younger woman and a social subordinate. Rather, she used it to cast herself as a polite and educated person in an effort to live up to the interview context.

Prima varied her use of contact features to fit different situations. In transcript 7, she makes suggestions about how to improve the cooking stove that she obtained from an NGO. On this occasion, we sat outside near her woodstove while my husband replaced some metal parts that had deteriorated on the NGO-supplied stove. He was within earshot but did not participate in the conversation. I played the role of a representative of the NGO, running through a cooking-practices questionnaire with her. In transcript 7, she responded to the question, "How could the stove be improved?"

Transcript 7: P (Prima), A (Anna)

1. P: Y yo decía, **Anita, sabís** que decía?	1. P: I was thinking, **Anita, you know** what I was thinking?.
2. A: ¿Mhm?	2. A: Uh-huh?
3. P: Que si no hubiera tenido el ladrillo, **fuera** solamente el **fierro**.	3. P: What if it didn't have the brick, if it **were** just the **metal** [ring].
4. A: Mhm.	4. A: Uh-huh.
5. P: Eso más bien quería yo Anna decir. Que tenga solamente ese **fierro**, y tenía las **patitas**, ¡que no tenga el ladrillo para que, tenga más **campito** adentro! ¡Si **asicito** es el **campito**!	5. P: That's what I was thinking, instead, Anna. That it should just have the **metal** [ring], and the **feet**, and not the brick so that it, has more **space** inside! It's this **tiny**, that **space**!
6. A: Mm, ya ya ya.	6. A: Mm, yeah, yeah, yeah.
7. P: ¿No ve? Mientras más campito, más **ponimos leñita** y más bracea, más calda va.	7. P: Right? When there's more space, we **put** more **wood** and it burns better, it heats more.

Although Prima had a number of serious complaints about the stoves, she was worried that direct criticisms might be offensive or might place me in a difficult position. She invoked our close relationship through an intimate address form, using the vos conjugation of the verb *sabís*, the diminutive *Anita*, and a pronounced [φ^{w}] in the words *fuera* and *fierro* (turns 3 and 5). She used the raised-vowel form of *sabés* [sabís] 'you know' and *ponemos* [ponimos] 'we know' (turns 1 and 7). She also used negative politeness strategies, focusing on the fact that it is "just me" that is giving this advice, using subjunctive verb forms in turn 3 and a proliferation of diminutives in turns 5 through 7: *patitas* 'little feet', *campito* 'little space', and *leñita* 'little sticks'.

Prima used these features to index a close personal relationship, one that was rooted in tradition and in traditional values of respect and politeness. While the features themselves are very similar to those found in the speech of Quechua-dominant speakers, Prima's varying use of contact features over different social contexts is part of her construction as a more skilled speaker.

VALLUNOS: ANTONIA

Antonia, an elderly woman, lived just outside of town, across the river. She dressed in the traditional, hand-sewed pollera and black fedora of the valleys. She understood Quechua and could speak it when necessary but said that she did not speak it well, and she spoke exclusively Spanish with her family members. While Antonia's close associates knew that she was a Spanish speaker, people who had seen her about town or knew her only casually sometimes expressed surprise to me that she does not consider herself a Quechua speaker. I surmise this had to do with not only linguistic but also other types of social factors, such as her style of dress and her longtime residence in an area that was considered isolated from Saipina. In addition, her heavy use of contact features could lead to this conclusion.

Antonia used Quechua contact features such as [φ^w] and alternation between *v* and *w*. She used penultimate stress marking more frequently than other Spanish speakers I recorded. As can be seen in transcript 8, she also used grammatical elements linked to Quechua influence such as *pues*, *también*, and *deciabámos* (turn 1), and she used the contraction *ande* in turn 7, where normative Spanish would have *dónde* (see Babel 2011, 2014c). In turn 5 she preposed the subject, "Marciana," where more standard or more formal varieties of Spanish would have placed it at the end of the sentence for focus.

On this occasion, a group of close family members were seated around the kitchen table in my home, preparing to have a meal. Antonia addressed this group of close family members in this transcript.

Transcript 8: A (Antonia), J (Juana), F (Francisco)

1. A: Dirá pues, ella también, "Tu tía es," le **deciabámos** al finado Germán, que es, el Gabriel.	1. A: She must be saying, too, "She's your aunt," we **used to say** to the deceased Germán, I mean Gabriel.

2. J: Ha a, ha a.	2. J: Mm-hmm, mm-hmm.
3. A: "Qué va a ser mi tía pues. Qué le voy a decir tía yo. Si yo soy más grande, ella que me esté diciendo tío a mí."	3. A: "I don't believe she's my aunt. I won't say aunt to her. If I'm bigger, she should be saying uncle to me."
4. F and J: [laugh]	4. F and J: [laugh]
5. A: La Marciana era esa.	5. A: That was Marciana.
6. J: Nunca más se ha sabido esa mujer, ¿no? Otra que no quiere parientes es.	6. J: We've never heard anything else about that woman, have we? She's another one that doesn't want relatives.
7. A: ¿**Ande** ha dicho que está? Ha hecho estudiar, en la—	7. A: **Where** did they say she is? She studied, in the—
8. F: No, ha—	8. F: No, she—
9. A: En Belén.	9. A: In Belén.

The signs that place people as lower class or "country" and open them to rude treatment and discrimination extend to practically everything about them, including their name. In transcript 9, the speakers continue talking about Marciana, a distant relative who has moved to the city. Juana opens a discussion of name changing.

Transcript 9: A (Antonia), J (Juana), N (Nolán)

1. J: No dizque se llama Marciana ahora, ¿no? Que dizque que se llama?	1. J: Apparently she's not called Marciana now, right? What do they say she's called?
2. A: Que se—	2. A: That she—
3. N: **F(φ^{w})austina** se llama ella.	3. N: She's called **F(φ^{w})austina**.
4. A: ¿**F(φ^{w})austina**?	4. A: **F(φ^{w})austina**?
5. J: No es Faust— ¿Qué dice que se llama? Vi-cki, no sé qué dice, ¡ha cambiado de nombre! Ya no es Juliana. No, la Juliana, la Juliana es la que se ha cambiado de nombre. La Marciana creo que sigue nomás con ese nombre.	5. J: It's not Faust— What is she called? Vi-cki, I don't know what they say, she changed her name! She's not Juliana anymore. No, Juliana, Juliana's the one who changed her name. I think Marciana still has the same name.

In this segment, Antonia's daughter, Juana, ridicules people who try to change their names as a sign of being modern people, making fun of Juliana's transformation into Vicki, a very trendy, almost teeny-bopper kind of name. Nolán, Antonia's adult grandson and Juana's son, jokes that the woman changed her name to Faustina, a name that is even more indexical of old-time country ways than her original name, Marciana. To add color to the joke and emphasize the name's country-ness, he pronounces Faustina with the [φ^w] variant. In turn 4, Antonia, who uses this variant consistently, misses both the iconic [φ^w] feature and the indexical linkage of the name Faustina to the idea of being traditional, rural, "backward," and rooted in the countryside; in short, she does not get the joke.

For Antonia, an elderly woman from the rural countryside, using the [φ^w] variant is not an index of anything. By mocking older styles of language use with his use of [φ^w] on the old-timey name Faustina, Antonia's grandson creates an indexical layer that his mother, but not his grandmother, recognizes and responds to. However, he did not intend to target his grandmother with this joke; while Antonia was a traditionally oriented older woman with roots in the countryside, her position as a native Spanish speaker and close family member exempted her from the negative evaluations that were commonplace for collas.

VALLUNOS: BRAULIA

Braulia was in her seventies, and she lived in Saipina, close to her children. However, she continued to own land in the high rural regions surrounding the town. Until the year of my fieldwork, when she bowed to pressure from her children and decided she was too old, she used to walk the six to eight hours to visit her estancia on a regular basis. Braulia wore pants and skirts, not the pollera, and she was a native speaker of Spanish. She said she did not speak or understand much Quechua. Braulia used enregistered features such as the [φ^w] variant of /f/ on a regular basis, as in transcript 10, where she discussed her (lack of) schooling.

On this occasion, Braulia had stopped by our house to chat on her way to gather firewood. She took a chair to our patio and spoke at length with my husband and me about her childhood as children and dogs played at our feet.

Transcript 10: B (Braulia), A (Anna)

1. B: De habilidad era. Igual era yo p'. Con él. Los únicos éramos los dos que sabíamos mascito de eso. De eso la Catoco una vez haya ido él, le dijo, "¿Por qué no ha puesto a la escuela? Así como yo elay no he aprendido, hace **falta**." De esa manera le haya, le haya venido . . . un añito nos ha puesto a la escuela. Después otro año ya no ha querido.
2. A: Esos años pues las mujeres no iban, ¿no?
3. B: No. "¿Pa qué va a servir?" me dijo. "¿Pa qué, en qué les va a servir el estudio? No va a servir de nada," nos dijo. Y tanto hace **falta**. Es como si uno **fuera** ciego, ¿no? [**intake**] A mí me da pena y rabia me hace que, que tanto a ver no hemos aprendido. Yo era, de habilidad era.

1. B: He was good at it. I was, too. As good as him. We were the only two that were any good at it. About that Catoco once when he went, she said, "Why didn't you put [her] in school? Look at me, I never learned, it's **necessary**." That's how, he came . . . and he put us in primary school for just one year. Then the next year he wouldn't.
2. A: In those years girls didn't go, did they?
3. B: No. "What good does it do?" he told me. "For what, what is studying going to do for you? It it's not worth anything," he told us. And it's so **necessary**. It's as if one **were** blind, isn't it? [**intake**] It makes me so sad and it makes me angry that, that there was so much we never learned. I was, I was good at it.

Throughout the transcript, as on the words *falta* and *fuera* in this segment (turns 1 and 3, in boldface), Braulia uses the [φ^w] variant of /f/. She also uses ingressive airflow, a Quechua contact feature, to complement her expression of anger and regret that she was never allowed to go to school (turn 3).

In transcript 11, recorded on the same occasion, Braulia begins to tell a story about shepherding her parents' sheep when she was young; this is typically a job for a preadolescent child. She describes her frustration when the vultures came to steal her lambs.

Transcript 11: B (Braulia), A (Anna), N (Nolán)

1. B: La última lomita donde yo salía a cuidar las **owejas** arriiiba, una loma era, ahí el, el **witre** me quitaba los corderos.

1. B: The very last ridge where I would come out to take care of the **sheep** up hiiigh, there was a ridge, the, the **vulture** would take the lambs from me.

2. A: [laughs]	2. A: [laughs]
3. B: Cuidando.	3. B: Shepherding.
4. N: El condor se come los corderos.	4. N: The condor eats the lambs.
5. B: Eese condor grande que es.	5. B: Thaat's it, the big condor.

In the sentence reproduced here, Braulia uses [w] in *owejas* [owejas] (normatively [oβexas]) 'sheep', as well as for *witre* [Spanish *buitre*] 'vulture', shown in boldface. This is an especially interesting choice, because the Quechua loanword *sucha* 'vulture' is in common use in this area. The use of the Spanish word indexes her Spanish-language family background, while using the Quechua phonology indexes the "traditional" activity and setting. In a following turn, Nolán substituted the Quechua loanword *condor*, which Braulia picked up and used for the rest of the conversation.

Unlike [φ^w], alternation between *v* and *w* was relatively uncommon for Braulia. Indeed, later in the same transcript (not reproduced here), she used the normative allophone of /v/, [β], in *oveja* 'sheep'. These linguistic features contributed to the way that Braulia framed her description of this particular activity, with its strong associations with her past and with the traditional activity of shepherding.

The following segment of the same story, in transcript 12, also includes abundant enregistered features, such as the Quechua-origin loanword *mark'a* '[held in] one's arms' (turn 3) and the *-abámos* verb form, indexing a nostalgic past (turn 9; see Babel 2014c). In addition, Braulia uses *ya* (turns 3, 5), causative *hacer* (turn 3), and singular mass noun *harto oveja* 'lots of sheep' (turns 3, 7) in this segment of discourse.

Transcript 12: B (Braulia), A (Anna)

1. B: De mi delante se lo alzaba. El corderito, en su pata lo alzaba y lo llevaba. Balaaaando.	1. B: Right in front of me he would pick it up. The lamb, with his foot he would pick it up and take it away. Baaaaa-ing.
2. A: [laughs]	2. A: [laughs]
3. B: Iba en su patita así un trecho, de ahí lo largaba al suelo, ya se moría el cordero. Ya yo alzaba, ya no servía ya. Pa que ande. Tenía que llevar en mi **mark'a**, a la casa **hacía** llevar. Mi mama	3. B: He would have it in his foot like that a little ways, then he would drop it to the ground, the lamb would be ready to die. When I picked it up, it was no good anymore. To walk. I had to carry

me pegaba, p' me decía, por qué no [pause], si las ovejas eran **haarto**, desparramadas, p' uno por alla arriba, ¡uno no va a estar en seguida, amontone y amontone!	it in my **arms**, I would **have it** taken to the house. My mother hit me, she said, why didn't you [pause], but there were **so many** sheep, spread all over the place, one way up there, one can't be right behind, herding and herding!
4. A: Mhm.	4. A: Mm-hmm.
5. B: Hasta que corríamos enton' no había, estaba leeejos ya, corría, hasta eso el condor venía ya. Ya me quitaba. Grave he sufrido ahí, cuidándoles a esas ovejas. Tanto.	5. B: By the time we ran up they were gone, they were far away, I would run, by then the condor would come. He would take them away. I suffered awfully there, taking care of those sheep. So many.
6. A: Hartos eran [entonces].	6. A: There were lots [then].
7. B: **Haarto** eran. De ahí nos hemos venido, vendido toditas las ovejas. El patrón nos ha vaqueado, de ahí, el patrón era de todo ese terreno ahí. Nos vaqueó el patron. "Váyanse a otro lado," nos ha dicho.	7. B: There were **loooots**. Then we came this way, sold all the sheep. The landowner ran us off, from there, the owner of all that land up there. The landowner ran us off. "Go somewhere else," he told us.
8. A: ¿Por que?	8. A: Why?
9. B: Es que ya teníamos oveja harto, ganado **teniabámos**; se molestó de eso. Se molestó de eso.	9. B: It's that we had too many sheep, we **had** cattle; he was offended by that. He was offended by that.

Braulia used some features linked to rural speakers, such as $[\varphi^{w}]$, consistently in her speech. Others, such as the *v/w* change, she used selectively. In transcript 12, we can observe that Braulia uses increased semantic, morphological, and phonological contact features when talking about traditional activities in the past. In Braulia's speech, like Emilia's, there is an emergent, higher level of indexicality (Silverstein 2003) that draws on linguistic features to evoke characteristics of her past in the rural countryside. Listeners indicated that they understood these uses of contact features as an acceptable sociolinguistic strategy, in contrast to their evaluation of Emilia as antisocial or of Beatríz as ignorant. Indeed, my husband suggested that I record this conversation as a historical record of the olden days.

VALLUNOS: SUMMARY

In this section, I have described the way that three speakers used Quechua contact features to mark traditional activities, to voice speakers from the past, and to manage a polite, intimate register in contrast to a formal one. These speakers were all older women, much like the colla women described in the previous section. Their use of contact features was not identical to that of colla speakers, but it was similar in many ways. Antonia, like Lorenza, seemed to be unaware of the indexical value that the phonological contact features she produced held for other listeners. Braulia, like Emilia, used contact features in order to invoke a time and an activity in the rural past. The major difference was in the way that speakers were evaluated by their audiences. While Emilia was characterized as a poor speaker and a poor neighbor in part because of her use of contact features, Prima used contact features in order to construct a polite relationship. While Beatríz was framed as a person who had no business speaking in a meeting, Braulia's audience listened to her attentively and suggested that her narrative should be recorded for posterity.

For local valley speakers, unlike the Quechua speakers, contact features were not linked with a lack of ability or a lack of neighborliness. Rather, they were interpreted as indices of a traditional orientation. Contact features in the mouths of vallunos were understood by their interlocutors to index the cluster of ideas that included rural life, women's sphere, traditional crafts, and occupations. The meanings attached to these features were not predetermined and common across all contexts and speakers but rather came out of contrast with typical patterns of use for particular speakers and groups.

LOCAL POLITICIANS

In this section, I turn to men in the context of community meetings—a more formal and more metalinguistically regulated form of speech. In the following transcripts, local politicians make claims to positioning as particular types of people through their linguistic practices. These claims are evaluated and then accepted or rejected based on expectations and evaluations of the speakers' claims to particular identities and stances.

Silvio was a highly educated *profesor* (teacher) originally from the highland regions. An able bilingual, he was a teacher and the director at one of the local schools. He was an accomplished orator and tended to dominate meetings with long speeches. He was a board member of not one but two neighborhood associations during the year of my fieldwork and also held an administrative office within the school district. In meetings, Silvio usually spoke in a sophisticated and relaxed oratorical style with few phonological or morphological contact features. The only consistent contact feature that I noticed in his speech was the tendency to raise vowels in confusing adjacent-syllable cases such as *pesimista* 'pessimist[ic]' > *pisimista*. (This feature was not restricted to bilinguals; monolingual Spanish speakers from this area did it, too, especially when they were trying out fancy, somewhat unfamiliar words.)

In one meeting, however, Silvio was challenged by his own *vocal*, a minor officeholder in charge of notifications, who accused Silvio of delaying and failing to carry out his duties. The vocal was young and fairly inarticulate; Silvio had demolished him on a previous occasion by pointing out his failure to follow correct procedure and protocol in lodging his complaint. However, at this point in the recording, the vocal's complaint (which he elaborated on after it was read from the *libro de actas*, or minutes of the previous meeting) was picked up by one of Silvio's main opponents, a young *autonomista* named Raúl. Raúl and all his family were politically active in the autonomy movement. On several previous occasions, Silvio had pointedly mentioned the inconsistency of being part of his organization, which was formed in order to request a housing project from the current government, while being a fervent autonomista, a member of a movement working to undermine said government. Silvio also liked to respond to Raúl by pointing out his relative youth and inexperience, on one occasion referring to him as "don señor joven Raúl" (Sir Mr. Master [lit., "youth"] Raúl).

Transcript 13: S (Silvio)

1. S: Yo no puedo dedicarme [absoluta] mente, parece que no, no me dejo entender, o [pause], no sé.	1. S: I can't dedicate myself entirely, it seems I don't, I don't make myself understood, or [pause], I don't know.
2. Yo trabajo y mi trabajo casi no permite. No, no permite, **curro** yo peligro de sanción, abandonar, e, mi trabajo. Porque hay que viajar a Santa Cruz, hay que hacer.	2. I work and my work nearly doesn't let me. It, won't allow it, I **run** the risk of censure, of abandoning, um, my job. Because I have to travel to Santa Cruz, there are things to do.

3. Y parece que de acuerdo a lo que hemos hecho, ¿no? Tal vez será el apoderado otro que tenga tiempo tal vez podría ser. ¿No? Porque de lo contrario, yo soy el que tengo que firmar. ¿No?

3. And it seems to be in line with what we've done, doesn't it? Maybe the person with power of attorney should be someone else who has more time. Right? But if not, then I'm the one who has to sign. Right?

4. Entonces me toca viajar a mí, o algo así. Entonces, en ese sentido, n—, un poco, n—, no tan **fácil**, la, no? hacer estas tareas, para, de acuerdo al trabajo que yo tengo.

4. So I have to travel, or something. So, in this sense, n—, a little, n—, it's not so **easy**, the, right? to do the work, for, in accordance with the job that I have.

5. Pero, [al contrario] si no **estuviera**, yo voy, cualquier dia, y dispongo. Me dedicaría a eso. Pero no es algo así.

5. But, [if things were different], if I **weren't**, I [would] go, any day, and make myself available. I would dedicate myself to this. But it's not like that.

6. Yo quisiera que me entiendan, bueno, Uds. beneficiarios, que no quiere, no van a entender, bueno, no sé.

6. I would like you to understand me, well, ladies and gentlemen, beneficiaries, [if there are some that] don't want to, that are not going to understand, well, I don't know.

7. Entonces, eso.

7. So, that is that.

Here, Silvio again began his argument by criticizing his opponent, commenting, "E, yo respeto a las personas, no somos de, de a misma altura. No? Conozco, e, he estudiado, conozco como se debe manejar, conozco parte de normas" (Um, I respect people, [but] we are not of the same stature. I know, um, I have studied, I know how this should be managed, I know the rules). In a lengthy reply, he once again criticized his opponent for failing to understand the rules of meeting organization, for hastiness and impatience, for (youthful) lack of respect. Then he began to elaborate the reasons why the process had been long and difficult, highlighting the difficulties that had already been overcome. Finally, he reminded everyone of his other commitments and of the time that he had already dedicated to this organization. Implicitly, he was reminding them that, even if he had failed, none of them was volunteering to lead the organization. He stated, "No, no permite, curro yo peligro de sanción, abandonar, e, mi trabajo (It's, [my work] won't allow it, I run the risk of censure, of abandoning, um, my job)" (turn 2). In transcript 13—highly unusually for this speaker—he raised the first vowel of the verb *correr* 'to run', making it /kuro/ rather than the normative /koro/. In later sentences, he raised a vowel in another common word, *istuviera* (cf. *estuviera* 'if I were', turn 5) and also used the [φ^{w}] realization of /f/ in the word *facil* 'easy' (turn 4; contrast this with the normative realization of the same phrase in turn 5). Silvio's voice was raised in a high, uneven pitch, giving the impression that he was emotionally moved.

What was Silvio doing in this segment? Consciously or unconsciously, he selected a few key contact features to insert into his speech while maintaining an overall formal register of speech. These features, as we saw in the examples above, are usually present in the speech of second-language (L2) Spanish speakers, especially those with fairly low Spanish proficiency—not highly educated bilinguals like Silvio. However, these features are also present in the speech of highly proficient or monolingual Spanish speakers who wish to build empathy, indicate affect, or evoke an intimate relationship. Silvio picked only a few, highly salient moments to insert these contact variants into his speech.

By the use of a tiny change in vowel height, Silvio delivered a complex, multivalent message. First, he himself was a highlander, a Quechua speaker, and (unlike his young opponent, Raúl) affiliated with the MAS political party of indigenous western highlanders. In this, he aligned himself with his audience, most of whom were poor, new immigrants, and Quechua speakers. Second, he was a highly educated and highly able Spanish speaker, a person who knew the ropes and knew the rules, as he stated explicitly in this excerpt (again, in contrast to his opponents). Third, he had dedicated his personal time, his personal commitment, to the group, and he was emotionally invested in the group and its outcome.

ESTEBAN AND STRESS SHIFTS

The type of positioning that Silvio used in the previous section could also be deployed unsuccessfully. In this section, I describe how a speaker who was ordinarily oriented toward education, urban spheres, and modernity unsuccessfully attempted to use a feature that was associated with the traditional local rural identity.

In order to invoke nostalgia, Spanish-dominant speakers shifted the main stress on first-person plural forms of -er/-ir verbs to a penultimate pattern: *ibámos* [íbamos] 'we went', *quisierámos* [quisiéramos] 'we would like', *estuvierámos* [estuviéramos] 'we would have been', *conociámos* [conocíamos] 'we knew', *queriámos* [queríamos] 'we wanted', *erámos* [éramos] 'we were' (instead of normative antepenultimate stress; see Babel 2014c). Speakers used the stress shift variant either to highlight longing or desire or to mark something from the long-ago times, from past experiences and traditions. Here, a young, highly educated, Spanish-speaking *legítimo* Saipineño attempted to use stress shift to build solidarity through a rousing oratorical performance before a group, and it fell flat.

Transcript 14: E (Esteban), F (Froilán)

1.	E: E, sí, yo creo que para terminar esta tema y no estar en polémica, uno de los bondades nuestro grupo que tenemos, los que estamos trabajando como dijo Don Froilán, es que somos bien unidos.	1.	E: Um, okay, I think that to finish this topic and not have controversy, one of the strengths that our group has, those of us who are working, as Don Froilán said, is that we are united.
2.	Todo reglamentamos por falta de [cuota cuotas]. Así funciona.	2.	We all regulate because of lack of [payment plan]. That's how it works.
3.	[Increasing audience noise]	3.	[Increasing audience noise]
4.	Si no **estuvierámos** unidos nosotros, ¿cuántas veces las personas que [unintelligible] hecho propietarios, nos hubieran estropeado, nos hubieran cerrado?	4.	If we **weren't** united, how many times would the people who [unintelligible] the landowners, would they have ruined us, would they have shut us down?
5.	Ya estamos construyendo pero. Nosotros hemos sido firme en la directiva [hemos dado] la reunión, es mucha la propuesta, ¡no se puede perjudicar, a una, a esta organización es solidario!	5.	But we're already building. We officers have been firm, [we've had] meetings, the goal is great, but you can't mess with a, this organization is *solidario* [all for one and one for all]!
6.	La gente necesita, no pueden Uds. imponer o [hincar], pero ¡la gente nos ha entendido que no nos van a perjudicar! ¡Sea quien sea dueño! ¡La bondad es que somos unidos! Y ¡adelante vamos a salir! Como dice Don Froilán, no nos vamos a dejar—	6.	The people have needs, you can't impose or . . . , but the people have understood that we will not be messed with! No matter who the property owner is! The virtue is that we are united! And we will overcome! As Don Froilán says, we will not be left—
7.	F: Y Uds. . . . ¡espantar *farna*!	7.	F: And you . . . to scare *farna*[?]!
8.	[laughter]	8.	[laughter]
9.	[Profe C tries to talk, people totally talk over him, the rest is completely unintelligible.]	9.	[Profe C tries to talk, people totally talk over him, the rest is completely unintelligible.]

Esteban was the young but politically ambitious brother of the mayor, an agronomist by profession and educated in the city. In this segment, Esteban trotted out a variety of clichés: "the people are united," "we shall overcome," "the goal is great." He used an oratorical structure that began with problems or issues (turn 2), built through rhetorical questions (turn 3), and ended with exclamations about the power of the people to overcome oppression (turn 5).

This speech came at the end of a long and contentious meeting. But rather than serving to rouse the group, it turned into a joke (which certainly dispelled tension but was not at all what Esteban intended). People were clearly not listening, and the noise of people laughing and talking started to rise, as noted after turn 2. In the end, Esteban was cut off by a mocking remark from the very person he invoked in turn 1, a highly respected valley farmer.

In this segment, we see Esteban making an effort to use populist discourse of a type that is widely and effectively employed by community leaders throughout Latin America. One feature that Esteban employed as part of this effort was the stress shift on "Si no estuvierámos unidos" (If we were not united) (normatively "Si no estuviéramos unidos"). This indexical association depended on the feature both as an index of populist discourse and as an index of the kind of person that Esteban claimed to be (Agha 2007a; Silverstein 2003). However, he did not have the wherewithal to pull it off successfully; instead, he became the butt of a joke. The stress shift, like other features of the discourse, were meant to index a man of the people, which Esteban was not—precisely by virtue of his standing as a member of the native-born upper classes and as an individual who had strongly aligned himself with modernity in other arenas, such as his education, his spouse, the home he lived in, and his political and professional activities. The use of the enregistered features to an audience of people who were not considered his peers in most social circumstances led them to evaluate him as laughably fake.

CONCLUSION

Social meaning—in particular, the value of linguistic indexes as markers of social categories—is produced in relationship with context (Babel 2014; Eckert 2008). Language use is a creative practice in which speakers not only respond to identity categories but also actively engage in creating and interpreting those social categories (Bucholtz 2010; Bucholtz and Hall 2004, 2005; Eckert 2000; Kuipers 1998). In this process of interpretive work, signs are meaningful only in relation to the context in which they are produced. This context includes language users' preexisting notions about the social categories to which particular speakers belong, and it affects the interpretation that listeners give to any particular instance of linguistic practice.

The semiotic field gives us a lens through which to view the place of contact features in a landscape of meaning that encompasses particular language features, as well as other categories such as social class, language dominance, and affective stances. Language use is broader than what we can measure through the production of linguistic features; it is also embedded in an interpretive system across the community.

Studies of language contact have recognized the importance of social identities in producing contact outcomes, but it is also important to interrogate their role in the perception of contact influence. There is no single contact feature or even group of contact features that distinguishes the linguistic practice of collas from local vallunos. Rather, it is a combination of large-scale patterns of language use and, especially, social expectations and stereotypes about language users that guide the interpretation of any given feature for a particular interaction in a particular context. Speakers learn language not with or in but as context. The semiotic field that I describe throughout this book provides this social context for listeners who evaluate particular instances of language use with respect to social categorization.

INTERLUDE

On Being a Near-Native Speaker

ON MY recent trip to Bolivia, my mother-in-law looked at me curiously, then commented, "You know, Anna, you sound almost just like us. But there's always something; there's always some little thing . . ." She shook her head, as if trying and failing to put her finger on what, exactly, made me different.

In the preceding chapters, I discussed the way that social identification and positioning affect the interpretation and uptake of the Quechua contact features by local audiences. But how do these linguistic features sound when taken out of the context of Saipina? As a second-language speaker of Spanish and a highly educated white American woman, what did it mean for me to speak a variety of Spanish that has significant Quechua contact influence, a variety that I learned primarily from rural Bolivian women?

The dialect of Spanish that I speak, and the one that my consultants use in everyday interactions, is one that I often euphemistically describe in my publications as a "nonprestige" variety. To be more precise, it's a manner of speaking that educated Spanish speakers hear as rural, uneducated, lower class, and, above all, "incorrect." Despite the fact that I'm a Spanish professor, this is the variety that I'm nearest to being native in. I have struggled to acquire the educated variety that my colleagues speak and that my students often expect, and I speak this prestige variety very imperfectly. Spanish-speaking academic audiences, including many of my own graduate students, find my accent "cute" or quaint. For many years, the first comment after my academic conference presentations in Spanish was not about the material I presented but about the dialect I used to deliver it.

This attitude was not limited to academic audiences. In daily interactions in urban areas of Bolivia, I had to be careful how native-like I sounded; though I am tall and light complexioned for a Bolivian, my manner of speaking meant that it was easy for people in positions of petty authority (airline clerks, shopkeepers, minor government functionaries) to perceive me not as speaking like a peasant but as being a peasant and to treat me carelessly, rudely. The signs that marked me as belonging to one category or another were physical but also malleable: habits of dress and posture, the muscle movements of the tongue that produce language, the presence of my dark-eyed, dark-haired children, the color of my passport. When I was recognized as a foreigner, suddenly doors were opened, flight attendants smiled, official wheels were greased.

When my husband and I traveled together in Bolivia, we cultivated the signs of the urban middle class, such as his intellectual-looking glasses and my blue passport, which hotel clerks photocopied and registered for official purposes. But when we traveled with his family, who did not have access to these signs, they were uniformly ignored, mistreated, and quite literally marginalized. On one trip that we took with Doña Antonia and Don Francisco, we complained to a hostel manager about being assigned a storage closet to sleep in instead of a guest room. As if it explained everything, the manager told me, gesturing at the elderly couple, "But you were supposed to give that room to them." When my mother-in-law traveled with me as a paid guest in order to help care for my infant son on a university-sponsored student exchange trip, Bolivian restaurant wait staff, hotel managers, and even our professional tour guides acted as if she were invisible, passing over her when they distributed souvenirs, talking around or above her, and failing to serve her food at our common meals.

The fact that I could opt out of this treatment by putting on an American accent and by wearing typical tourist clothing such as T-shirts and sneakers—my position of privilege—meant that no matter how well I spoke this variety of Spanish, despite speaking it on a daily basis for fifteen years, despite being able to "pass" under certain circumstances as a native speaker, despite the fact that it was a language of intimacy that I spoke in my home, I could not claim it as "my" variety without encountering reactions ranging from skepticism to indignation to derision.

At the same time, my use of the local variety of Spanish made me a member of a community that put language at the center of local identity. When I approached a friend by the thaco tree in the center of town during my last visit, a bystander who had not seen me for several years suddenly recognized me. He stared, mouth agape, and then exclaimed, "¡Saipineñísima!" (As Saipineña as they come!) before shaking my hand and walking away without another word. When people in Saipina said, "You sound just like us," this was a way of claiming me, erasing my foreignness, and making me a conocida, a member of the community, drawing me into a shared frame of reference.

As blurry as the categories "insider" and "outsider" can get, being "near native" is a little like being a number approaching infinity—no matter how far I go or how near I get, I'm never going to lose that tell-tale little thing that sets me ever-so-slightly apart. I am not, and can never claim to be, a "native"; yet I am near enough that many of the complications of being a native spill out into my life, even as the hurdles of being an outsider remain. Anyone who has done long-term fieldwork has experienced this in-between state to some degree, and I don't think that I'm unusual among anthropologists in feeling a displacement in my own identity. The lines blur; the categories break down. But if there's anything I've learned as a linguistic anthropologist, it's that the words we use to talk about our experiences matter. When we say near, how near? And when we say native, of what?

CHAPTER 3

QUECHUA AND SPANISH LANGUAGES AND SPEAKERS

THE QUESTION of whether people spoke Quechua in Saipina was at the front of my mind the first time I heard of the town, in 2002, during my Peace Corps training. Peace Corps volunteers went through several weeks of training in a major city before they were assigned to their permanent sites. This training included information on language, culture, safety, local politics, and development projects in the areas where the volunteers were assigned. In my case, I had afternoon sessions on agriculture in Bolivia and the types of projects that might be available in my permanent site. Since I was already fluent in Spanish, I studied Quechua in the mornings along with two other volunteers. A few weeks before site assignments were made, the staff circulated short descriptions of each of the available sites to the group. In my group, one site description elicited great interest.

The site description had been written by the current volunteer, whom the new volunteer would replace. She was clearly in love with the place. While most of the dozen or so descriptions that were circulated consisted of three or four dry lines written by the project director who had chosen the site, she had written two long paragraphs. In them, she described the pleasantly warm weather, the fertile valley conditions, the welcoming, outgoing people, the delicious food, and the local obsession with amateur sports, which she listed as including basketball, volleyball, and indoor and outdoor football. Everyone could see themselves playing sand volleyball with Bolivian friends while wearing comfortable clothing and going out for dinner and drinks afterward.

In the end, after several weeks, a couple of different reshuffles, and some major disappointments for volunteers who had their hearts set on particular sites, I was assigned to the coveted site. I had only one question for my project director: Do they speak Quechua there? I had entered the Peace Corps wanting to learn a new, preferably obscure language, and I couldn't imagine anything worse than being assigned to a site where people only spoke Spanish.

He paused a moment and looked at me carefully. "Sure," he said. "There's plenty of Quechua in Saipina."

But when I visited the site briefly prior to moving in I heard the opposite. Everyone emphasized to me that Saipina was a Spanish-speaking town, and everyone I spoke to spoke Spanish to me. I was disappointed. I assumed that my project director had prevaricated so that I wouldn't be unhappy about my placement.

It wasn't until I had lived in Saipina for several weeks that I realized that he had been telling the truth. Not only was Quechua spoken in Saipina, but after I had lived there for a few weeks, I heard it all over the place. I heard it at the ancient tree in the main square where people gathered to gossip, buy bread, and look for work in the mornings. I heard it in the plaza, where people gathered in their free time. I heard it in the market among the buyers and sellers. I heard it in the fields where people worked. I heard it between mothers and fathers and children at home, walking out to take care of animals, on the street where people paused to chat. Even the local dialect of Spanish, which I sometimes found rather difficult to understand, was liberally sprinkled with Quechua-sounding words. That tree in the plaza was called the *thaco* (a type of acacia tree). In the gardens, people went to *khorar*, a word that I knew from my Quechua classes sounded a lot like the Quechua *qhora*, the word for "weed." My host mother worried that her food was *k'ayma* (bland). And when my bike tire went flat, I was told it had *ch'usuyado* (gone flat). My neighbor was called El Mich'a (the cat) because of his light-colored eyes. This didn't sound like any Spanish I had learned.

And yet my first impression wasn't entirely wrong either. Everyone I spoke to reiterated the same thing: in Saipina, people speak only Spanish. And they weren't lying to me. Everyone I spoke to was in agreement. Saipina was a Spanish-speaking town. When I asked around for someone who could give me Quechua lessons, they directed me to the Quechua teacher in the local schools.

They assured me that she was the only person who would be capable of teaching me Quechua.

This wasn't as contradictory as it sounded. Saipina *was* a Spanish-speaking town, and people could point to other towns nearby that were predominantly Quechua-speaking towns—where the elite, the oldest settlers, the town fathers were bilingual or Quechua speakers, even though some people, maybe many people, also spoke Spanish. The only people in Saipina who were Quechua dominant were first-generation migrants. Their children switched to Spanish as soon as they began public school, if not earlier. And yet the idea that people spoke Spanish in Saipina was not only something that people claimed but also something that they believed and made true through their actions. The fact that people spoke Quechua was simply erased in local discourses. Maybe it was the wrong kind of setting or the wrong kind of people. Maybe it was someone who could and would speak Spanish under most circumstances. Maybe it was just someone who spoke the local, mixed-up variety of Spanish, which, crucially, was not Quechua. But the fact was, when people spoke Quechua, it didn't always *count*.

WHEN DO PEOPLE USE QUECHUA?

In most cases, people did use Spanish. They certainly used Spanish when talking to outsiders and foreigners. When they chose to use Quechua, people didn't just come out with it randomly, whenever they felt like it. So why, and under what circumstances, was Quechua spoken in Saipina?

Walking down the street one day, I passed by a tire repair shop on the main dusty road through the center of town. One young man was cleaning out the inside of a dirty white taxi, his head stuck inside the interior. A slightly younger man, perhaps of high school age, was standing outside, carrying on some joking banter with him. The younger guy was clearly getting the worst of it. As I walked by, the he said, "Mana intindiygichu Queshua." This sentence was not good Quechua. What he said was garbled, something like "I don't understand you Quechua." The Quechua word *intindiy*, a commonly used word for "understand" in Cochabamba Quechua, is a loan from Spanish *entender* and as such is relatively easy for Spanish speakers to remember and produce. At the same time, the way he pronounced the words indicated that he had learned them from a native speaker: he pronounced the *k* as a *g*, something that I often heard younger Quechua speakers do; and he pronounced *Quechua* as *Queshua*, softening the *ch* so that the word sounded like the word for "valley," from which the name of the language is derived.

The other young man responded in fluent-sounding Quechua, but since his head was inside the car, I couldn't hear what he was saying. Then the second young man, clearly having just been insulted in Quechua, turned to Spanish as a way to dominate the encounter. He replied in Spanish, "Please speak Spanish. We're in Saipina, not in Aiquile." Aiquile was a town in Cochabamba that was well known as a Quechua-speaking town. Many of the Quechua-speaking migrants in Saipina came from the Aiquile area.

This was a desperate jab, however. The first guy replied mockingly in Quechua that he didn't speak Spanish—a phrase that his interlocutor was sure to understand even given his apparently limited Quechua proficiency. This ended the exchange; the Quechua-speaking participant had successfully asserted that Quechua was the court on which this game was being played. The younger man was miserably ill equipped to follow, despite his attempt to move the conversation back into Spanish by appealing to the idea that Saipina was a Spanish-speaking town.

People often told me that the reason it was necessary to speak Quechua was that if you didn't know it, people would make fun of you in public, and you would have no way to answer them. You wouldn't even know what they were saying. The younger man's failure was related to the context in which the exchange took place. In Saipina, Quechua was reserved for very intimate family domains, jokes, teasing, stories, and certain types of activities. If he had been on the floor of a meeting in the town hall, the young man probably could have successfully held the floor by insisting on speaking Spanish or challenging his opponent's right to speak Quechua. But Quechua rightfully belonged to spheres that included the home, play, and joking contexts between friends such as the encounter that I describe above. The younger man was unable to assert that Quechua was inappropriate for this particular interaction because of the informal context in which the conversation took place.

Stories and anecdotes often contained crucial phrases in Quechua. For example, my husband, a monolingual Spanish speaker, told a story he heard from his grandmother about a man whose horse was running away. The protagonist, a monolingual Quechua speaker, was sitting with a group of Spanish speakers. One of the Spanish speakers noticed that the Quechua speaker's horse was running away. The joke consists of the following exchange between the two speakers:

¡Se va tu caballo!	Your horse is running away! (Spanish)
Ben, ben.	Good, good. (Monophthongized Spanish *bien*, emblematic of Quechua speakers)
¡Se va tu caballo!	Your horse is running away! (Spanish)
Ben, ben.	Good, good. (Monophthongized Spanish *bien*)
¡Kaballuyki ripushan!	Your horse is running away! (Quechua)
¡Ay, caraste!	Darn it! (bivalent Spanish/Quechua)

Exclaiming "Darn it!" the Quechua speaker gets up and races after his horse, now far away in the distance.

While this joke pokes fun at a Quechua speaker with little knowledge of Spanish, it also demonstrates that speakers who consider themselves Spanish monolinguals are often capable of producing well-formed Quechua phrases when needed. This is true within the framework of the anecdote, in which a Spanish speaker shifts to Quechua in order to convey a crucial bit of information once it becomes clear that the Quechua speaker does not understand him. It is also the case in the telling and retelling by speakers like my husband who assert that they have no knowledge of Quechua. These kinds of jokes and stories, and the ability to respond to jokes and insults, were a central part of life in Saipina.

Through these kinds of performances, speakers who positioned themselves as Spanish monolinguals revealed (perhaps limited) Quechua competence. Yet they used Quechua to represent Quechua speakers, Mock Quechua (following Hill 2001) to respond to Quechua discourse, and Quechua contact features to position themselves as local speakers. Spanish speakers were also aware of variation within Quechua. Several people told me that the Quechua spoken in neighboring Cochabamba was *más ch'uwa* (more clear), a phrase that incorporated a Quechua loanword, compared to the Quechua spoken in the highland department of Chuquisaca, which they told me was *cerrado* (closed).

When people from Saipina spoke of Cochabamba Quechua as being más ch'uwa, they also iconically drew the residents of the Cochabamba valleys closer to their own experience. People from Saipina had strong trade and kin relations with people from the Cochabamba valleys. Before the existing roads were developed in the 1960s and 1970s, it was much quicker to walk to population centers a little west of the main town in the Cochabamba province than it was to travel east. As a result, many children born in the areas surrounding Saipina were baptized and issued birth certificates in the West. Agricultural relations surrounding seed, production, and marketing of the potato, the most important cash crop in Saipina, were also centered in Cochabamba.

Was it any wonder, then, that Cochabamba Quechua speakers, even monolinguals, were described as speaking a language that was "clear"? I think it would be a mistake to suggest a purely functional explanation, that is, these speakers were clearer because of their high level of Spanish contact effects in Quechua. Rather, Cochabamba Quechua contained Spanish contact features for the same reason that Saipina Spanish contained Quechua contact features: speakers had a high degree of interaction with each other. They sought to differentiate themselves through different language orientations (monolingualism vs. bilingualism, camba vs. colla accents), but they shared kin relations, work relations, economic relations, common religious and symbolic understandings, and common festivals and rituals. They shared ways of greeting and referring to each other. They even shared intralingual jokes, nicknames, and puns.

Through these interactions, Quechua played multiple functions as an icon of Quechua speakers, an index of local identity, and a symbol of outsider identity. It also drew neighboring populations of Quechua speakers recursively closer through emphasizing their perceived similarity or distanced them through perceived differences between the Spanish spoken in Saipina and particular varieties of Quechua. At the same time, these phenomena contributed to the blurring of the boundaries of what constituted a language speaker. Using the right kind of Quechua at the right time marked people as competent local speakers. Using the wrong kind of Quechua or using it at the wrong time marked them as outsiders or possibly cultural incompetents.

People in Saipina held strong opinions about when and where Spanish and Quechua were appropriate to use. Ideologically speaking, people said that Saipina was a Spanish-speaking town even as they acknowledged that there was a large community of Quechua speakers who lived there. However, these categories were complex. For one thing, being a Quechua speaker and being a Spanish speaker were identity categories, not descriptions of linguistic ability. Most people spoke at least some Quechua, and most people spoke at least some Spanish. Furthermore, the variety of Spanish that was spoken in Saipina had significant influence from Quechua, and vice versa.

The question of linguistic borders is not a simple one. Rather, we must question and analyze the ideological clarity of these borders and examine the ways in which they are culturally constructed (Urciuoli 1995). As Bonnie Urciuoli points out, the understanding of language as "communicative competence" rather than as a bounded system of rules has a long history in linguistics and linguistic anthropology (Haugen 1966; Hymes 1972; Weinreich et al. 1968). Precisely because of the way that speakers play with the fuzzy boundaries between codes, code-switching has been recast as "translanguaging" by scholars in the field of second language acquisition (Canagarajah 2011; García and Wei 2014; Hornberger and Link 2012). Yet this research also shows how codes are marked as separate and bounded. Like other types of social meaning construction, codes—what we call "languages"—are defined through contrast (Abbott 1995; Irvine 2001). In this case, Spanish and Quechua form a binary opposition that also has productive room in the middle for language mixing and other types of language play that ultimately affect that way that the languages are spoken and experienced by speakers (Thomason 2001).

HISTORY AND STRUCTURE OF SPANISH AND QUECHUA

Quechua is a language family that is spoken principally in the Andes. Regrettably, we have no historical records of the Quechua language before the arrival of the Spanish. For this reason, even in the earliest colonial documents, we always see Quechua through the lens of Spanish.

We don't know that Quechua was the only or even the most widely spoken language in the Saipina region before the arrival of the Spanish. However, it was certainly spoken after their arrival. This pattern is widespread in the Andes (Adelaar and Muysken 2004). While the Inca appear to have used Quechua largely as an administrative language, the Jesuits adopted it as one of their principal languages of evangelization, following a policy of using local languages (Durston 2007). This spread Quechua as the dominant lingua franca even to areas where other indigenous languages may have been spoken previously. Perhaps ironically, Quechua became a widely spoken common language in part because of Spanish colonial language policies (Mannheim 1991).

These days, varieties of Quechua (or Kichwa, as the varieties spoken in Ecuador are known) are spoken by populations in Colombia, Ecuador, Peru, Bolivia, and northern Argentina (Coronel-Molina and Grabner-Coronel 2005; Hornberger and Coronel-Molina 2004). Quechua is also spoken wherever there are large Andean migrant communities (Klee 2009; Larson and Harris 1995). Some of the largest Bolivian expatriate communities include Arlington, Virginia; Barcelona, Spain; and Buenos Aires, Argentina (Bastia and Busse 2011; Escandell and Tapias 2010; Fernández García 2009; Martínez 2009; Price and Singer 2008; Rockefeller 2010; Sassone 2007; Yarnall and Price 2010). Increasingly, Chile has become an attractive destination for Bolivians, who settle both in northern Chile near the Bolivian border (Fernández 2014) and in the outskirts of Santiago.

Quechua is a linguistic isolate. As far as we can tell, there are no other languages that are related to it. However, it shares many features with Aymara, a language spoken in northern Bolivia and southern Peru (Cerrón-Palomino 1994). Though the languages cannot be said to be related with any degree of confidence, Quechua speakers have clearly shared close, long-term cultural contact with Aymara and Aymara speakers (Howard-Malverde 1995). In scholarly work, Bolivian Quechua is generally grouped together with southern Peruvian Quechua, which has a common history, as well as similar relationships with other languages (Torero 1964). The variety of Quechua found in Bolivia and southern Peru is the variety that has the closest relationship with Aymara (Torero 1964). Relatively little work has been done on the internal distinctions between regional dialects within Bolivian Quechua, though there are several different varieties spoken in the country (King and Hornberger 2004).

In some ways, Quechua is as different from Spanish as a language can be. It has a very different sound system, with exotic-sounding ejective and aspirated consonants (Babel 2016a; Babel 2017). It does not have grammatical gender. Adjectives come before nouns rather than after them. The order of sentence constituents is different from that in most European languages. And rather than separating sentences into words, Quechua is an agglutinative language that expresses grammatical complexity primarily by adding suffixes—up to seventeen on a single word, according to one of my Quechua teachers. (see, e.g., Adelaar 1977; Cusihuaman 1976; Herrero and Sánchez de Lozada 1978; Kusters 2003; Lara 1991). It is quite possible to have a full sentence expressed in a single word. One very important difference between Quechua and most Romance languages is both pragmatic and grammatical: Quechua grammar encodes obligatory categories for responsibility and information source (Faller 2002; Floyd 1999; Sánchez 2004). That is, speakers modify their sentences to include information about whether what they're saying is something that they attest to personally or not.

Linguists and historians would tell us that Quechua and Spanish are very different languages. Perhaps common sense would dictate this as well. However, people in Saipina, as in much of Bolivia, do not necessarily experience the two languages as being vastly different. This is due to the fact that for centuries, Quechua and Spanish speakers have lived and worked side by side. They have intermarried and traded. Much of Bolivia is characterized by a high degree of Spanish-Quechua bilingualism. This is especially true in the Cochabamba valleys, which border the Santa Cruz valleys that I describe in this chapter (Pfänder et al. 2009).

The high degree of contact between Spanish speakers and Quechua speakers might not inevitably have led to this closeness in the languages, but it certainly facilitated it (Thomason 2001). A person who grew up hearing both Spanish and Quechua on a daily basis would surely notice parallels and similarities between them (Babel and Pfänder 2013). This is all the more true because both Spanish and Quechua have changed over the course of their long relationship with each other. Quechua structure seems to have remained largely the same, but the Quechua language has many, many loanwords from Spanish, and its phonology has been affected by the Spanish vowel and consonant systems. Conversely, Spanish not only includes Quechua loanwords and phonological influence but also has been deeply structurally and pragmatically affected by contact with Quechua (Escobar 2011; Klee 1996; Sánchez 1996). The variety of Spanish that has resulted from this deep contact is known as Andean Spanish in the scholarly literature (Boynton 1981; Camacho et al. 1995; Escobar 1994; Klee and Caravedo 2006; Manley 2007; Muntendam 2011; Paredes 1992; Sánchez 1996). It has been shown that Spanish has been affected at every level by Quechua—its pronunciation, its syntactic structure, the meaning of certain elements, and even the ways by which people assign responsibility (Babel 2012; Calvo Pérez 2000; García Tesoro 2015; Nino-Murcia 1988; Olbertz 2005). Cognitive metaphors such as the directionality of time have passed from one language to the other (Hintz 2007; Núñez and Sweetser 2006).

For example, in most of the Spanish-speaking world, as in English, the future lies ahead of one. In the Andes, though, if I say someone was here "en delantito" (just a little ahead), it means that that person was here just a minute ago. This mirrors Quechua, in which the past is metaphorically located in front of the speaker (because you can see it). Speakers also calque, or copy, expressions such as "en su encima" (lit., "in its topside" for "on top of"), "no seas malito" (lit., "don't be a meanie" for "please"), and other ideas from Quechua semantic structure (de Granda 2001). When they want to focus on a particular part of the sentence, they move that part to the beginning, snubbing their noses at normative Spanish word order (Escobar 1994; Muntendam 2011). And despite the fact that Spanish generally is not considered to have aspirated consonants, many native Spanish speakers have phonemic differentiation between word pairs such as *tapa* 'lid, top' from Spanish and *thapa* 'nest' from Quechua (Babel 2016a; Babel 2017).

The linguistic relationship between Spanish and Quechua in the Andes can be traced back as far as the first contact between the Spanish invaders and the Inca in the Cuzco region in 1532 (Andrien 2001). The Spanish presence rapidly expanded throughout the region, reaching the region that encompasses the present-day Santa Cruz valleys in less than a century (Finot 1978; Julien 2008). Most of the towns in the Saipina area were founded between 1615 and 1620 by Spanish settlers and have been continuously inhabited by descendants of the Spanish and indigenous peoples since then (FORTEMU 2004).

Because the area is part of the stretch of land to the east of the Andes that was claimed by the Inca before the Spanish, we can infer that Quechua was spoken there—by at least some residents—before the arrival of the Spanish. Place-names, many of which are clearly of Quechua origin, support this assumption. For example, the name Saipina is a Hispanicized version of a place name derived from the words *sayay* 'stopping place' and *phiña* 'angry'—the angry place. Quechua speakers who are not familiar with the town sometimes try to correct the Hispanicized pronunciation, calling the town Saipiña. All over the Santa Cruz valleys, the use of Quechua place-names was well established by the time the historical record is available (Rivera 2015).

WHAT MAKES A PERSON A QUECHUA SPEAKER?

One of the relevant pieces of information that circulated in descriptions of people was whether they were Quechua speakers or Spanish speakers ("You know, Doña Rosa, the Quechua speaker who lives on the corner"). The terms for these categories in the local dialect of Spanish were *quechuista* and *castellanista*. These were labels that people were generally able to use to classify others with relative ease, though in some cases they might express surprise about who was a native speaker of one language or the other. It was a category analogous to knowing who had a high-school education, or who owned their house versus renting. Language dominance, an important dimension of social meaning in Saipina, was related to other social and economic measures and tied up in all the complexity of the broader semiotic field. What wasn't immediately clear to me, though, was what made a person qualify as a Quechua speaker or not.

I found that people who were described to me as Spanish speakers often spoke Quechua, while people who were described to me as Quechua speakers generally spoke Spanish as well. This distinction went beyond language dominance or status as a native speaker. A pair of middle-aged brothers I knew, Don Andrés and Don Jacinto, had different language identifications and practices. Don Andrés told me on numerous occasions that he was a monolingual Spanish speaker, and his language practices bore this out. I never heard him speak Quechua. His accent in Spanish sounded like he came from lowland Santa Cruz, where he had lived for several years. I was somewhat surprised to find that his brother and best friend, Don Jacinto, who lived in the same house with him and worked in the family business, was an avid fan of a Quechua radio station. Don Jacinto, it turned out, was a fluent Quechua-Spanish bilingual, as were the two men's mother and Don Andrés's wife. All four of these individuals had lived in the same house for years. Yet Don Andrés himself did not identify as a Quechua speaker, and he claimed not to understand or speak the language. Likewise, his children all identified as Spanish speakers and told me that they did not speak or understand Quechua.

Similarly, my friend and landlady, Doña Felipa, was a Spanish speaker even though she spoke fluent Quechua and used it often. She told me that she was a second-language speaker of Quechua. She had learned Quechua as an adult, when she spent several months in the highland capital of Sucre because her husband needed medical attention there. However, her sister Doña Benedicta was a native Quechua speaker. The two women were raised by a Spanish-speaking mother and a Quechua-dominant father, who died when they were both relatively young. They explained the difference in their language identification to me by saying that Doña Benedicta had been older when their father had died and therefore had more exposure to Quechua as a young woman. Still, I heard Doña Felipa use Quechua on a daily basis with her *peones* (day laborers) in the fields and friends around town, while I seldom heard a Quechua sentence pass Doña Benedicta's lips.

Exposure to Quechua at a young age was not enough to make a Quechua speaker, however. My husband's grandmother Doña Antonia spoke fluent Quechua. She was born to a Spanish-speaking family but was orphaned in her preteen years and was sent to live with an aunt. The aunt was a Quechua speaker. Though Doña Antonia stayed with her aunt for several years, she never considered herself a Quechua speaker and was identified as a Spanish-dominant speaker by members of both language groups. Conversely, several women whom I never heard speak anything but perfectly fluent-sounding Spanish were identified as Quechua speakers. One woman, Doña Eugenia, told me that she had not used Quechua in so long that she was forgetting how to speak it and that her friends were sometimes surprised to learn that she was a Quechua speaker. Her husband and children were monolingual Spanish speakers. Nevertheless, she identified herself to me as a quechuista.

As suggested by the descriptions above, some Spanish speakers spoke fluent idiomatic Quechua, but others spoke very little beyond a few rote words and phrases. Like the idea that Saipina was a Spanish-speaking town, individuals' language identification was less a matter of linguistic ability than it was a matter of social identification (Ahmad 2011; Firestone 2013). But being a Quechua speaker or a Spanish speaker didn't excuse one from using the right kind of language in the right kind of situation. If you couldn't speak formal Spanish, you were expected to be quiet in formal meeting situations. If you didn't know any Quechua, you could expect to be teased on the streets.

More than anything, being classified as a Spanish speaker or a Quechua speaker placed people within a social universe. This social universe was not only linguistic but also spatially coordinated and organized. In the town of Saipina, the neighborhoods with the highest concentration of Spanish speakers were in the center of town, while the neighborhoods with the highest concentration of Quechua speakers were around the periphery—the "new" neighborhoods. This spatial configuration helped to contribute to the conception of Saipina as a Spanish-speaking town and to the construction of Quechua speakers as recent migrants.

Language use was also linked to migration. Many of the people I knew in Saipina came from small towns in the surrounding valleys. These towns were mostly on the Cochabamba side of the border but had strong ties to the Santa Cruz valleys, especially to the cultural center of Vallegrande. As rural rainfall-dependent agriculture became less sustainable and transportation to and from the city became more important, many families moved to Saipina. This migration pattern affected their linguistic competence and identification. Many of the people who came from these towns were originally Quechua speakers or fluent bilinguals. After settling in Saipina, however, all these families switched to Spanish. Their children grew up as Spanish speakers, but Quechua didn't disappear completely.

WHERE QUECHUA IS SPOKEN

Quechua and Quechua contact features were most common in particular social contexts. One of the easiest ways to identify the contexts in which Quechua influence was apparent was to listen for loanwords in the local variety of Spanish. Over my first couple of years in Saipina, I compiled a list of Quechua loanwords in common circulation in the Spanish of Saipina. When I left off, the list had more than two hundred word roots and many more entries that were variants on those roots.

This vocabulary list clustered around certain topics. I noticed this especially when I became a mother. There were a wealth of Quechua terms related to child-rearing. Beyond *wawa* 'baby', which is used all over the Andes, people in Saipina used words such as *ch'eti* 'little guy', *chʰila* 'little one', *imilla* 'young girl', and *lloqhalla* 'young boy or man'. Women offered children their *chuchu* 'breast'. Illnesses, too, were often described using Quechua words; diarrhea was called *khechalera* and malaria was *chukchu*. All of these words are Quechua roots used with Spanish grammatical frames.

As this may suggest, Quechua influence on local Spanish is not evenly distributed throughout the language but is most common when people are talking about certain topics. The contexts in which I heard more Quechua spoken were also the contexts in which I heard more Quechua mixed with local Spanish. Since I was an agriculture volunteer during my Peace Corps service, I spent a lot of time in the fields or traveling around with agronomists. Many of the words relating to agriculture came from Quechua, such as *khora* 'weed' and *thamir* 'to loosen soil'. Names for common local pests were also often Quechua loanwords; farmers lamented the *itha blanca* 'white fly' and the *khuru* 'potato worm' that damaged their crops.

My secondary project involved weaving, and here too I heard many Quechua words. People spun wool on *phuskhas* 'drop spindles'; hand-spun yarn was known as *k'aytu*. You would *iskaychar* 'double' (or 'ply') two strands of yarn. Warp yarns were threaded on an *awanero* 'loom', and a bone tool called a *wich'una* was used to pack in the weft yarns and pick out patterns in the warp. When yarn was old, it would break into little bits, *p'itir*. These, too, were Quechua roots.

I also heard many Quechua loanwords related to making and drinking chicha, an alcoholic beverage made of corn (Jennings and Bowser 2008). Chicha manufacture was alive and well, but at the time of my fieldwork it was seldom practiced in the most traditional form, which involved chewing corn into smaller bits, using the saliva to start the fermentation process. Cakes of chewed-up corn were called *muk'u*. My contacts told me that in the old days of the *hacienda*, part of the tribute owed by tenants was a certain number of cakes of muk'u to the landowner. Chicha was used not only to drink but also in ritual offerings, which are known as *ch'allas*.

Chicha manufacture was a subset of cooking vocabulary, which also included many loanwords. Women cooked over a *khoncha*, an open cooking fire. They used a *kaywina*, a long-handled wooden spoon, to stir the soup. The things they cooked included *ch^{h}arullas*, toast-like dried pancakes; *lawas*, watery soups; and *phiris*, or porridges. Lawa and phiri were often made of corn but could also be made of wheat or other grains. One of my favorite foods was *thaco lawa*, a sweet breakfast porridge made from the protein-rich bean pod of the acacia tree.

Much of the vocabulary describing plants and animals came from Quechua. This included not only familiar foods such as *quinoa* and *habas* 'fava beans' but also most native plants. The *uma-uma*, from the Quechua word for "head," described a little head-shaped cactus; the *nina-nina* was a dangerous wasp with a sting that was sometimes lethal. Animals that were left orphaned were known as *wajchas*, and children chased after *chiwacos* 'little birds' and *k'entes* 'hummingbirds'.

Quechua words were plentiful in colorful sexual imagery, especially jokes and insults. I seldom managed to get these on tape, but I heard people refer insultingly to another's *p'itu* 'string' or 'dick', or *k'ajllu* 'vagina-shaped opening'. A dog in heat was said to be passing through *k'alinchería*. Women sometimes talked about their husbands being *khewa* 'stingy' or their children *khello* 'lazy'.

Jokes and insults also sometimes relied on onomatopoetic words, taking advantage of the ejective consonants—a *lap'o* imitates the sound of a slap or blow, while *lak'ar* 'to plaster' imitates the sound of plaster being thrown against the wall before being smoothed out. People accused each other of being obtuse or stupid using the word *opa*, meaning "deaf and dumb."

Although many of the contexts in which I encountered Quechua were associated with women and the feminine sphere, they could also be used to enact a masculine working-class identity. Indeed, one of the first contexts in which I became aware of the use of Quechua loanwords was nicknames, particularly among men. I knew men who were called El Tiluchi, a kind of bird; El Mich'a, "The Cat"; El Itha, a kind of moth; El Sucha, "The Vulture." One neighbor was known as Don Kusi, "Mr. Happy," because of his wide smile. The prevalence of Quechua loanwords may have been related to the class of words that often became nicknames. The Spanish forms of these nicknames often referred to animals: El Pollo, "The Chicken"; El Oso, "The Bear"; El Zorro, "The Fox"; El Pato, "The Duck." There were nicknames for almost everybody, though they were generally not respectful. Sometimes women were called by the feminine version of their husband's or brothers' (nick)names.

The contexts in which I heard Quechua were generally informal, even intimate social contexts. They involved both men's and women's work, but there was a strong tendency for this kind of mixing to appear most around traditional activities such as agriculture, construction, weaving, making chicha, domestic affairs, sex, raising children, and talking about plants and animals. As I suggest in the previous paragraph, men also used them to construct a working-class identity—when talking about shop work or mechanical matters or when joking around. These were the contexts in which Quechua was easiest to use, closest to the surface. When people were in more formal contexts—interviews, community meetings, from time to time participating in a study that I was running in town—they would be startled to hear me mention these words and might even claim not to recognize them (Babel 2011).

While words are the aspect of language contact that is perhaps the easiest to identify and the easiest to understand, structural influence from Quechua in Spanish followed similar patterns to the distribution of loanwords. Structural convergence between Spanish and Quechua was greatest in the same situations in which I heard many loanwords. Though speakers might be aware of loanwords and could try to control them, in general, speakers were not aware of the structural elements to the degree that they could suppress them consciously (Babel 2016d).

IDEOLOGIES ABOUT MIXED LANGUAGES

The use of loanwords and mixed language was not neutral. Eva, a college-educated young woman, told me that she didn't like hearing her mother use Quechua loanwords and that she tried to correct her and get her to use the Spanish equivalent. "Why?" I asked, and she replied, "It's that sometimes people think it's an insult, you know, when you say 'el ch'eti, ese ch'eti' [the boy, *that* boy] or 'la imilla, la imilla esa' [the girl, *that* girl]." The use of Quechua loanwords could index a rural agricultural identity, in the case of Eva's elderly mother; however, it could also index a critical or pejorative stance.

While eating lunch one day at a *pensión*, a small local restaurant, I heard another patron jokingly ask the waitress for some *runtuphiri*, a Quechua word meaning "egg porridge." "What's that?" she asked. "Fuera [Get outta here]," he exclaimed in mock indignation, explaining that it was a dish of scrambled eggs fried with onions. "Back in the highlands she used to eat runtuphiri, and now she doesn't know what it means," he said mockingly. "She's gotten refined. I'm not like some people. I don't run around pretending not to know what runtuphiri is." The waitress giggled. In this context, my fellow diner used the loanword runtuphiri to index a local, working-class identity in contrast to "refined" people who pretended not to understand Quechua loanwords. At the same time, foregrounding the use of Quechua loanwords placed the conversation into a joking genre, a mocking exchange that was not to be taken seriously.

People referred to the local variety of Spanish using the words *mezclado* 'mixed', *cruzado*, and *atravezado* 'crossed'. The "mixing" and "crossing" refer to the mixture of Spanish with Quechua. While mezclado has very similar connotations to the English gloss "mixed," cruzado and atravezado have additional shades of meaning. Cruzado not only can refer to crossings but also is closely related to the word for breeding animals. Atravezado means lying crossways, like logs crossing a stream, but an alternate definition in the *Diccionario de la Real Academia Española* (Real Academia Española 2009) reads "Que tiene mala intención o mal carácter" (Having bad intentions or character). People used these words to refer to the local variety of Spanish in comparison to "good" or "pure" Spanish, but they were used just as often to describe the way that native Quechua speakers spoke Spanish. If I heard with no further context that someone spoke "medio atravezado" (kind of crossways), I understood that that person was a Quechua speaker.

These terms were not complimentary. Teachers in the schools criticized and disciplined children whom the teachers perceived to be speaking "mixed-up" language, and children took these attitudes home to their parents. More than one mother confided to me that her child, after starting school, had criticized her for speaking "bad Spanish." Yet even schoolteachers were not immune from criticism. For a time, I studied the local variety of Spanish with a schoolteacher in a nearby town. Though she was a perfectly fluent native Spanish speaker, people told me disapprovingly that her Spanish was not good and that I should find someone else to study with. When I told people that my research concerns Spanish-Quechua contact, they were quick to acknowledge that everyone in

Saipina spoke this way, but they laughed when I give them examples and told me it was bad Spanish.

A person could use words and structures borrowed from Quechua and still be a perfectly good Saipineño, as long as they only used them in Spanish (or maybe a *little* Quechua, if they were really drunk or really angry). In fact, being able to use these words with ease and appropriateness was part of being Saipineño. It was very Saipineño to say that one's bicycle "se ha chhusuyado" (went flat) rather than "se ha pinchado" (got a puncture).

On the flip side, people who spoke Spanish that had very few contact features were characterized as being boring, pretentious, or fake. I attended one meeting that was run by a wealthy individual who had lived in the area as a small child but settled permanently in the business community in Cochabamba. This person was investing a large amount of money in local industry and engaged in the unrewarding task of trying to get the small producers of the Saipina area to form a cooperative in order to demand higher prices. This endeavor was viewed with suspicion by most local producers; while they liked the idea in theory, they suspected that they were being taken advantage of for the personal profit of the Cochabamba businessman. The businessman dominated the entire meeting, with practically no back-and-forth from the audience. His speech was Cochabamba accented but slick and educated sounding, and he used a lot of marketing terminology. Later, people who had been at the meeting described him to me as a fake and an outsider, a person who thought he was better than everyone else. They pointed out that he supported the elite politicians in Santa Cruz who opposed the MAS government (see chapter 5), even though he was, in their view, clearly a colla himself—in other words, a hypocrite.

Through these commentaries, my consultants described a complex and sometimes contradictory landscape of ideologies surrounding Spanish and Quechua. Spanish was understood to be the best marker of local prestige, acting as an icon of racial superiority, but at the same time educated, western varieties of Spanish were felt to be alienating. Quechua, on the other hand, was a marker of outsider status, characteristic of western bilinguals but also a familiar code used in jokes, insults, and nicknames. In contrast, a particular style of Quechua contact influence in Spanish was presented as a convincing marker of local identity. These patterns are congruent with language dynamics involving power and solidarity (Brown and Gilman 1960), or "substrate" and "superstrate" languages, all over the world (Bakker 1997; Jaffe 1999; Lefebvre 2006).

NATIONAL LANGUAGE POLICIES ON THE LOCAL SCALE

Where did ideologies that privileged pure varieties of Quechua and Spanish and disparaged mixed varieties come from? In large part, they were spread by educational institutions. One day during my dissertation fieldwork, I brought a questionnaire that I had translated into Quechua to my friend Isabel, a fluent bilingual, and asked her to check my translation. As I read through it, she frowned in concentration and, rather than commenting on the translation, responded in Quechua to the questions that I read to her. I found that she was unable or unwilling to correct my Quechua. It was a long and frustrating meeting; she was clearly annoyed with me. Finally, I asked her if there might be someone else, one of her nieces perhaps, who could help me. She told me that there were very few people in town who would be able to do this work for me. She herself, she told me, only knew some of the words that I was using because she had for some years attended an *internado*, a "boarding school," where Quechua literacy was taught. She pointed to one of the words on my sheet—*qilqay*, which I was taught in my language classes was the word for the verb "to write"—and told me that nobody around here used that word. Instead, they used the Spanish loanword *iskribiy* from Spanish *escribir*.

School Quechua was not the Quechua that was spoken on the streets. As the tides of different educational reform acts washed through Saipina, there was sometimes a place for a Quechua teacher and sometimes not (on the Educational Reform Act, see Albó 2004; Comboni Salinas and Juárez Nuñez 2001; Gustafson 2009a). The Quechua teachers that I knew were fluent, educated speakers of Quechua, generally from the altiplano highlands rather than the Quechua-speaking valleys. Most of them were well-meaning teachers who cared about their students, but they held purist language ideologies about both Quechua and Spanish and explicitly denigrated language mixing (Luykx 2003, 2004). Since most of the children in their class identified as Spanish speakers, the Quechua instruction was presented at a very basic level—memorization of lists of vocabulary words, spelling tests, pronunciation drills. Emphasis was placed on purist, sometimes arcane vocabulary, such as numbers and the days of the week (as Hill and Hill 1986 describe for Mexicano). In the living spoken language, these classes of words have been entirely replaced by their Spanish equivalents in most varieties of Bolivian Quechua. The Spanish-speaking students that I knew found the classes teeth-grindingly dull and felt they were there to be punished for not speaking Quechua. Quechua speakers who were placed in the same classes were told implicitly and explicitly that the language that they spoke was not a valuable or educated variety. This attitude persisted throughout the course of the educational process. A college student I knew who was required to take Quechua as part of her teaching degree told me that even though she had grown up a fully fluent speaker of Quechua, she could barely understand the Quechua that was taught in her class.

National language policies influenced the way that people in Saipina perceived Quechua. The Educational Reform Act of the early 1990s under Gonzalo Sánchez de Lozada mandated that children should be taught in their native language (Gray-Molina et al. 1999; Sánchez de Lozada 1994). While this was surely meant to be a progressive step, in Saipina it meant that Quechua language instruction was eliminated, since the town was officially and ideologically classified as a Spanish-speaking area. Later, Quechua classes were reinstated, but the quality of instruction was not improved. In towns slightly to the west of Saipina, which were understood to be Quechua speaking, bilingual teachers were assigned to classrooms. In Saipina, however, even teachers who were themselves bilingual taught in Spanish. Later, Evo Morales's administration eliminated bilingual education entirely for several years before moving toward a more progressive education policy (on Bolivian education policy, see, among others, Hornberger 1997; Hornberger and Coronel-Molina 2004; Hornberger and López 1998). The resistance to the Reforma Educativa was not entirely the fault of national policies; both teachers and parents supported traditional educational policies, such as monolingual Spanish instruction, rather than the more progressive policies of the Educational Reform Act. When I asked parents what languages they thought their children should study in school, the answer was overwhelmingly "English." Only a few families mentioned Quechua.

Another language policy decision that affected the perception of indigenous languages in Saipina was the decree of the Constitutional Assembly, convened by Evo Morales in 2006, that all government employees were required to speak at least one indigenous language of Bolivia (Rojas and Pablo 2006). "Competence" was identified through a government-administered language evaluation. In the case of Quechua, the most commonly spoken indigenous language, this meant not just any kind of Quechua but the purist variety of Quechua that was taught in universities. Morales's policies had perhaps unanticipated effects in an area with a linguistic situation as complex as Saipina's. After the policy took effect, long-time municipal employees were challenged for not speaking an indigenous language and replaced by highly educated bi- or multilingual highlanders. I knew of no local people and only a few people from Cochabamba who managed to defend their right to their job based on their Quechua competence. Instead, government positions were increasingly held by highly educated individuals from the highland urban centers of La Paz, Potosí, and Sucre. Naturally, this exacerbated long-standing resentments between locals and outsiders, Spanish speakers and Quechua speakers.

Language policies, like language ideologies, function on a variety of scales and may have unanticipated effects or interpretations in local contexts (Hornberger 1997, 1998). To be a speaker of a language—Spanish or Quechua—in the Santa Cruz valleys means something different from what it does in the judicial capital of Sucre or in the executive capital of La Paz, where such policies are generally made (on minority language politics, see Jaffe 1999; Meek 2012).

CONCLUSION

Discussions about language in Saipina were structured around a binary opposition between Quechua and Spanish. At the same time, these poles were not simple or absolute. People recognized different dialects or accents of each language, and they were aware of mixing and code-switching between languages. Quechua and Spanish as distinct languages and identities were constructed by and through practices that people engaged in. Like the other categories that I discuss in this book, "language" is not a simple object in the world that can be easily named and identified; instead, it is a complex set of understandings and behavioral norms embedded in a semiotic field that structures the system of meaning (Duranti 1994; Hill and Hill 1986; Kuipers 1998).

Quechua and Spanish existed in a symbiotic relationship in Saipina. There was no firm, clearly defined line between the types of people or the types of contexts in which one language or another was used, although I have identified tendencies of use in this chapter. Despite ideologies reinforcing the dominance of Spanish, Quechua was alive and well, in part because of continued migration of Quechua speakers but also because of the way that people used a Quechua-Spanish mixture to index a local identity (Babel 2012, 2014b). The ideas that people in Saipina held about Spanish and Quechua might be clear and distinct, but the way that they used the languages told a different story.

Quechua was seen rather differently in Saipina from how it has been described in other parts of the Andes. Most people spoke a mixed variety of language; if they spoke Spanish, it was Spanish mixed with Quechua; if they spoke Quechua, it was Quechua mixed with Spanish. The mixture of Quechua with Spanish indexed a local identity, intimacy, agriculture, child-rearing, and a host of other concepts. Even Spanish speakers who identified themselves as monolinguals were able to understand and produce Quechua words and phrases. Even siblings who grew up together might have different linguistic identifications. This positioning came into conflict with the national rhetoric that made Quechua—*pure* Quechua—a state symbol and the related assumption that the Quechua language was tied to an indigenous identity (Albó 1979, 2004; Hornberger 1997, 1998; Luykx 2004; Mannheim 1984).

While Spanish and Quechua formed a binary relationship, like the colla/camba dichotomy, my consultants felt most comfortable locating themselves somewhere in between the two poles. This in-between positioning reinforced the existence of Quechua and Spanish as opposite poles in a dichotomy and reflected the East/West, camba/colla dichotomies that I described in chapter 1. The interrelationships between all these dimensions of identity and meaning created the structure of a coherent semiotic field. In turn, the semiotic field was used to interpret social meaning through language or other signs, as I describe in chapter 2. The fact of being a Spanish speaker or a Quechua speaker affected the way that people interpreted and evaluated meaning produced within this system of signs.

INTERLUDE

The New Neighborhoods

DOÑA JUANA was my key informant throughout my years of fieldwork in Saipina. I first encountered Doña Juana as a neighbor—she lived right across the street from the first house that I lived in as a volunteer. Some time later, I married her son, and we entered into a new kind of relationship, as daughter-in-law and mother-in-law. Doña Juana's house, tiny and crowded and ramshackle, was where I went anytime I had nowhere else to be. I spent countless hours squatting on a low wooden beam outside her open-air kitchen, watching her cook, eating her food, and playing with the younger children in her household. When I was sick—as I often was—Doña Juana took care of me, giving me herbal teas to treat my fever and soothing me with her healing hands. She was fond of foreigners, plants, and animals, all in approximately the same nurturing and slightly amused way. There were always dogs and cats and for a long time a parrot living in her yard, and she talked to her recalcitrant papaya trees—which never bore fruit—as if they were people. She was always picking up strays, human and animal, and took care of quite a few of my pets and friends over the years. I greatly admired Doña Juana's natural graciousness and courtesy in dealing with people from all walks of life.

Doña Juana knew everything about everyone in Saipina. She had an absolutely encyclopedic memory for births, marriages, deaths, relationships, and all things relating to families. The location of her home in the center of town meant that she could open her front door and see everything worth knowing about passing by. Doña Juana worked for wealthier families, lending a hand with cooking for large events or sometimes cleaning and child care. She was also a reliable participant in the Club de Madres (Mothers' Club), a Catholic Church–supported organization that brought together all the mothers of families who lived in downtown Saipina. These pathways of gossip and knowledge placed her at the center of the Saipineño elite.

We were all happy when Doña Juana landed a job cooking and cleaning at the brand-new municipal hospital. Though it was hard work, with long hours and few vacations, she was well qualified for the job, and she enjoyed working with doctors and nurses and around sick people. It also gave her a stable source of income and state-supported health insurance. At the hospital, she found a group of colleagues and friends among the doctors and nurses, and as her children grew older and more independent, she became an indispensable part of their social gatherings.

The difficult part about working at the hospital was its location, far up in the tierras nuevas (new neighborhoods). It was a long walk uphill to work in the morning and a longer walk back after lunch break in the blazing sun. In the evenings, Doña Juana came home well after dark, and the long walk through scrub brush where stray dogs wandered was sometimes unpleasant. Doña Juana, who had participated in the group petitioning the government for new housing, was assigned a house lot and eventually a house in one of the "new neighborhoods," far from the center of town, across the quebrada (ravine). The new house was located conveniently close to the hospital, only a few minutes' walk away and in fact within sight of the hospital complex. However, even after other people started moving out to the new neighborhoods, Doña Juana was reluctant to leave her home. It wasn't just the hassle of moving or her fond memories of the old house—it was also the symbolic step of moving from the center of town to the periphery, to a new neighborhood where many outsiders—colla immigrants—lived. The hurdle was psychological and social—though the new houses were clean and modern and in good repair, convenient to the hospital, and offered more space for Doña Juana and her family, they were not nestled in the bosom of Saipina society the way the old house was. She would no longer be able to look out onto the main street to watch everything that mattered passing by, would not be able to gossip with her old neighbors. Instead, it would be a long walk to the center of town, and she wouldn't belong there in the same way.

At the urging of her son, Doña Juana eventually moved out to her new house, and I think she was more or less happy there. It didn't have the same homey spirit of the old house, though, and people didn't hang about as I and others used to. The Mothers' Club was a long walk away, and Doña Juana's attendance fell off. She no longer worked for other matrons, since she was busy at the hospital. Moving to a new neighborhood didn't make Doña Juana a different person—she was still welcome and beloved and conocida (known) among families from the center of town and just as generous and nurturing as ever—but it changed the people she spent time with and the groups that she was most firmly integrated in.

CHAPTER 4

LEGITIMATE SAIPINEÑOS AND STRANGERS

Race, Language, and Migration

On my way to buy bread one afternoon I noticed a woman sitting outside her house on the sidewalk, crocheting. I said hello, and she invited me to sit down. Her name was Doña Aleja, and she was a part-time teacher in the schools. She also told me was that she was a *legítima Saipineña* (legitimate person from Saipina). As we talked, she told me all about her family, saying that they lived here when the town wasn't much more than the central plaza, a block from where we sat. Gesturing at her own dark eyes and curly hair, which contrasted with her light complexion, she explained that she was the darkest person in her family. All the rest of them were fair and blue-eyed and curly-haired, her great-grandfather was a Spaniard, and her father and grandfather came from towns to the east, from the monolingual lowlands.

Without prompting, she told me that she didn't like more recent immigrants, and she hoped that her children, who were studying at the prestigious public university in Santa Cruz, wouldn't marry anyone from bilingual Cochabamba. I asked her why not, and she explained that people from Cochabamba were mean, that they weren't like people from Saipina. "Te hablan muy lindo pero si les niegas algún favorcito ya no te miran" (They talk pretty, but if you deny them the tiniest little favor, they never look at you again), she said. In contrast, she spoke about the generosity and friendliness of people who were *real* Saipineños.

Legítimos Saipineños were an endangered breed. Doña Aleja told me this, and so did everyone else whom I talked to about migration and Quechua-Spanish contact. "I can count the number of legítimos Saipineños on my fingers," said Blanca, an older woman from one of Saipina's founding families. She held up her fingers as she flipped through mental genealogies aloud, commenting on who had died and who had moved to the city.

Two generations ago, Saipina was a tiny town—but it wasn't quite as tiny as people implied. In Spanish as in English, the word *legítimo* (legitimate) is connected to birthright; a legitimate child is one whose father's name appears on his or her birth certificate. The word "legitimacy" contains a fascinating overlay of birthright, institutional recognition, and race (de la Cadena 2000). An illegitimate child is one who is not acknowledged by his father; an illegitimate citizen is one who is not recognized by the state. Historically, many Bolivians have been illegitimate both personally and institutionally. It is no coincidence that discussions of Saipina's roots also revolve around European heritage and that the families that are identified as legítimos Saipineños are all owners of large tracts of land, and most of them are wealthy. Language was also an integral part of the construction of legitimacy; over and over, I heard that real Saipineños were monolingual Spanish speakers.

I explored this question with my friend Doña Mónica. Mónica ran a small business, and when I talked to her she was forty years old and enormously pregnant. She was hot and uncomfortable and irritated, and she spoke more directly than she might have otherwise. She talked openly about her dislike of Quechua speakers, characterizing them as both ignorant and arrogant. "These people don't even know how to dial a phone, but they think they're something special," she said.

Mónica explained that being Saipineño meant being born, being brought up, and living in the town of Saipina. She mentioned her parents, who came to Saipina at the age of ten and thirteen, respectively, and formed their family there. Unlike Doña Aleja, Mónica could not consider herself part of a founding family. When I asked whether she still considered them Saipineños, she told me, "They came here when they were very young." We talked about a neighbor who had lived in Saipina for nearly sixty years, who was a fixture in town and—for me at least—an icon of Saipina. She hesitated. "He's *almost* considered to be a Saipineño," she said with the manner of giving a generous compliment.

But this neighbor in question was a proud bilingual, and though he had not lived in Cochabamba in many years, he enjoyed speaking Quechua on the streets. Being born and raised in Saipina was not the only quality involved in being a Saipineño. In the transcript below, Mónica responded to a question about whether all her friends spoke alike or whether there were some who spoke better than others.

Transcript 15: M (Mónica), A (Anna)

1. M: Yo creo que los Saipineños que somos Saipineños, hablamos todos iguales.	1. M: I think that Saipineños, those of us who are Saipineños, all speak alike.
2. A: Mhm. Mhm. Todos son iguales.	2. A: Uh-huh. Uh-huh. All alike.
3. M: Sí. Los Saipineños que *somos* Saipineños, ¿no?	3. M: Yes. We Saipineños that *are* Saipineños, right?
4. A: Y ¿qué quiere decir, *ser* Saipineño?	4. A: And what does it mean, to *be* Saipineño?
5. M: Bueno, que, e, por, somos nacidos aquí, somos criados aquí, digamos. ¿Ya?	5. M: Well, that, um, because, we're born here, and we're raised here, let's say. Okay?
6. A: Mhm.	6. A: Mm-hmm.
7. M: Todavía vivimos aquí desde que hemos nacido, digamos.	7. M: We've lived here since we were born, let's say.
8. A: Mhm.	8. A: Mm-hmm.
9. M: Y somos todos conocidos porque ya no somos muchos.	9. M: And we all know each other, because there aren't many of us anymore.
10. A: Ah, pocos son.	10. A: Oh, there aren't many.
11. M: Sí, ya somos pocos los Saipineños. Entonces, clarito, el Saipineño, que, que vive, aquí.	11. M: Yes, there are very few of us Saipineños now. So it's very clear, the Saipineño that lives, here.
12. A: Hm.	12. A: Huh.
13. M: Pero no es, desde, bueno, viven muchos años pero no es Saipineño.	13. M: But it's not, since, well, they [can] live here for many years, but they're not Saipineños.
14. A: Mhm, mhm.	14. A: Uh-huh, uh-huh.
15. M: También hay muchos Saipineños que desde, han llegado niños y se han criado aquí.	15. M: There are also lots of Saipineños that since, they arrived as children and they grew up here.
16. A: Mhm.	16. A: Mm-hmm.
17. M: Casi ya son considerados Saipineños, no, porque hasta su forma de este, ya, son, son como un Saipineño, no como las personas que decimos [que] estan llegando.	17. M: They're almost considered Saipineños, right, because even their manner of um, they're, they're like a Saipineño, not like the people we say are arriving.

18. A: Mhm.	18. A: Mm-hmm.
19. M: No, o por lo menos no sabe el Quechua.	19. M: No, or at least they don't speak Quechua.
20. A: Ah ha.	20. A: Uh-huh.
21. M: Pero el Saipineño siempre casi poco sabe. No sabe Quechua.	21. M: But a Saipineño doesn't know practically anything. S/he doesn't know Quechua.
22. A: M, ya, ya.	22. A: Mm, okay, okay.
23. M: No, el Saipineño no sabe Quechua casi.	23. M: No, a Saipineño basically doesn't know Quechua.
24. A: No sabe.	24. A: S/he doesn't know it.
25. M: No. No, no sabe. O tal vez ha aprendido, ya, con el tiempo, pero yo creo que no sabe siempre bien el Quechua.	25. No. S/he, doesn't know it. Or maybe s/he has learned, now, with time, but I think that [a Saipineño] will never speak Quechua well.

In this conversation, Mónica began by describing Saipineños as people who were born and raised in Saipina (turns 5, 7). She elaborated, mentioning that all Saipineños were by definition *conocidos* (known). This put a slightly different spin on the definition; a "familia conocida y decente" (known and decent family) is a designation used since colonial times to denote white families in contrast to nonwhite families (de la Cadena 2000:44–85); something like the overtones that the phrase "he comes from a good family" can take on in English. If Saipineños were legítimos and conocidos, then the idea of being a Saipineño was tied not only to place of birth but also to station in life, tying this concept to race, class, and language, as Mónica went on to explain.

In turns 13, 15, and 17 Mónica allowed for some doubt in the cases of people who lived in Saipina from a very young age, that is, who were raised in Saipina but not born there. She began to mention that even their manner of speaking sounded like a Saipineño (turn 17), contrasting people raised in Saipina with recent arrivals. She linked recent arrivals with Quechua, emphasizing in turns 19, 21, and 23 that a real Saipineño could not speak Quechua, although she hedged this statement, saying *casi* 'almost'. Mónica concluded that a being Saipineño and being a Quechua speaker effectively contradicted each other. In turn 25 she seemed to say that it was acceptable for a Saipineño to try to learn Quechua; but she concluded that a person who was serious about being a Saipineño would never be serious about learning and speaking Quechua. In Doña Mónica's opinion, legitimate Saipineños don't speak Quechua.

Between Doña Aleja and Doña Mónica, some clusters of ideas began to emerge. Being a Saipineño–or at least a Saipineño legítimo–was connected not only with birthplace but with being of European descent (fair, curly-haired, with light eyes), speaking Spanish, and being friendly and generous; new immigrants, on the other hand, were described not only as Quechua speakers but as interlopers who were two-faced, ignorant, mean, and arrogant. By definition, a Saipineño was a monolingual Spanish speaker, or at least knew very little Quechua. A person who was raised in Saipina but not born there could be considered a Saipineño–as long as they were not considered to be a Quechua speaker. Ideas about legitimacy—and, through legitimacy, race—were closely integrated with the ideologies around collas and cambas, Quechua and Spanish speakers, through their participation in the semiotic field.

In these commentaries, Spanish was presented as an index of belonging, and not only belonging, but of belonging to a select group of people from Saipina who were of European descent and of recognized families—families that could be counted on the fingers of one hand. Or, perhaps more accurately, the fact of speaking Quechua openly was a symbol of outsider status. A person who was openly proud of being a bilingual would never really be a legítimo Saipineño. In telling these stories and making these claims, Mónica and Aleja policed the borders of polite society, using language identification as a litmus test. The problem with bilinguals was not that they were able to speak Quechua; it was that they were proud of being able to do so.

The term *conocido* was often associated with being legítimo. While legítimo referred to birthright, conocido referred to being a local person, to being well known, to being recognized as a resident of the local area (somewhat in contrast to de la Cadena 2000:44–85). Unlike the term *legítimo*, this term wasn't limited to the Saipina elites. It could also be used for people who had established their residence in Saipina and who were well known in town. It was used by and for many families who were not in the upper echelons of Saipina social life; it had something to do with permanence and rootedness, as well as race and class. A person who was conocido was someone you could trust, even if you didn't know them very well. When we were looking for a renter for our house, we were repeatedly urged to look for someone who was conocido. This, it was implied and sometimes stated, would exclude Quechua-speaking recent immigrants—in a word, collas. The issue was centered not just on race or class but on language and place of origin.

A *desconocido* (stranger), on the other hand, was not to be trusted. The term *desconocido* was often used as a synonym for collas or for recent migrants. During one period of fieldwork, there was a rash of burglaries around town—people's electronics and valuables were stolen out of their houses while they were away. Around the same time, a neighbor warned me about some suspicious characters, desconocidos, she had seen hanging around. She told me that there were two of them and that they were Quechua speakers. One of them was of very small stature, almost childlike, and she had seen him inspecting the area around our house. She described them both as being dark-complexioned. She worried that they had been planning to rob our house. In comments like these, desconocidos were connected to Quechua-speaking immigrants from the west who had physical characteristics like small stature and dark skin that were linked to indigeneity. At the same time, they were characterized as lawless people who were not integrated into local society and who were potentially dangerous or threatening.

Through these discourses, disparate categories such as race, migration status, familiarity, rootedness, and morality were drawn together into a single complex of ideas with multiple overlays. By referring to someone as desconocido—or by complaining that Saipina had been overrun by desconocidos and that there were hardly any conocido families around anymore—people invoked multiple simultaneous layers of meaning. Conocido and desconocido formed two poles in a binary that could be superimposed on other binary poles (Spanish/Quechua, eastern/western, camba/colla) through its participation in the semiotic field that provided a structure to organize these concepts. Conocido/desconocido contained perhaps the most explicit moral overlay of all the binary pairs, forming a link between migration history, regional origin, language use, and integration into society.

In contrast to desconocidos, people who were born and raised in Saipina could claim to be Saipineños, people from Saipina. When I asked people what made a Saipineño, answers varied. Many people told me that Saipineños were people who were born and raised in Saipina. But others appealed to more intangible measures. "It means having the culture of this area, keeping our traditions," Ana María told me. "An agricultural lifestyle." Glover, who had moved to Saipina as a ten-year-old with his parents, Quechua-speaking migrants from the west, told me that he absolutely considered himself a Saipineño. On the other hand, Serena, who lived in Saipina and came from an old Saipineño family but spent the first six years of her life in Santa Cruz, hesitated when I asked her whether she was Saipineña. "I'm more Saipineña than I am anything else," she told me after a long pause.

When I asked people how they would characterize a Saipineño, they described a friendly, outgoing personality and a good sense of humor. "A Saipineño, if you see them on the street, they'll say, 'Good morning,' and if they have a minute, they'll come up and shake your hand," Vladimir told me. Noemí, describing urban migrants disapprovingly, said, "People I know, people I went to high school with, they would just pass me on the street. They didn't say hello, they didn't greet me, nothing." "Saipineños are good folks," Tomás told me. "They're always ready with a joke, they're funny, they help each other out." Serena told me that this outlook had gotten her into trouble when she studied in the highland city of Sucre. "Sometimes one says something, just as a joke, and people take it seriously," she said. "Around here we're always kidding each other, but other people get offended."

The definitions of conocido and of Saipineño are historically malleable. In the 1970s, after the river shifted and the roads were improved, migrants began arriving from the highlands and valleys surrounding Saipina. The highland farms were small plots dependent on rain. Unlike the farms around the river, they didn't produce large crops suitable for commercialization. They were often inaccessible during the rainy season and unproductive during the dry season. Young men and women from the highlands began to move closer as Saipina turned into an economic boom town in the 1970s and 1980s. There was an enormous demand for labor and large potential profits.

The young families who migrated to Saipina in the 1970s and 1980s had children who could claim to be Saipineño by birth and by upbringing. During those years, one of the main environments for producing Saipineños was the school system. Beginning in the mid-1980s, as Saipina grew large enough to support a *núcleo escolar* (school district), children could attend school in Saipina from kindergarten through high school. As schools do everywhere, this institution produced close relationships and friendships, and people felt a close connection with their classmates throughout their life (on the role of schooling in producing Bolivian citizenry, see Canessa 2012:184–215; Luykx 1999).

BACKGROUND AND THE BIG PICTURE

Descriptions of Bolivia often claim that 60 percent (or some similar number) of Bolivians are "indigenous" and that this number is the highest in Latin America. This statistic reflects the number of people who identify themselves as "indigenous" on the census. For many Bolivians, this is largely a political stance, and people's ethnic identification can shift through changes in social status or political orientation (see de la Cadena 2000 on Andean ideologies of race). The category does not necessarily reflect genetic heritage, divergent language or cultural practices, or a sharp division between "indigenous" and "mestizo" ethnic groups (Canessa 2005, 2012). Indeed, even among people who identify as indigenous, there is a sharply politicized distinction between Andean and Amazonian indigenous groups (Albro 2010; Emlen 2016; Fabricant 2012; Gustafson 2009a; Postero 2007, 2010).

In Saipina it is safe to say that practically all local residents have mixed native South American and European ancestry. In all the time I have spent in Saipina, I have seldom heard anyone use the term *indígena* or *mestizo*, and I don't think I have ever heard my consultants use the term *criollo* or *Europeo* to describe either themselves or other Bolivians (Canessa 2007; Howard 2010). Words like *negro* (black), *blanco* (white), *choco* (light-complexioned), and *moreno* (dark-complexioned) were used to describe skin color, but generally not in a racialized way. The word *indio*, however, was used as a racial slur. This is not to say that Saipineños did not have sharp divisions between racialized social categories. While factors such as ancestry, physical characteristics, and family history were important, they were used as part of a system that layered social and ethnic differences with the camba/colla distinction and with histories of migration.

The semiotic field structured the way these features played into social categorization in Saipina. Racialized categories included ancestry, histories of migration and geographical origin, and physical characteristics such as hair texture and eye color, body build, and skin color or complexion. They were also connected to social class, family histories, and power through racialized terms such as conocido, decente, and legítimo. While race was seldom invoked explicitly, racialized interpretations of categories like conocido, decente, and legítimo provided a framework for differentiating between "insiders" and "outsiders," extending the reach of these binary poles into other social categories.

AGRICULTURE AND MIGRATION

Perhaps the most important dimension of social differentiation in Saipina was migration history, and migration was driven by the agricultural economy.

Products were transported in and out; workers migrated to and from the highlands in different seasons. Families maintained estancias in the upper reaches of the valley or farmed rainfall-dependent plots on the upper slopes during the rainy season. People maintained relationships with their seed suppliers, truckers, and *mayoristas* (wholesalers, middlemen, or, more often, Quechua-speaking middle*women*) in the city markets. There was movement in the transfer of land from traditional landowning families to new generations of workers. Young people emigrated from Saipina to the city, whether to study or to work, after high school. These migration flows, particularly the West-to-East pattern, have obtained for decades, if not centuries, in the Saipina valley (for the broader context of Andean migration, see Larson and Harris 1995).

Because of its fertile soil, dry climate, and year-round irrigation, Saipina produced an array of crops, the most reliable of which were tomatoes, potatoes, and sugarcane. Onions were also popular, and watermelons and other fruits were produced in season. All of these were primarily cash crops, though people also grew other crops, notably corn, for their own consumption. Farmers engaged in a cycle of ever-increasing costs due to the application of chemical fertilizers and pesticides, which caused resistance in common pests. Many families also cared for livestock such as chickens, pigs, and free-ranging goats, sheep, and cattle as a fallback when profits were meager.

In 2004 a German-funded development project dammed a river upstream from Saipina and opened hundreds of acres of previously barren land to irrigation and agriculture. Anyone with collateral rushed to secure a loan on newly arable parcels of land. This caused some upheaval in traditional social categories, as recent immigrants who were able to raise enough money to buy a plot suddenly became landowners. These new arrivals brought their friends and neighbors from the highlands to help them work the new lands. A new neighborhood populated mostly by Quechua-speaking migrants from the West grew up on the side of Saipina nearest to the new lands. This neighborhood was baptized San José de la T'ajra, a *t'ajra* being a Quechua toponym describing an infertile, rocky piece of land, and José the given name of the landowner.

One day I asked my comadre, a Quechua-speaking migrant from the West, whether she would ever return permanently to her home in the highlands. She shook her head. "When we lived there, I had to go out in the fields [to herd livestock] every day. I was gone from daybreak to sunset. The children were always hungry. They would cry from hunger. I would come home and make dinner, and sometimes they would fall asleep before they could eat it." Speaking of their childhood, her sister told me, "We were poor. To make soup, we would boil water and add salt, rice, and potatoes. That was all. Or we would make corn gruel. When we were able to milk the goats, that was when we had milk. When we butchered a kid, that was when we had meat."

The arid highlands in the West yielded just one crop a year, seldom enough to feed a family; if they were lucky, women herded sheep and goats and kept scrappy chickens to make up for the caloric difference. In the dry season, men traveled to irrigated regions like Saipina or other nearby towns to make some money as day laborers or to an urban center to work in construction. Some men and women traveled away from their families for weeks and months as peddlers. Still, agriculture was seen as the most desirable occupation for a family.

The opening of new irrigated lands in Saipina created a year-round demand for work and offered an economically attractive alternative to families who already participated in the migration cycle. Many workers who had been seasonal residents moved to Saipina permanently, bringing their families with them. They came in family groups that partly replicated their support structure in their hometowns; other relatives stayed behind to care for now uninhabited tracts of land and groups of homes.

Within a generation or two, Saipina underwent massive and constant population growth. At one time, it was a sleepy hamlet of only a few hundred people. Shifts in the river, improved transportation, the availability of chemical pesticides and fertilizer, greater irrigation capacity, and the opening of new cultivated lands all contributed to this agriculture-related economic growth. When I arrived in Saipina in 2002, the official estimate of the town's population was 2,998 residents. By the time I returned for my dissertation fieldwork in 2008, a town council member told me that though official population figures registered only a modest increase, she calculated that the population had grown to at least 10,000 and probably more. My own observations supported this claim. New neighborhoods had sprung up all around the edges of town. Most of the houses were constructed by hand, and land arrangements were informal: landowners allowed people to live on their land for free, but with the understanding that they could be turned out or required to pay the current land value at any time. Because the rapid expansion of these neighborhoods stressed the already weak public services, many houses went months or years before they were able to install utilities such as water, electricity, and gas.

The economic power of the agricultural economy drove migration from the western highlands to Saipina, making the presence of highland Quechua-speaking migrants one of the key axes of social differentiation in Saipina. The rapid growth of the town over a relatively short period of time made these distinctions even more salient than they may have been in the past. One of the ways in which more and less recent migrants were distinguished was by their use of language.

LANGUAGE PRACTICES: MIGRANTS FROM THE LOCAL VALLEYS

I found Doña Sofía and her husband, Víctor, sitting in chairs on the dirt road outside their house, as they sat every evening, watching the sun set and the people walk by. I squatted down in the dirt to talk to them, and after a while Don Víctor offered me his chair, going back into the house to bring back a stool for himself. Their grandson played in the street with his friends.

Doña Sofía told me that she came from Cochabamba and was a Quechua speaker. Her mother was a monolingual Quechua speaker, and although her father spoke Spanish, she didn't learn the language until she enrolled in school. "My mother spoke to me in Quechua because she didn't know how to speak anything else," she told me. She said that her friends were sometimes surprised to learn that she spoke Quechua. She had lived for almost forty years in Saipina, and her accent was indistinguishable from that of other Spanish speakers in the area. Sofía claimed she was forgetting Quechua because she hardly used it; none of her children learned Quechua, although the grandson playing nearby had learned to count to ten in school.

When I asked Doña Sofía and Don Víctor about language instruction in the schools, they both talked about English. They said that there should be more English taught because so many young men and women were going to foreign countries for work. They told a story about how their son was swindled by a person who claimed to be able to obtain a visa for the United States. When I asked about Quechua, Don Víctor said it was useless to teach it in school; Doña Sofía said it might be useful if children had to go to Cochabamba or Potosí, to the west, where people spoke Quechua. She said that her children sometimes met people who spoke Quechua and didn't understand, didn't know how to respond. Through these comments, Sofía and Víctor supported the idea that Quechua was something that was only useful in other parts of Bolivia, not in Saipina. The language that they desired for their children was not Quechua but English, which would lead to upward social mobility.

This pattern was widespread among families that emigrated from the local highlands in the 1970s. Many of these individuals came from families with a mixed Quechua and Spanish background; often women were monolingual Quechua speakers and men were Spanish bilinguals, or some branches of the family were Quechua speakers and some were Spanish speakers, or neighboring towns were known as Quechua-speaking towns or as Spanish-speaking towns. Patterns of migration, adoption, and family changes due to death and remarriage also resulted in widespread mixing between Spanish speakers and Quechua speakers.

After settling in Saipina, all these families switched to Spanish, and their children grew up as Spanish speakers; yet Quechua didn't disappear completely. It was this group that came up to me on the street and, speaking Spanish, admired my daughter's *chheros* 'curls'; they squeezed her little legs and called her *thusuda* 'big-calved' and *chaskañawicita* 'star-eyed' (having long, curly eyelashes); they suggested that I squeeze her nose every night so that she wouldn't grow up *ñata* 'broad-nosed', and they carried her around in their *markha* 'load carried in the arms' or *khepi* 'load carried on the back'. They scolded me for letting her run around *chuta* 'naked bum' in the cold weather, and they told me when the *thantakhateros* 'peddlers' were in town selling cheap baby clothes. They came to her *thiluda*, the hair-cutting ceremony, where she was given an *iwacha* 'animal still in the womb'.[10] These linguistic markers of Quechua influence, linked to child-rearing practices, demonstrated the close links between Quechua-Spanish contact and intimate spheres. They served as evidence of recent language shift from Quechua-dominant homes to Spanish-dominant ones.

LANGUAGE PRACTICES: RECENT MIGRANTS

One day I went to visit my friend Doña Lorenza. Doña Lorenza and her husband, Samuel, had moved to Saipina from the Quechua-speaking area to the west nearly two decades earlier, when their daughter Damiana was still a young child. Samuel was a day laborer and sometime sharecropper; Lorenza cared for a wide variety

10. The *thiluda*, also known as *rutucha*, is an important Andean rite of passage for children after their first birthday. Guests at the ceremony give money or gifts to the child as they cut locks of hair. One of the most valuable gifts is livestock, and the *iwacha*, after its birth, could grow into a significant asset. The extent of the value of this gift depends on the luck of the child: if the animal is stillborn, the child gets nothing; if the animal is male and survives, the child has a source of cash; if it is female and survives, the child might have the beginning of his or her own herd of cattle. *Padrinos de cabello* (godparents of hair) are equal in importance to the child's *padrinos de bautizo* (godparents of baptism).

of livestock. They joined family members who had moved to Saipina a few years before. Damiana and her younger brother Tomás grew up and went to high school in Saipina. The family owned a house not far from the center of town.

Doña Lorenza's husband was bilingual, and she herself spoke Spanish with a strong Quechua accent (see also chapter 2). However, most of their interaction at home was carried on in Quechua. Damiana spoke fluent Quechua, although she preferred to speak Spanish with her friends.

On this day, Tomás was making *bico*, a paste used to intensify the mildly stimulant effect of chewing coca. He would sell this bico to workers in the city for a profit. In addition to Tomás, his mother, his sister, and his cousin Isabel were all at home. As we talked, I noticed that Damiana and Isabel were the barometers of language choice; both fluent bilinguals, they accommodated Doña Lorenza by speaking Quechua and me and Tomás by speaking Spanish. The two young women used mostly Spanish when addressing each other but would switch to Quechua to elaborate an argument or clinch a series of thoughts.

At one point, Doña Lorenza and I were telling the group about the interview that I had carried out with her a few days before. I mentioned (in Quechua) that I didn't speak well but that I could understand. Tomás challenged me in Spanish, "How can you understand but not speak?" Without thinking, I countered, "But you understand and you can't really speak," forgetting that this might be insulting or inaccurate.

He responded, "It's like if I was trying to say a word in English. I might not say it perfectly or pronounce it well, but I still say it." By this statement, Tomás positioned himself as a nonnative speaker of Quechua. His mother, too, sometimes insisted that Tomás could speak and understand just fine, but she also commented that he almost never spoke to her in Quechua.

On that particular afternoon, he spoke to Lorenza in Quechua only once. They were packing the loaves of bico into a cardboard box for his bus trip that afternoon. He wanted to pack them in groups of five, but Lorenza's hands were too small to pick up groups of five at a time. After asking her several times to pass him groups of five, frustrated, he said, "Phishqamanta phisqaman" (Five by five) to her in Quechua, framing her failure to respond to his request as a lack of understanding by switching into a code that he seldom used.

When I spoke to the family several years later about language practices, Tomás confidently identified himself as a Quechua speaker. "How could I not be, when you know that my mother speaks Quechua?" he asked me. Yet Lorenza told me that Tomás, who was born in Saipina, had refused to speak Quechua as a small child. "I would say to him in Quechua, 'Riy, chayta apamuy!' [Run, go get that!], and he would just stare," she told me. "Then, 'Andá, traé eso!' in Spanish, and he would run off right away to pick it up." She told me that he had learned Quechua when an older female cousin who was a monolingual Quechua speaker came to stay with the family. Tomás confirmed this account, saying that his cousin had taught him Quechua. However, his willingness to speak the language shifted over the years that I knew him.

Families such as Lorenza's constituted a second wave of migration to Saipina, after the influx from the neighboring highlands in the 1970s. Most of these more recent immigrants were Quechua-dominant families from the western highlands. The "new" neighborhoods around Saipina were full of Quechua-speaking women wearing pollera, and it was these new neighbors whom many of my older, more established consultants complained about when they used terms like *colla* and *desconocido*.

Children of this second wave of migrants attended school, and in school they were inculcated with the dominant-language ideology; despite the growth of several new, largely Quechua-speaking neighborhoods, language shift from Quechua to Spanish was still in process. Yet there was also room for change and shift over time, and not always in the direction of language loss; while Tomás positioned himself as a Spanish-dominant speaker in his youth, as he grew older he identified more strongly as a Quechua bilingual.

INDIGENOUS IDENTITIES: *RUNITA* AND *PROFESORES*

When a truck carrying bags of cement drove off the road near Saipina, several passengers riding in the open bed, mostly men coming from the highlands to work as migrant laborers, were killed. Their families came to Saipina to claim those that were identifiable. The families were mostly women, monolingual Quechua speakers who came from rural regions in the western highlands around Chuquisaca. They wore not the mass-manufactured pollera common in the Saipina region but hand-woven and embroidered skirts and jackets that were typical of indigenous groups. One of my neighbors in Saipina was overcome with pity while talking about how these women struggled to navigate the Spanish-language bureaucracy and unfamiliar instruments such as the public telephone across from her house.

While bilingual Quechua speakers from Cochabamba were called collas and characterized as aggressive, hostile, mean, and a host of other stereotypes, monolingual Quechua speakers from the rural highlands of Chuquisaca were characterized as *runita*, from the Quechua word *runa* 'person' and the Spanish diminutive suffix. In Spanish, the word sounded patronizing, derogatory. People often related it to the physically small stature that was understood to be typical of highlanders, to the Quechua language, and, implicitly at least, to the low socioeconomic power that these groups commanded. People whom I heard referred to as runita generally came into town as seasonal laborers and spoke very little Spanish. The use of the word *runita*—literally, "little people"—placed them within a foreign realm of indigenous highlanders. One man, a long-term resident of Saipina who was a Quechua monolingual of very small physical stature, was referred to by the nickname El Ch'ullpa, a Quechua loanword used for precolonial burial sites. While exchange and intermarriage with collas was a part of daily life, interactions with runita were generally limited to their seasonal appearance as agricultural workers. I was often told that the "real" Quechua, "pure" Quechua, was spoken by these speakers from the Chuquisaca highlands (on Quechua linguistic purism, see Howard 2007; Niño-Murcia 1997).

At the other end of the social scale in Saipina were a small cohort of educated and wealthy teachers and merchants from the altiplano regions of Sucre, Potosí, La Paz, and Oruro. *Profesores* 'schoolteachers' were highly respected in rural regions of Bolivia, and Saipina was no exception. Teachers from these altiplano regions were among the most highly educated and respected townspeople, despite their outsider status. All the altiplano profesores I knew were bilingual in Quechua and Spanish, and many were Aymara speakers as well. One had studied at a Catholic seminary in Venezuela; he read Latin and Greek, as well as several European languages. One day on a bus ride we had a long philosophical conversation about the role of women in the clergy. Another, the late Jorge Mamani, had studied the work of Swiss linguist Ferdinand de Saussure and knew the basics of linguistics, and he and his wife, Nora Flores, shared many thoughtful conversations with me about indigenous language education. These conversations about intellectual topics were unusual in my daily life in Saipina.

Another professor, Profesor Quispe, chatted with me one day about language practices in the area. In the conversation excerpted below, Profesor Quispe and I spoke while sitting outside his store while his wife sat nearby, listening. Profe Quispe spoke Aymara at home with his wife, Quechua with other friends, and Spanish at school and in business interactions.

In the transcript below, I asked Profe Quispe how he would characterize the way people spoke in Saipina. He turned the conversation to a contrast between East and West, urban and rural, moving beyond language to physical characteristics and, later, behavior and discipline. He discussed complexion, asserting that people from the highlands (which he refers to as the *interior*) were darker than people from the eastern areas.

Transcript 16: Q (Quispe), A (Anna), S (Quispe's wife)

1. Q: Y por otro lado se les caracteriza porque la gente de aquí son mas blancones, y la gente del interior somos mas morenos.	1. Q: And on the other hand, they can be characterized because the people from here are whiter, and [we] the people from the interior are darker.
2. A: Mm . . . [laughing].	2. A: Mm . . . [Laughing].
3. Q: [Laughing]	3. Q: [Laughing]
4. A: Pero Usted no es muy moreno.	4. A: But you're not very dark.
5. **Q: Yo soy feo carita de barro como Atahuallpa.**	5. **Q: I'm an ugly mud-face like Atahuallpa.**
6. A: [Laughing] Lo que dice!	6. A: [Laughing] The things you say!
7. Q and S: [Laughing]	7. Q and S: [Laughing]
8. S: Lo que dic—!	8. S: What he sa—!
9. [Laughter]	9. [Laughter]
10. Q: Ayy . . . se va reir la . . .	10. Q: Ayy . . . she's going to laugh . . .
11. A: Y yo, que será pues?	11. A: And what about me?
12. Q: Puuucha, Usted es simpática como una virgen!	12. Q: Daaarn, you are beautiful like a virgin [saint]!
13. A: No pues!	13. A: No way!
14. G and S: [Laughing]	14. G and S: [Laughing]
15. . . .	15. . . .
16. A: Otros dicen . . . color del gusano ese.	16. A: Others say . . . the color of that worm.
17. Q: Como khuru.	17. Q: Like the khuru worm.
18. A: El gusano blanco.	18. A: The white worm.

Profe Quispe began by saying that "we," people from the highlands, were darker-complexioned than easterners. In response to my comment that he didn't have a very dark complexion, he made the joking remark "Yo soy feo carita de barro como Atahuallpa" (I'm an ugly mud-face like Atahuallpa).[11]

11. Atahuallpa was the Inca leader whose internecine war weakened the Inca Empire at the time of Spanish conquest.

At this deadpan remark, his wife and I burst out laughing, and she half-repeated my turn 6 in turn 8. Up to this point Quispe's wife had not participated verbally in the conversation, although she was sitting close by and listening attentively. After this remark, in turns 7, 9, and 14, she laughed out loud and made a few remarks as the interview frame was interrupted by Profe Quispe's jokes in turns 5 and 12 and my visible embarrassment at being told that I was "beautiful like a virgin." I defended myself in turn 15, referring to myself as "the white worm," a mild taunt commonly aimed at white foreigners.

In this exchange, Profe Quispe positioned himself as a phenotypically dark, indigenous person from the highlands and simultaneously as an educated person through his reference to Atahuallpa, a historical figure. He teased me by comparing me to a *virgencita* 'saint'. His remark was both self-deprecating, referring to himself as "ugly" and "mud-faced," and self-elevating, comparing himself to Inca royalty. Through these comments, Profe Quispe positioned himself as an indigenous highlander while at the same time claiming a high social status by linking his indigenous heritage to Inka royalty.

Runita, monolingual Quechua-speaking seasonal laborers from the highlands, and profesores, highly educated, wealthy, multilingual teachers, stood at opposite ends of the social scene in Saipina. Profesores lived permanently in the town, their children growing up and going to school with local children. Runita were largely transitory, making a little money before returning to their own lands. Despite their widely differing socioeconomic status, both of these groups were explicitly characterized as indigenous people in comments that I heard in Saipina. Likewise, both were characterized as outsiders to the local area, migrants who could have Saipineño children but would never be fully naturalized themselves. These comments draw racial and linguistic categories into the context of the semiotic field, linking race, language, and migration status.

A NICE BOY

As soon as I arrived in Bolivia, mothers and aunts, aware that I was a young single woman without a family structure, tried to set me up with their sons and nephews. "He's a nice, good-looking boy," they would tell me. "He's tall, light-complexioned, chubby, and he has a university degree." We joked about how I would make a tall chubby young man fit in my suitcase when I carried him back to my country.

After it became common knowledge that I was romantically involved with the man who would become my husband, these conversations changed. Strangers introduced themselves as distant relatives of my *novio*, tracing family trees that involved marriage and cousins and complicated generational relationships. Women would ask me whom I was dating, and when I told them, many of them were surprised that he was not a chubby, light-complexioned, highly educated member of the elite. I vividly remember sitting with two women one day in the plaza. I didn't know either of them well, nor were they close friends or relatives of my boyfriend. After I explained who he was, one of them turned to the other and said, "Es un negro flaco y feo, ¿no?" (He's an ugly skinny black guy, right?).[12] The other woman responded, "No, es moreno pero no es tan feo" (No, he's dark-complexioned, but he's not that ugly). While this sticks in my mind as the most overt comment, it was only one in a series of repetitious allusions and innuendos that circled around the same themes. Over and over again people told me I was wasting my time dating a thin, dark-complexioned man who had not gone to college (and often added that they had a son or a nephew who would be more suitable).

These conversations made it clear that certain kinds of bodies and physical qualities—white, tall, and chubby—were tied to class and race categories. Desirable bodies were European-looking, tied to prestigious social categories and to education and wealth. Undesirable bodies were poor, dark-complexioned, and indigenous-looking. When Profe Quispe joked about being an ugly mud-face like Atahuallpa, he drew on these stereotypes while simultaneously challenging them by referring to a contrasting concept of indigeneity as educated, wealthy, and high status. This comment challenged and formed a counterdiscourse to stereotypes of indigenous people as rural, uneducated, and poor while acknowledging the systemic racism against bodies marked by characteristics linked to indigeneity.

LEGITIMACY, DECENCY, AND RECOGNITION

In the preceding sections of this chapter, I described three major social categories in Saipina and linked them to language practices and ideologies. I have characterized my speakers in terms of three principal social groups: legítimos Saipineños, long-term residents who owned valuable tracts of land, were

12. *Negro* (black) in the local context generally refers not to African heritage but to a very dark skin tone.

politically and socially prominent, and claimed European heritage; migrants from the local valleys who arrived within the prior thirty to forty years and who were from conocido families; and recent immigrants, often poor and landless, from the western highlands of Cochabamba and the nearer reaches of Chuquisaca. These groups were distinguished not only by migration history but also by language practices. Legítimos Saipineños were understood to be primarily Spanish monolingual speakers. Migrants from the local valleys often spoke Quechua and used Quechua loanwords in their speech, but they used primarily Spanish in the home. Finally, more recent immigrants from the western highlands were generally Quechua dominant, but their children shifted rapidly to Spanish in the ideological surroundings of Saipina.

In contrast to these three groups, indigenous people were characterized as outsiders, though runita and profesores stood at opposite ends of the socioeconomic landscape of Saipina. While profesores were characterized as distinct from locals because of their multilingualism and high level of education, runita were treated as radically foreign in part because of their illiteracy and Quechua monolingualism. Saipineños stood somewhere in between these two poles.

While I didn't hear much about racial categories like "indigenous," "white," and "European" with reference to people in contemporary Saipina, I heard the word "legitimate" everywhere I turned. A legitimate Saipineño was someone who was Saipineño by birth or upbringing; but it was also defined as someone who talked like a Saipineño, joked like a Saipineño, someone who was tied to the agricultural lifestyle of the valleys. These people were conocidos, known or recognized by their neighbors, in contrast to the dangerous and mistrusted desconocidos. While there were overtones of racialization in these designations, it is hard to consider them essentially racial. Rather, they contained an element of traditional Andean culture—the strong identification with one's birthplace and the importance of working the land where one lives—combined with a colonial system of value—institutional and societal recognition.

Much of the literature on race in the Andes has focused on highland indigenous groups and on the relationship between rural indigenous people and urban mestizos (Allen 1988; Harris 1980, 2000; Larson 1988; Stephenson 1999). Saipineños saw themselves as belonging to neither of these groups. They observed traditions linked to indigeneity such as the ritual hair-cutting around a child's first year, honored the dead by baking bread and making flowered arches for Todos Santos, blessed new endeavors with a *ch'alla* or ritual sacrifice, told stories about *vírgenes* (saints) and *duendes* (imps) in the wilderness, and honored sacred places, particularly on the high slopes of the mountains. However, they positioned themselves as racially unmarked and treated indigenous people as outsiders and potentially threatening foreigners. These positions are certainly linked to a colonial system of value such as the one described by Marisol de la Cadena (2000) in Cuzco. At the same time, Saipineños placed high value on agricultural practices, on owning and farming land, and on rootedness and relationships within the community—qualities that are linked to indigenous systems of value (Canessa 2008b).

As the stories I have recounted above demonstrate, people were closely attentive to color, social class, and the colla/camba division, which in turn was tied to identification with indigenous versus European heritage. The use of terms like *legítimo* and *conocido* were far from innocent of racial overtones, and there was explicit and implicit racialization through contrasting discussions of physical characteristics. Yet race as a category was difficult to pin down in Saipina, as in other regions of the Andes (Canessa 2005, 2012; de la Cadena 2000; Sanjinés 2004; Weismantel 2001), because it was so deeply intertwined with language and migration, two categories that are profoundly malleable.

These disparate characteristics were organized through their participation in a larger semiotic field that links binary oppositions across types of social attributes. On the one hand were people who unquestionably qualified as being conocido and legítimo: large-scale property owners and members of the elite who claimed European heritage. On the other pole were desconocidos: strangers and outsiders who were not permanently rooted in town and were often characterized as western highlanders. The great majority of Saipineños fell somewhere between these two poles. They were not wealthy or large landowners, but they were small-scale farmers. They claimed neither European nor indigenous heritage. They might or might not speak Quechua, but they were Spanish dominant in a variety that had strong contact influence from Quechua.

These complex concepts wrapped together ideas about race, physical appearance, participation in a community, European versus indigenous heritage, histories of migration, and structural, genealogical recognition. Like the other oppositions discussed in this book, they were structured around binary oppositions: legitimate, illegitimate; conocido, desconocido. The semiotic field allowed people to "jump" between sets of binaries, as Doña Mónica did in the transcript at the beginning of this chapter; legitimacy was not only about legitimacy but also about migration history and language use. Through these processes, complex sets of characteristics were organized into coherent systems of meaning.

INTERLUDE

Civil Disobedience and Belonging

ONE OF the first things I did after moving to Saipina was to attend a blockade. I happened to arrive during a tumultuous time in local politics. A few weeks after I arrived, the mayor and the town council members were driven out of the town hall by force, and the door was locked with chains by the official in charge of investigating corruption. Someone hung a banner over the door with a hand-drawn cartoon of the town council members sucking from the teats of a giant cow—an accusation of corruption. The mayor and many of the members of the town council fled, some to the city of Santa Cruz, and some as far away as Argentina and Mexico. Shortly afterward, a group of citizens organized a blockade of the major national highway that ran through town and required all the stores to close.

I walked out to the blockade one night with a friend. (Though I didn't know it at the time, he would later become my husband.) There was a festive, relaxed atmosphere. People walked around, offering plates of food for sale; there were campfires scattered along the road; someone strummed a guitar. It was the calmest scene of civil disobedience I had ever seen. Yet there was an undercurrent of anarchy. Earlier in the evening, the blockaders had managed to dynamite a section of the steep hillside over the road, and as I approached, they sent another rock the size of a small bus thundering down among the crowd in the road. It made me nervous, but nobody else seemed to be worried, and nobody was hurt. Immediately, a group of young men climbed on top of the giant rock and started laughing and talking. I squatted down by my friend and listened to music through one side of a set of headphones. People were drinking all around. Someone ran through screaming "La vaca! La vaca!" (The cow! The cow!) as a large mass with prominent horns thundered through in the dark. I jumped and everyone laughed—the "cow" was a couple of teenagers stomping around under a tarp with a cow's skull held up before them, trying to scare anyone timid or gullible enough to believe them.

When I went back in the daytime, I could see a caravan of trucks stretching as far along the curves of the road as I could see. People told me they were backed up for a kilometer, for three kilometers. Some of the trucks carried livestock, and as the days went on the truckers begged to be let through—the animals were dying of thirst and hunger. A couple of trucks tried to bypass the blockade, rolling down a steep slope to the river, but they got bogged down in deep water. In town, the streets were eerily quiet. Nobody went out in town during the day, although work went on in the fields as usual. All the shops were shuttered. My host, Doña Laura, like other women in town, was able to buy supplies by knocking on back doors and buying stealthily.

Later, I heard that the blockade was organized in order to protest the high prices that were charged for the electrical utility. At the time, though, people told me contradictory things. They were protesting corruption. They were asking for a paved road. They wanted progress and more of a say in central government. They were a bunch of hooligans who were just screwing around for the fun of it. The underlying theme, though nobody expressed it in precisely this way, was that people were angry and they felt disenfranchised and removed from power. In the mountainous topography of the Andes, where there were few possible routes for heavy traffic, blockades were an effective way of drawing national attention to local demands and dissatisfactions.

This anger was sometimes directed at Americans. Some years later, during my dissertation fieldwork in 2008, the U.S. dollar was in a nosedive because of the worldwide economic depression. Nobody in town would exchange or accept dollars because of the rapid devaluation of the currency and the impossibility of exchanging the dollars quickly in the city. In the wake of allegations of espionage and disagreements over drug policy, the American ambassador was asked to leave the country, and the Peace Corps and other development institutions evacuated immediately. I went in to speak to the mayor, wondering if I should be worried. He left me waiting for a long time outside his office. When I was finally admitted, I asked him simply, "Do we have a problem?" He immediately assured me that there was no problem, saying, "Todos somos conocidos aquí" (We're all known to each other here). In other words, my status as a member of a local family in good standing would override the political turmoil at the national level. By casting me as a conocida, he assured me that I would be treated, and protected, as a legitimate member of the local community—a designation that my national ID card and Bolivian passport alone would not have guaranteed.

Over the years that I lived in and returned to Bolivia, blockades and civil disobedience were a fact of life, especially around urban centers. When people were angry—over low salaries, over inflation, over environmental degradation, over political disenfranchisement, over corruption, over the simple fact that their lives weren't getting better or weren't getting better fast enough—they took to the street in marchas and demonstrations, blocking roads, seeking attention in any way they could get it.

CHAPTER 5

THE GREENS AND THE BLUES

National Politics, Local Scale

AS THE first decade of the 2000s crawled on, the blockades and civil unrest grew worse and worse. Sometimes barely a week passed without a blockade somewhere in the country. Often there were three or four major blockades, showing up on the nightly TV news as red slashes across road maps of the country. I learned that the Santa Cruz valleys were relatively calm and that blockades were infrequent between Saipina and Santa Cruz. The roads to Cochabamba and between Cochabamba and La Paz, however, were constantly disrupted. Saipina lies on an alternate route to the main road through the tempestuous Chapare region between Cochabamba and Santa Cruz. Whenever there was a blockade on the main route, large semitrucks would start to run heavily through town, one after another, struggling to make the tight curve by the plaza and scattering dust, engine noise, and exhaust fumes through the center of town. The town market filled up with truckers, some of whom would sell extra produce off the back of their trucks. When the blockade lifted, we knew it first from the sudden silence and confirmed it later by watching the TV news.

In 2003 growing political unrest led to President Gonzalo Sánchez de Lozada being forced out of office (Vanden 2007:22–25). "Goni" had not been a popular president; perhaps the least of his defects was that he had grown up in Chicago, and people said that he spoke Spanish with a pronounced American accent. Both before and after his exile, he was accused of genocide by the

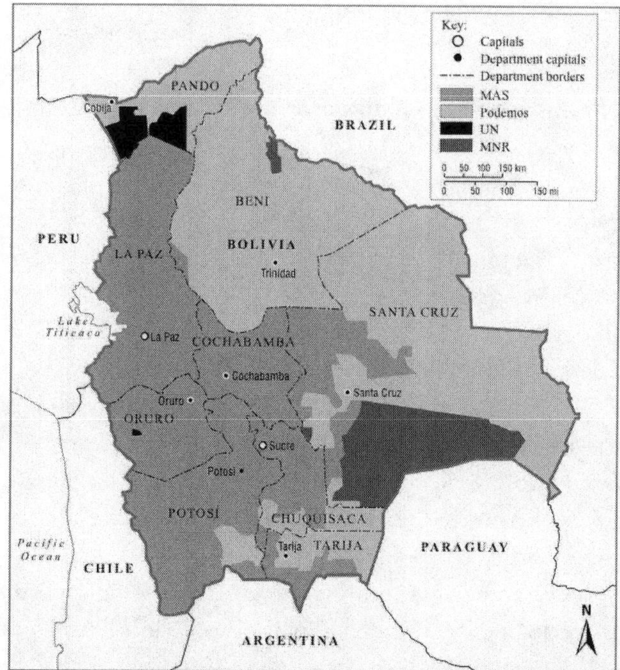

FIGURE 5. 2005 election results. *Source*: *Fixing Fragile States: A New Paradigm for Development* by Seth D. Kaplan (Praeger Security International, 2008).

popular press because of violent military responses to peaceful protests (see Mamani 2003). He was succeeded by his vice president, Carlos Mesa, and then in quick succession by the head of the Supreme Court, Eduardo Rodríguez.

Evo Morales of the Movimiento al Socialismo (Movement for Socialism) party was the favored candidate when elections were finally declared again (Kohl and Bresnahan 2010; Webber 2010). When I asked friends in Saipina whether they would vote for him, they shrugged fatalistically and told me that they were afraid the blockades, strikes, and general "paralyzation" of the country would go on forever unless he were elected. Despite their lack of enthusiasm for Evo's politics or for his party, people told me that they were hopeful that something would change, that the country had been dominated for too long by politically powerful elites.

Evo was elected in 2005 with 54 percent of the vote. This was a major victory. Since Bolivia has multiple competing political parties, there is generally a runoff election—often a coalition—between the two highest finishers. Evo was the first president to win an election outright since the military dictatorships (for an analysis of the historical and cultural context of this victory, see Postero 2010).

Despite opposition in Santa Cruz, Evo won several of the small provinces on the Santa Cruz–Cochabamba border, including Saipina. The lowland states of Pando, Beni, Santa Cruz, and Tarija voted largely against him. People started talking about the tension between the lowland medialuna states and the western highland provinces (Assies 2006).

As Bolivia moved through a series of votes in the aftermath of Evo's election, it became clear that Evo could consistently deliver a majority of votes. MAS won 54 percent of the seats in the Constitutional Assembly in August 2006. Evo won a recall election in 2008 by 64 percent. This was followed by a referendum on the constitution, approved by 61.7 percent. Evo won the 2009 general election with 64 percent. He again won 61.4 percent of the 2014 elections, after modifying the constitution to allow himself to run for a third term.

Evo's 60 percent was his strength: it enabled him to fight off the opposition during the autonomy crisis and to push his socialist agenda in the face of opposition from traditional elites (Eaton 2007, 2011; Flesken 2012). It was also his weakness, because it meant he had little need to compromise or to modify his political positions, which were often extreme (Pineo 2016; Webber 2016). His 2008 break with the American diplomatic mission, which resulted in the expulsion of the American ambassador and the suspension of American aid to Bolivia, is only one example of the results of Evo's strong political positions. Throughout these tempestuous political times, the western Santa Cruz valleys were on the front lines of the struggle between Evo's MAS political party and supporters of the autonomy movement in urban Santa Cruz.

AUTONOMY

There is a post planted in the middle of the plaza in Saipina. It is made of heavy wood and is about five feet tall, and it has writing burned into it on four sides. Two sides bear the name of the town, Saipina. The other two sides bear the word *AUTONOMÍA* (autonomy). Similar posts stand in plazas everywhere in Santa Cruz, including the main square in the center of the capital city (Gustafson 2006:368).

The rather unenthusiastic support for Evo in the Santa Cruz valleys during his first election in 2006 quickly morphed into loud opposition as the election failed to produce a miraculously invigorated economy and an immediately notable improvement in the standard of living. Even people's hopes for less political unrest were dashed, as the Santa Cruz elites quickly mounted an opposing political campaign. The governor of Santa Cruz and many powerful business and economic leaders demanded regional autonomy, a rallying cry that *cruceños* (people from Santa Cruz) of all social classes responded to (Fabricant 2009; Gustafson 2009b). The autonomistas argued that Santa Cruz and the other lowland provinces were "producers," while the highland provinces were poor "consumers" of the country's wealth. They argued for decentralization, regional control of funds, and regional economic autonomy (Eaton 2007; Fabricant and Postero 2013; Perreault and Valdivia 2010). My acquaintances in Santa Cruz, deeply invested in this ideology, justified these means by arguing to me that this was in fact the model that the United States followed. They were surprised when I explained that, in fact, in the United States we pay *both* federal and state taxes and that the relationship between the federal government and the states is both complex and deeply contested. The free-market economy that they argued for was, however, closely connected to the "shock therapy" model that the United States promoted in Latin America and other developing countries (Larraín and Sachs 1998), a model that led to runaway inflation and major economic devastation in Bolivia in the 1980s.

The autonomy movement was not only an economic ideology, however. It was couched in explicitly racialized and racist terms. The Unión Juvenil Cruceñista, a social club for the youth of the Santa Cruz elites, quickly morphed into a gang, provoking violent confrontations in the streets (Fabricant 2009:777–778; Gustafson 2006:371). On the television, we saw footage of the Unión Juvenil patrolling the streets in jeeps and yelling racist slogans as they marched. These images were frequently paired with a swastika, and the group seemed to encourage the neo-Nazi label. This imagery brought back the fact that Bolivia was a prime resettlement zone for Nazi war criminals; Santa Cruz has a large and thriving German expatriate community that dates back to the postwar era (Fabricant 2009:773, 78). This history was laminated onto the discourses in which the leaders of the autonomy movement painted themselves as unfairly burdened by the demands of the poor, majority indigenous departments of La Paz, Oruro, and Potosí (Lowrey 2006; Mura 2016; Valdivia 2010).

Given the strong existing national division between colla and camba, those who identified as cambas quickly jumped on the bandwagon. The Unión Juvenil swelled in membership, and their demonstrations began to be commonly accompanied by tear gas and riot police, who beat back any resistance to the gang's patrols. The leaders of the autonomy movement dismissed these aggressive actions in "boys will be boys" terms, dissociating themselves from responsibility for the actions (Fabricant 2009:777–778; Gustafson 2006:371; Mura 2016).

In the discourses, race, class, and politics were tightly integrated into a single cluster of signifiers. While the autonomy movement claimed to champion

FIGURE 6. Autonomy vote boycott flyer. Text in bright green reads "DON'T VOTE ON MAY 4TH—NO LODGES—DO NOT VOTE FOR THE STATUTE OF THE LODGES." "Lodge" refers to secret societies or brotherhoods, such as the Caballeros del Oriente (Knights of the East), of the powerful elites of Santa Cruz. In this flyer they are linked to racism through the appearance of the Nazi swastika on the depiction of the "statute" flyer.

lowland indigenous groups who were marginalized by Evo's focus on Quechua and Aymara, they also explicitly appealed to a "majority mestizo racial makeup" (see figure 7) that subsumed indigenous identity through mestizaje (Flesken 2012, 2013; Gustafson 2009b:1008–1009). When indigenous groups were mentioned, lowland groups like the Chiquitano, the Ayoreo, the Mojeño, and the Guaraní were acknowledged, but "immigrant" Quechua and Aymara people were not included in the proposed model (Lopez Pila 2014; Weber 2013). News stories pitted the "oligarchs" of Santa Cruz against the poverty-stricken

FIGURE 7. In this page from a booklet explaining the proposal for regional autonomy, the "five native peoples" of the Santa Cruz department are named: Chiquitano, Ayoreo, Guaraní, Guarayo, and Mojeño. Conspicuously absent are Quechua and Aymara. In the bottom right, the man on the left says, "Guess what race I am? I'm Chiquitano, Guaraní, Guarayo, Ayoreo, Mojeño, Aymara, and Quechua. Neither more nor less! Score!" The bearded man on the far right says, "You are a mestizo of Santa Cruz!" The text in the bottom left reads, "The people of Santa Cruz recognize with pride their primarily mestizo racial makeup, as well as the obligation and responsibility of conserving and promoting the autonomous and integral development of the five peoples native to the department."

highlands, neo-Nazi whiteness against indigeneity, and free-market policies and regional autonomy against centralist, socialist MAS (Fabricant 2009).

The western Santa Cruz valleys served as the front lines of this struggle as both political parties vied to consolidate control of the hotly contested "in-between" zone. Saipina was papered in flyers like the ones reproduced above. There was an unusual concentration of visits from national-level politicians. Even among those who had voted for Evo, there were many who were now hotly opposed to him and who argued that Saipina, like Santa Cruz, was being overrun by outsiders, westerners, immigrants.

CUMPA OSO, THE "BEAR MAYOR"

In national votes, the western Santa Cruz valleys leaned first one way, then the other, waving the rainbow-colored flag of the Andean indigenous movement with one hand and the green-and-white flag of the Santa Cruz department with the other.

For more than a decade, the *alcalde* (mayor) of Saipina was a popular local high school teacher who belonged to the MAS political party. Despite being a member of the local elite, from one of the oldest families in Saipina, he cozied up to the president, accompanying him on trips to Cuba and Venezuela and even making visits to Miami. Universally known by his nickname, El Oso, "The Bear," the mayor attracted large development projects to the Saipina valley. He embraced his nickname, campaigning as Cumpa Oso, "Compadre Bear," in an appeal to the figure of an authentic valluno. In campaign photos, he always sported the black fedora iconic of the local valleys (see chapters 1, 4).

My contacts in the city of Santa Cruz complained about the deterioration of basic infrastructure, the large projects left abandoned, the increasing crime rate, and the inadequate measures against corruption. They complained about laws that restricted exports of agricultural products and natural resources and that disproportionately impacted Santa Cruz. They complained especially of the highlanders who were taking over all government offices, taking advantage of the decree that all federal employees must speak at least one indigenous language.

In the rural valleys, though, a series of development projects left their mark. A group of Cuban-trained doctors staffed a new hospital in town. Bridges spanned many of the roads where yearly floods had stopped traffic, sometimes for weeks on end. There were two cell phone towers, and a "repeater" made the national news directly available to homes. Most of the schools were renovated or rebuilt, and the valley was dotted with huge tin roofs for *canchas polifuncionales*, athletic courts that could be used for basketball, volleyball, indoor football, or other sports. People joked, "Hay tinglados hasta pa los khuchis" (There are tin roofs even for the pigs), pointing to a giant structure that was intended to shelter a *sede* (seat, club) and athletic court for the teachers' union but that was for the time being enjoyed by free-range pigs, which made their homes in its shade. People also pointed to the installation of *gas domiciliario*, gas lines that were installed directly into people's homes, eliminating the necessity of buying heavy and expensive tanks of gas for cooking. "We used to have to go out and gather firewood on the outskirts of town," Angel told me. "I don't know how many trees I must have killed, just on my own account. Now almost everyone cooks on gas, and the *monte* [bush] is starting to recover."

In part, these development projects were evidence of careful maneuvering on the part of the mayor. When Santa Cruz governor Rubén Costas arrived to promote the autonomy movement, there was a parade through the town that was carefully planned to avoid the building projects that had a prominent MAS logo on them. Costas was taken to the stadium, which received funds from the departmental government in Santa Cruz. In contrast, a visit from the MAS leadership was celebrated at the high school, rebuilt with government funds. For Costas's visit, people were given little flags in the colors of the Santa Cruz department to wave, and a band played traditional tunes of Santa Cruz as the delegation paraded through the town. When MAS came to town, supporters turned out en masse, waving *wiphalas*, the checkered rainbow flag of the highland indigenous movement.

Seen in this light, El Oso's apparently contradictory decision to run as a MAS political candidate despite his place in the Saipina elite was a brilliant political strategy. He was able to attract votes and support from even the oldest Saipina families because of his personal and family networks; he was a quintessential conocido, a native-born son of Saipina. At the same time, as a MAS candidate he was able to secure the votes of the recent migrants from the highlands who increasingly controlled the electorate in the region. As Don Simón, a local musician, put it in a *copla*, a satirical rhyming verse, "El Oso es muy listo, y muy inteligente. / Se consigue del prefecto, y del presidente" (The Bear is very smart, very intelligent. / He gets things from the governor and from the president).

Just before the 2008 vote to recall Evo from the presidency, I went to a *concentración*, a political rally, for MAS in Saipina. The event was advertised all afternoon on a bullhorn that was driven around town on a taxi, an effective way to communicate with people who didn't listen to the radio or TV. Though it was the mayor's political party, and the rally was held practically on the steps of the town hall, he didn't attend the rally. He needed to walk a delicate line, and these were not his people; they would vote for MAS regardless of the candidate. The crowd there looked gaunt and dark and scarred, their clothes worn thin with washing and the sun, most of the women in pollera, overwhelmingly agricultural migrant workers from the western part of the country. I heard quiet conversations in Quechua all around me. Some people were shooed off by downtown homeowners, members of the local elite, who wanted to park their cars. Nobody protested, though it was a public sidewalk; they just moved away, averting their eyes. I tried to make conversation with a woman next to me, and she turned around and walked away, pointedly not answering.[13] It took an eternity to get the projection equipment set up, and then there was a dark and frightening documentary about child workers in the mines, followed by lots of shots of Evo meeting with *campesinos* (peasants) in working-class neighborhoods. I saw no familiar faces in the audience, not even children who would usually show up for any public showing of a movie. They were *puros desconocidos*, all strangers.

HORDES AND CHIEFTAINS: RACIALIZATION OF LOCAL SPACES

One day during the tense times in 2008, I went out to find the town buzzing with scandal. A wealthy businessman had taken out an advertisement on the local television that stridently supported the autonomy movement. The advertisement used the phrase "las hordas del MAS" (the MAS hordes). The MAS supporters in town were enraged. I stopped in to chat with Andrés, a MAS supporter, Saipineño, and respected high school teacher. Andrés looked at me carefully and asked me if I knew what that phrase meant. I admitted that I did not. "*Hordas* means from a time when brothers slept with sisters and fathers with daughters," he explained to me. He pointed out the irony of the fact that the man who wrote the advertisement was originally from a town just to the west of Saipina—in Andrés's eyes, colla territory. He also asserted that despite

13. Probably because I was a gringa. A central tenet of MAS ideology is resentment of North American interference in Bolivian national politics.

his enormous wealth and big house in the city, the businessman still talked like a colla.

In this exchange, Andrés clearly positioned the national political debate along East/West, camba/colla lines. He implied that the businessman's origins in western Bolivia stood in contradiction to his political positioning, despite his current wealth and residence in urban Santa Cruz. Moreover, Andrés interpreted the language of the advertisement not only as a slur but as a racialized attack on the decency and morality of MAS supporters, casting them as premodern and uncivilized. Finally, the businessman's western accent became an important signifier that negated his positioning as a lowlander and an autonomy supporter.

Around the same time, a meeting between the Padres de Familia, the parent organization, and the school board generated another scandalous example of language use. In the course of a contentious and well-attended meeting, the school superintendent, a wealthy native Saipineño, accused the representatives of the Padres de Familia of acting like a bunch of *caciques* (chieftains). It seems that he meant to accuse them of acting impulsively and illogically, with a pack mentality rather than civilized due process. Like the word *hordas*, this language was interpreted as a racial slur, and the superintendent was openly accused of racism and disrespect to the *padres* (parents). Juana explained to me, "I understood this to mean that he was calling us ignorant, uneducated. *Cacique* is a word for a leader of a group of people, back when people didn't study or have an education." Though this was a local issue rather than a national one, the use of the term *caciques* indexed a premodern time that was associated not only with indigeneity but with ignorance. In parallel with these accusations, a recent scandal involving the superintendent's personal life was recirculated and recontextualized in local gossip: Who was he to judge other people's morality? The bivalency of the term *educación*, meaning both "education" and "manners," perfectly conveyed the overlapping semantic fields of education (which the superintendent had and many of the parents did not) and morality or manners (which the parents had but, they asserted, the superintendent did not).

Like the businessman who used the term *hordas*, the superintendent's use of the term *caciques* was understood to be explicitly racialized and having moral overtones—an accusation of acting uncivilized, ignorant, like an indio, a savage, with all the negative stereotypes that the words invoked (de la Cadena 2000). There was no room in this discussion for the superintendent to assert that he didn't "mean" to be racist in his use of language. In the highly politically charged atmosphere of the town, the fact that the superintendent was a member of the local elite and a political supporter of the autonomy movement was enough to position him as racist.

In these examples, racial categories were superimposed on political positioning and language use through their shared participation in the semiotic field. MAS and Evo were understood to be strong among recent Quechua-speaking immigrants from the West, while the autonomy movement in Santa Cruz was understood to have strong support among people who positioned themselves as Saipina natives—legítimos Saipineños. In these discussions, political sympathies were aligned with patterns of migration, race, social class, and legitimacy and debated on a field in which morality and accusations of amorality or uncivilized behavior were interpreted along these lines.

The national political tensions between East and West, autonomistas and MAS, were transposed onto local spaces in ways that followed the structure of the meanings constructed through the organization of the semiotic field. MAS voters were understood to be indigenous, western, and Quechua speaking, while autonomistas were racially unmarked, eastern, and Spanish monolinguals. These associations held even when the individuals in question could have been interpreted through other categories—for example, the local superintendent was a legítimo Saipineño, and the autonomista supporter was from the Quechua-speaking highlands. Given the considerable ambiguity attached to social categorization, the ways that people cast themselves and others within these frameworks held a considerable amount of wiggle room. Saipineños balanced between political extremes, generally positioning themselves somewhere "in between" but occasionally flaring up into scandals and accusations. At the same time, the politically charged atmosphere at the national level leaked into local spaces, imbuing public discourse with racial and moral tension.

FAST FORWARD TO 2014

The 2014–15 election cycle was once again fiercely contested in Saipina. By this time, few people talked about autonomistas. Instead, they referred to the anti-Evo lowland political group simply as "the Greens." The use of green in campaign materials was tied to the green-and-white colors of the flag of Santa Cruz, an implicit reference to the party's stance of pride in its eastern, lowland heritage (Fabricant 2009). In contrast, Evo's MAS political party used the color blue. Leading up to the elections, political parties painted supporters' houses in their color, adding the names of their candidates in white. This resulted in a landscape of blue and green houses around Saipina, painting neighborhoods with the color of the candidate with the broadest base of local support.

In this election cycle, for the first time, I saw local political debates that were removed from face-to-face, in-person contact and from the town of Saipina. Instead, the Internet emerged as a major arena for debate and political discussion, and a set of Facebook pages that focused on Saipina as part of the Santa Cruz valleys sprang up. Most of the participants on these pages were migrants from Saipina who now lived in the city, and they were also generally young people who were comfortable using the Internet on their cell phones.

As Evo came up for his third election, I watched a discussion unfold on one page in which urban migrants were urged to register to vote in Saipina regardless of their current place of residence. The explicit aim of this campaign was to defeat MAS in Saipina with an influx of urban voters who could be assumed to be anti-Evo. The group shared the date by which voters must register and urged them to gather in a local business whose proprietor was known to be a Green supporter. There followed outraged posts when the voter registration table was shut down by the mayor, El Oso, who claimed it was unauthorized.

As in the example below, criticisms of the local slate of electoral candidates centered largely on the contrast between local and migrant (see chapter 4), adding accusations of corruption and outright lies. In this Facebook post, the writer contrasted "a town with traditions, customs, typical of the valleys, the common people" with *sindicateros* (unionists) and accusations that the candidates were unqualified for their positions. The closing phrase, "peguita peguita," uses a slang word *pega* 'work' to refer to positions that are created for supporters by a corrupt party boss.

> EL **MAS** Y SU SINDICATO EN SAIPINA[14]
>
> SAIPINA **ANTES** UN PUEBLO CON TRADICIONES, COSTUMBRES, TIPICO DE LOS VALLES. . . . **AHORA** QUIEREN VOLVERLO UN PUEBLO SINDICATERO, SIN DEJAR LA MAMADERA, APROVECHANDOSE Del voto De GENTE HUMILDE. . . . **QUE PENA, QUE VERGÜENZA** !!!

14. Here and below, I have preserved original orthography, capitalization, and punctuation in the Spanish text. The English text is my translation.

USTEDES COMO SAIPINEÑOS VOTARIAN POR ESTA GENTE ??????... QUE FALTA DE CEREBRO !!!! QUE PENA SI ESTO SIGUE !!!! LOS UNICOS QUE DEFIENDEN SON LOS FUNCIONARIOS DE LA ALCALDIA QUE VERGUENZA.... PEGUITA PEGUITA

Los unicos Saipineños de nuestra tierra y lo ponen de 4to y 5to consejal todavia de suplente.... Es saipina señores ... su pueblo por que se prestan para esto!!!!

MAS and its syndicate in Saipina

Saipina **before** was a town with traditions, customs, typical of the valleys.... **Now** they want to turn it into a syndicate town, without leaving the tit, taking advantage of the vote of the common folk.... **What a pity, what a shame !!!**

Would you as Saipineños vote for these people ????... What simple minds !!!! What a shame if this continues !!!! The only ones who defend [us] are the officials of the town hall What shame.... Peguita peguita

The only Saipineños from our homeland and they are placed as 4th and 5th delegate, even as substitutes.... This is Saipina, gentlemen ... why do you let yourself be used like this?

In closing, the accuser noted that the only native-born Saipineños were placed last on the ballot, as substitutes. In the comments, people agreed that it was a shame that these two were the only insiders on the ballot. They ignored the MAS mayoral candidate, the brother of the current mayor and, like him, a member of a prominent, unimpeachably legitimate local family.

These were not the only voices, however. On another page, a defender of MAS called out by name the person who she believed was responsible for these posts. She added, "You make your colleagues look bad, you're worse than a snake, you chose the wrong profession, you should have been a detective not a teacher, you created [name of page] and [name of other page] go back to your family." Another commented, "I'm sick of your stupidity, look around you and at least make accusations with some foundation and real proof, this is way too much."

The importance of being a Saipineño by birth regardless of current residence came up again and again. Shortly after MAS's victory in the province was announced, the following comments were posted:

Ganaron los del mas.... Ni modo esq. Somos pocos. Los Saipineños (MAS won.... Too bad. You see there are very few Saipineños left).

> Un día llegaremos a nuestro pueblo y nosotros seremos los desconosidos (One day we'll come to our town, and we'll be the unfamiliar ones).

> Por eso no tenemos que dejar de ir aponer presencia y que sepan que ellos solo son allegados nosotros y nuestras filas nacimos en nuestro pueblo hermoso !!!!! No dejemos de ir jóvenes !!!!!! (That's why we must not stop being present and let them know that they are the recent arrivals we and our families were born in our beautiful town !!!!!! Let's not stop going [to Saipina], young people !!!!!!).

> Si q se va ser ni modo, pero nosotros tenemos algo q esa gente jamás tendrá EL ORGULLO DE HABER NACIDO EN SAIPINA (Yes what can you do it's too bad, but we have something that those people will never have THE PRIDE OF BEING BORN IN SAIPINA).

> Si chicos ahí esta el tema no tiene q dejar de venir aunq sea un mmento pero no irse i olvidarse del pueblo en el q uno nase tambiem se les entiende por el trabajo q tienen pero hay q darse un tiempo y venir (Yes guys that's the thing you can't stop coming even if it's only for a moment but not leave and forget the town in which one is born one understands that it's because of the work they have [to go to the city] but you have to make some time and come [back to Saipina]).

In these comments, legitimate Saipineños were contrasted with recent migrants, who would never have "the pride of being born in Saipina." However, all native-born Saipineños, especially urban migrants, who were the primary audience for this page, were assumed to be supporters of the lowland elites. In contrast, recent migrants from the highlands—outsiders—were cast as MAS supporters.

The right to claim status as a Saipineño was fiercely defended by participants in these pages as they exhorted each other to maintain connections to the town by visiting regularly, even when living in the city. Status as a local person was tied to political positioning but also to ethics through accusations of corruption aimed at elected officials. These ethical and moral axes could be used to both exclude people from a group and include them; the mayoral candidate, despite his status as a native-born Saipineño, was cast as a traitor to nativist Saipineños because of his political affiliation. Through these posts, political affiliation was clustered with status as a native-born, or legítimo, Saipineño and contrasted with "outsiders" who did not respect Saipina's traditions (see chapter 6).

MODERATE *MASISTAS*

For the national election in October 2014, voting tallies were once again close in Saipina. My friend Reynalda was named as an electoral worker, and she manned one of the tables, helping count votes for the presidential election. "It was one for Evo, one for the Greens," she told me. They stayed until late counting and recounting the votes, but in the end Evo won by a small but clear margin. "There weren't enough of us," Carlos, an urban migrant and an ardent Green supporter, told me. "The outsiders won."

Following the 2014 national elections, the MAS Blues won easily at the local level in 2015, winning most of the seats on the town council. After gaining their comfortable majority, MAS supporters in Saipina positioned themselves as moderates. "We're MASistas, but we're not radical MASistas," Octavio, a town council member, told me. "We're the kind of MASistas that you can talk to. Not like some of those others." He shook his head, puffing out his cheeks and raising his eyebrows in a gesture of disapproval at the more radical elements of the party. While the Greens had suggested that MAS candidates were all outsiders and immigrants, Octavio characterized urban migrants as outsiders. "And what's happened to their mayoral candidate now?" he asked. "It was like he dropped in from a helicopter, and now nobody ever hears of him." Other consultants confirmed that the Green candidate had been born in Saipina but had grown up in Santa Cruz. Though they were familiar with his family, few people in the town of Saipina knew the Green mayoral candidate personally. In contrast, the MAS candidate was a well-established local who had lived in Saipina for many years, the brother of the current mayor, and an unquestionably legítimo Saipineño.

In the local elections, the Greens attacked the Blues, characterizing them as ignorant liars. They derided one of the town council candidates for not having gone to college and publicly posted a document that showed that the mayoral candidate had earned poor grades at the university. They even alleged that he went by the title *ingeniero* despite never having finished his engineering degree. Several people told me in hushed tones that they had "put ears" on the ex-mayor Oso, now a candidate for the National Assembly. Putting donkey ears on a person meant accusing him of being a burro, ignorant and uneducated. My consultants implied that this was going too far.

"It was way too personal," Octavio told me. "It was the dirtiest election I've ever seen." Juana, watching a large dog attack a smaller dog in the street, commented, "He's like the Greens." She giggled. "He knows who he can beat up. He's aggressive." There were rumors that the Greens had attempted to buy votes and that people refused, offended by the suggestion that their votes were for sale. This scandalous accusation underlined the perception that the Greens were high-handed, assuming that they could take the support of local people for granted.

Still, for some people, political affiliation came down to a matter of expedience. Noticing a blue campaign shirt on Reynalda, whose family had been firm autonomista supporters in 2008, I asked her, "Are you MASista now?" Her mother, who was also present, jokingly replied, "A la fuerza" (We're obliged to be). Both mother and daughter were employed by the municipal government, though not in directly political posts. "But surely your jobs don't depend on political appointments?" I asked. "The Greens said they would make a clean sweep if they won," Reynalda told me. "Everyone out, down to the janitors."

The political landscape of Saipina became a battleground that echoed the prejudices against westerners, outsiders, and Quechua speakers that I described in the preceding chapters. Status as a legitimate Saipineño or as a conocido was a crucial part of local political positioning, and both the Greens and the Blues claimed that their candidates had the more authentic claim to local identity. While the terms of these claims were up for debate, the centrality of the debate over status as a "legitimate" local resident was not. Through these discussions, status as a local versus an outsider was clustered with political affiliation and ultimately used to make claims to political legitimacy.

MIGRATION, POLITICAL ORIENTATION, AND CHANGE

When I asked Diana, a college student, how the town had changed in recent years, she sighed. "I don't want to talk about politics," she said. Yet it was precisely politics that people discussed when I asked them this question.

"I don't like this government," Doña Bertita, a small landowner, said, referring to MAS. "When aid came from abroad in the past, it came for everyone, for anyone who needed it. Now it only comes for people who are 'poor.' Evo just sends it to his *choladas.* They're trying to kill Santa Cruz by restricting exports of soy and other crops, with the laws about giving a double bonus to employees at Christmas. Where's the money going to come from? They're trying to kill

Santa Cruz, but I think Santa Cruz is doing just fine." By using the derogatory term *choladas*, derived from *chola*, a woman who wears pollera, Bertita linked MAS supporters to western immigrants and to the use of the pollera. Almost in the same breath, she complained about her neighbors, recent immigrants from the West. She told me that the woman hit her small daughter. "She yells at her in Quechua. I don't have any idea what she says, but there's no reason to hit a child. I don't like these new neighbors." In these comments, Doña Bertita linked disparate categories—styles of dress, political affiliation, migration history, and morality—as binary poles within the semiotic field, associating MAS supporters with the use of Quechua, the use of the pollera, and unacceptable social behavior.

Others told me that the town had changed for the better, pointing to the newly installed sewer system, the profusion of athletic courts that had sprung up around town, the small area of downtown that had been recently paved, a rural literacy campaign. "Saipina's doing well," Octavio told me. "We've benefited under Evo. I've never seen a politician who cares about people from the rural areas like he does."

In a separate interview, Zenón, a staunch Green supporter, disagreed, pointing out that the sewer system had never been hooked up and that other promises had not been kept. "This government only takes care of its own," he said, referring to Evo and to MAS.

"But isn't Saipina MAS territory?" I asked him.

"We may be MAS, but we don't speak Quechua," he told me, giving me a meaningful look.

Both Greens and Evo supporters agreed that while Saipina was MAS territory—indeed, had been solidly Blue for the past three election cycles—people in the area were not radical MASistas but, rather, moderates. Octavio positioned himself as "a MASista you can talk to," in contrast to other, presumably more rabid supporters of the party. Zenón used Quechua as an icon of MAS allegiance, suggesting that real MAS supporters would be Quechua speakers. Through these comments, my consultants once again set up a binary—Greens and Blues—and positioned themselves in the middle. At the same time, politics was enmeshed with race and morality in public discourses, crossing boundaries of social categorization. Through these discourses, people produced a semiotic field that crossed and aligned categories, producing binaries that crossed ethnicity, political affiliation, and language use.

CONCLUSION

The tension between the Greens and the Blues reflected the "middle ground" that Saipineños occupied in political terms, just as was the case for other types of social meaning. Political support of the Greens and Blues was tied to binary oppositions like free-market economy versus socialist control, the highland/lowland colla/camba divide, contrasts between the rural poor and lowland "elites," and positions of power and privilege that were also entwined with language use and migration history. Yet the way that these conflicts were experienced and interpreted was never a simple matter of one versus the other. Local actors maneuvered between powerful political outsiders in order to obtain benefits for their community and to benefit themselves and their families personally, and individuals used political positioning as a way of expressing other types of social affiliations and stances.

At the same time, national political tensions provided an environment in which particular examples of language use became flashpoints for accusations of racism and entangled in debates about morality and local identity. Words like *sindicatero* 'syndicalist', *campesino* 'peasant', *hordas* 'hordes', *indios* 'indians', and *caciques* 'chieftains' were drawn up into racialized local political landscapes in which identification with the Greens and the Blues was crossed and complicated by status as a local person, wealth, and language use.

The autonomy movement in urban Santa Cruz was often ugly and violent in the first decade of the 2000s (Fabricant 2009; Fabricant and Postero 2013; Gustafson 2006, 2009b). Though autonomistas claimed lowland indigenous identity and rejected highland indigenous claims, they subsumed that identity in privileged mestizo interests that held little real advantage for indigenous communities (Eaton 2007; Flesken 2013). The motivations behind this positioning were baldly economic and clearly benefited the elite cruceños who funded violent attacks (Mura 2016; Perreault and Valdivia 2010; Valdivia 2010). However, the use of camba identity was not just a cynical elite strategy (Lowrey 2006:82); outside of urban Santa Cruz, the ways that people understood their own ethnoracial, linguistic, and regional identity were intimately connected to their political positioning. Rural and indigenous cruceños throughout the country negotiated conflicting stances as they balanced regional affiliation with Santa Cruz with their identity as rural campesinos and marginal urban migrants (Kirshner 2010; Lopez Pila 2014; Weber 2013). In areas like the Santa Cruz valleys, political affiliation was a complex calculation that took on moral and ethnical overtones and participated in existing social groupings of migrants and legítimos Saipineños, among other categories. These complex relationships between categories resulted in affiliations that changed and shifted over time and depending on context. As was the case for other sets of binaries, both autonomistas and MAS supporters positioned themselves as somewhere between extremes. The binary structures of the semiotic field not only organized social categories but also formed the basis for claims to legitimacy and authenticity in political discourse.

INTERLUDE

"¡Que viva el Falange carajo!"

DOÑA JUANA'S mother, Doña Antonia, was a young woman in the mid-1950s when the Agricultural Reform Act was passed. Despite the progressive nature of the times, Bolivia was in the throes of political instability and conflict. The conservative, nationalist Falange Socialista Boliviana had been gaining political strength and was recruiting heavily in the Santa Cruz valleys for its nationalist (some would say fascist) "cells." The progressive Movimiento Nacional Revolucionario, the political party that was in power, struggled to cement its claim to political legitimacy. Among other actions, it sent paramilitary police to the Santa Cruz valleys to ferret out supporters of the Falange.

Doña Antonia's family, like other peasant families, had lived through the devastating Chaco War within recent memory. Peasant farmers were particularly hard hit by casualties, and the veterans who returned were psychologically scarred and often physically disabled. Though she did not participate directly in the conflict, Doña Antonia had lived through devastating events in her personal life. As a child, she lost both parents at a young age and was brought up by a relative. Her siblings were sent to different homes. Now the existing social order, the hacienda system, was about to be dismantled by the new Agricultural Reform Act. As exploitative as the hacienda system had been, the prospect of major social change and the slow, bitterly contested retreat of the hacenderos was profoundly unsettling.

Even in this atmosphere of extreme instability, daily life went on much as usual. There were chores to be done, animals to be cared for, crops to be processed and stored, food to be cooked, clothes to be made, water to be carried, and wood to be gathered for the fire. As she went about her chores one morning with her young son at her side, Doña Antonia saw a group of armed men walk into the clearing around her home. They demanded that she tell them if there were any Falangistas in the area.

Unsure which party they were from, Doña Antonia denied that she knew of any Falange supporters. Yet even as she spoke these words, her young son piped up in his little voice, "¡Que viva el Falange carajo!" (Long live the Falange, dammit!).

Doña Antonia was shocked and afraid. She supposed that her son had heard the words from groups of men in the community or perhaps on the radio; the members of her own household were in fact supporters of the MNR, like most peasant farmers. She hushed her son and repeated her denial to the men. Finally, after a long pause, they turned away and left.

Doña Antonia told me this story on many occasions. Each time, she mimed the soldiers' gruff demand, her own denial, and then her shock and fear at the child's words. Then she giggled at the thought of her tiny son piping up with the political slogan at the worst possible moment, repeating the words again as if they were burned into her mind: "¡Que viva el Falange carajo!"

When I lived with Doña Antonia, she was in her late seventies, and these days were long past. Still, whenever the national news came on the radio, she would stop our conversation and motion for me to be quiet so she could listen attentively to the broadcast. In 2005, when Gonzalo Sánchez de Lozada's successor, Carlos Mesa, was forced out of office, she spent all evening glued to the radio, listening to the accounts of mass protests, civilian casualties, and marches and protests by the opposing party. There were whispers of a coup. Yet even as the political system of the country was in evident crisis, daily life went on in a way that was so normal as to be almost surreal. We herded the goats out to pasture every morning and brought them back in the evening; we cooked and carried lunch out to the fields; we gathered and chopped firewood; we ground corn on the giant stone batán to make chicken feed and porridge for the dogs.

In contrast, in 2008 a family crisis superseded political unrest. Doña Antonia's son, Miguel, who had cried out the worst possible words to the armed men when he was a little boy, died suddenly of a heart attack in the city. He left behind a widow and two teenage daughters. The family observed his death with an elegant funeral at a funeral home in urban Santa Cruz, then accompanied the coffin to a niche in the cemetery. Don Miguel had lived in the city since he was a young man. He had died in his car at the airport, waiting to pick up his wife from a business trip to the United States. His widow, who had always struck me as poised and fashionable, commuting between her home and business contacts in Los Angeles and Miami, screamed in pain as her husband's coffin was fitted into the niche. They had both come from the rural countryside, and they had been married since she was sixteen, younger than her daughters were at the time of their father's death.

At the funeral in Santa Cruz, I heard the mourners from Don Miguel's wealthy urban social set whisper, "¡Es la mamá! ¡Es la mamá!" (It's his mother! It's his mother!) with pity and surprise as Doña Antonia, her sparse gray hair braided tightly down her neck, wearing a black fedora and a pollera dyed black for mourning, walked to the front of the room to say good-bye to her son. In this context she looked old and rural and poor, with none of the shiny jewels, modern clothing, and dyed blonde hair of the urban women. Don Miguel had been one of only three children to survive infancy, her only son to live to adulthood.

Following the funeral, we all crowded into a taxi to head back to Saipina—my husband, my mother-in-law, my two sisters-in-law, Doña Antonia, and me, in addition to the taxi driver. Blockades paralyzed all the major routes. At one point we left the road entirely to take a long detour around mud paths through agricultural fields and forded the river before returning to the road. It was midnight before we arrived in Saipina; we were lucky to arrive at all. In the following weeks, everything that came from the East—gas, chicken, cheese—ran short due to blockades. On the television, we saw that public institutions like the courts had been taken over by the Unión Juvenil Cruceñista, private shops had been looted and windows broken, that the military had been called out with orders to shoot if necessary. People were calling it a golpe de estado (coup), and there were rumors of a civil war.

As remote as national politics sometimes seemed in Saipina, the national political scene was interwoven with the experience of daily life; national confrontations were overlaid with personal tragedies.

CHAPTER 6

THE PAST AND THE FUTURE

Tradition and Modernity in Saipina

WHEN I visited Eduardo, an ardent Green supporter, he was eager to discuss politics with me. We spoke about the challenges and opportunities of local government, with which he had been deeply involved for many years. Eduardo had traveled widely within Bolivia, and he showed me a set of postcards that he had printed up at his own expense in order to publicize the town, handing them out to friends and acquaintances and inviting them to come see for themselves someday.

The cards that he showed me depicted a series of images of Saipina. One showed the giant thaco, an iconic acacia tree that stood in the center of town, a few steps from the town hall. Another showed the archaeological museum; another the cave paintings of El Buey, an archaeological site about an hour away from Saipina; and another the colonial-era *reloj de sol* (sundial) in the center of Chilón, a neighboring town within the municipality. Finally, there was a card showing a field being planted with potatoes behind a *yunta de bueyes* (yoke of oxen) and a card depicting a *molienda,* where cane was pressed and the juice processed into raw cane syrup and then blocks of raw sugar known as *chancaca*. Eduardo told me that Saipina was known as far away as the Bolivian capital of La Paz for its agricultural production; in the past, he told me, it was most famous for its tomatoes. As the quality of tomatoes had declined, it was becoming better known for its sugarcane, in particular *caña blanca* (white cane), which is meant to be cubed and chewed as a snack rather than processed into sugar.

Eduardo's framing of what made Saipina distinctive and interesting to outsiders drew on historical artifacts and agricultural practices and products. The cave paintings and archaeological museum referenced a prehistoric time period; the reloj de sol and the thaco tree in the center of the plaza represented different types of historical time that were closely connected to the colonial history of the area; and the agricultural practices referenced a tradition that could be understood to stretch continuously from prehistoric time, through the colonial period, to the recent nonindustrialized past, and up to the present.

Eduardo's postcards produced a vision of Saipina that placed "tradition" within a particular configuration of time and space (Bakhtin 1937; Blommaert 2015). Though the Greens and the Blues had strong political differences, they agreed on what constituted the right way to portray "traditional" Saipina and what, in contrast, was "modern" or outside of the category of tradition. In this chapter, I discuss the production of tradition, and an implicit contrast with modernity, through local practices that are entwined in other types of systems of meaning. Yet tradition also struck me as being something that was performed with an outside audience in mind (Graham and Penny 2014).

Recent literature on the Andes has demonstrated how actors as diverse as *tinku* (a style of dance that is also a ritual confrontation) fighters (Van Vleet 2010), cholita wrestlers (Haynes 2013), and early 20th-century archaeologists (Sammells 2012) represent themselves and their work as part of a continuous tradition that stretches into the past but also is projected forward into the future, a past, present, and future that are both traditional and modern. This vision of tradition and modernity, as qualities of time that are constructed and achieved through semiotic labor and that can be perceived differently from different points of view, stands in contrast to theories of tradition and modernity that see them as standing in juxtaposition with each other (García Canclini 1995). As I show through the examples in this chapter, tradition and modernity are produced and juxtaposed with each other through practice and in conversation with broader systems of social meaning (Bauman and Briggs 2003; Webster 2009). If tradition and modernity stand in contrast to each other, it is because that relationship is produced and historified, not because this is the natural or universal way of things (Gusfield 1967; Inoue 2004; Silverstein 1998). By producing "tradition" that is linked to the local landscape and to a continuous historical tradition, consultants constructed a particular type and configuration of time and space that was then linked to other types of local practices (Agha 2007b; Bakhtin 1937; Blommaert 2015; Carr and Lempert 2016). The production of "traditional Saipina" drew on existing discourses of region, ethnicity, migration status, and other qualities.

BRANDING AND TOURISM

The signs that constituted "traditional Saipina" were explicitly proposed, discussed, and sometimes contested. During the first and second decades of the 2000s, increased access to the Internet and a growing interest in attracting tourists and external grant funding spurred increased attention to the idea of Saipina as a brand or a commodity (Manning 2010; Manning and Uplisashvili 2007). The main actors in the production of the image of "traditional Saipina" were past and present municipal officials.

The most explicit markers of "tradition" were the official symbols of the municipality. Like Eduardo's postcards, these markers focused on agricultural production. The official town seal, redesigned sometime in the 2010s, had the name of the town in the center surrounded by agricultural implements (a hoe, a machete, and a shovel), a carapari cactus, the image of the thaco tree, a *trapiche* (press) from a cane mill, and an image of the German-funded dam project, La Cañada. Above the shield were the words "Tierra fertil de los valles cruceños" (Fertile land of the Santa Cruz valleys); below was the motto "Lo único que no produce es lo que no se siembra" (The only thing that won't grow is what you don't sow). The words "Tierra Dulce de los Valles Cruceños" (Sweet land of the Santa Cruz valleys), referring to sugarcane production, were also printed on the windshield of all municipal vehicles, proudly proclaiming their identification with Saipina and with an agricultural lifestyle.

These agricultural themes are repeated over and over in materials that represent the town. In the plaza, along with the autonomy post (see chapter 5), there was an old wooden oxcart of the kind that was once used to transport sugarcane to the mill and a wooden cane press with a long arm that would be harnessed to a horse in order to turn the mill. In another corner, a *cántaro de barro* (large clay pot) lay on its side against a tree. On a poster for the municipal Día de la Tradición (Tradition Day), I found images of the agricultural fields surrounding Saipina; raw sugar setting in molds at a cane mill; a man and a woman holding up handfuls of recently harvested onions; a bunch of workers sorting tomatoes

FIGURE 8. Saipina's municipal seal, including the phrases "Fertile land of the Santa Cruz valleys" and "The only thing that won't grow is what you don't sow." Images (*clockwise from top left*) depict agricultural tools, the thaco tree, a cane mill, and the Cañada dam.

FIGURE 9. Windshield of a municipal vehicle: "Sweet land of the Santa Cruz valleys."

after the harvest; and a plate of *biffe*, which consists of a tomato-and-onion salad, fried potatoes, and a fried egg—all products produced in the Saipina area. Even the local buses repeated these images; one had a *trapiche* icon on the back of the bus, along with the words "Tierra Dulce" (Sweet Land), while another was decorated with an enlarged reproduction of a photo of a farmer loading sugarcane from a cart harnessed to two oxen.

These agricultural traditions formed a continuity between the past and the future in Saipina. While most cane mills used gasoline-powered cane presses, and fields were increasingly plowed by tractors rather than by oxen, people pointed to the older agricultural ways as constituting something that was fundamentally Saipineño. Yet the big new dam at La Cañada and the high-tech export-quality cane mills were also presented as things that were fundamentally Saipineño, making agriculture a tradition that reached not only into the past but also toward the future (Haynes 2013; Sammells 2012).

These signs were drawn into performances and activities that were explicitly aimed at a public audience beyond the town of Saipina. In 2008 I attended a meeting of the organizational committee for the Día de la Tradición Saipineña

FIGURE 10. A large image on the side of this bus shows an oxcart and a farmer loading (or unloading) sugarcane.

(Traditional Saipina Day), which was framed as an event that would increase local tourism by appealing to Bolivian tourists, many of whom might be urban emigrants and their descendants. The event was being planned for the first time. During the meeting, a group of elected officials and community leaders discussed traditional foods and activities for a festival in which "traditional Saipina" would be showcased. The organizers, officials affiliated with the town hall, spent most of the meeting arguing about whether certain foods were traditional or not, convincing the teachers to agree to put on a series of "traditional" dances, and discussing the details of a beauty pageant with the mother of the previous year's Carnaval queen.

In the following excerpt, Esteban, the mayor's brother, twice referred to the event as a *vitrina* 'glass display window' for the town, comparing the event to a strawberry festival that was put on by a neighboring town.

Transcript 17: E (Esteban), L (Lucho)

1. E: Perdon, la palabra. Gracias. Disculpa por la tardanza. Este, e, yo creo que a lo mejor el año pasado hemos tenido una experiencia muy buena, digamos, ¿no? Día de la chancaca, le pusimos feria de la chancaca, y hemos . . . nuestros productos. Yo creo que, **es la vitrina para nosotros**, por ejemplo, ¿no? Esta feria. Se conoce, se encuentran los productos, e, artesanal, danzas, todo, y sería bueno invitar a, en este caso, la, ¿qué se llama? a la televisión, aunque sea a un canal, a una emisora, para que nos pueda publicar.	1. E: Excuse me, may I take the floor. Thank you. Please excuse my late arrival. Um, uh, I think that it seems that last year we had a very good experience, so to speak, right? For Chancaca Day, we had the Chancaca Fair, and we . . . our products. I think that, **it's a showcase for us**, for example, right? This fair. One learns, one encounters the products, um, artisanal, dances, everything, and it would be great to invite, um, in this case, what do you call it? The television, even if it's one channel, a station, so that they can give us publicity.
2. L: Eso era. La once, la . . .	2. L: That's right. Eleven, or . . .
3. E: Sería bueno, porque, por decir, se, en Comarapa se hace la feria, netamente se hizo, nacional de la frutilla este año, ¿no? Ahí se muestran todas las variedades, los productos, y **es una vitrina para uno** para poder, e, hacer convenio incluso con gente de instituciones tambien, no? Sería tan bueno, digamos, hacer eso.	3. E: It would be good, because, for example, in, in Comarapa they did a fair, they really did it right, a national fair for the strawberry this year, right? There you could see all the varieties, the products, and **it is a showcase for one** in order to, even to make agreements with people from institutions, right? It would be great, you know, to do this.

As Esteban explicitly stated in this excerpt, the planning of Tradition Day was a way to attract outsiders, particularly those who might have opportunities for external funding (underlined). Tradition Day was a vitrina where artisanal products and cultural events would be publicized by the news media (such as television stations, all centered in large urban areas) and attract investors from outside the community. The organizers were careful to plan the event on a date when many people from the city would be present. They settled on the weekend of Todos Santos, All Saints' Day, when many urban migrants came back to remember the dead and to spend time with living relatives. In effect, they saw the event as a branding opportunity (Manning and Uplisashvili 2007; Moore 2003).

The artisanal products discussed at the meeting included *chancaca,* a raw sugar product used primarily in the manufacture of alcohol; weavings; traditional foods; dances and poetry presented by the local schools; and the aforementioned beauty pageant (on the latter, see Canessa 2008a; Gustafson 2006). With the exception of chancaca, all of these events would be the primary responsibility of women in the community—individual artisans in the case of weaving, schoolteachers in the dance and poetry presentations, and mothers and daughters in the beauty contest. Through this framing, the role of women as guardians of tradition (Stephenson 1997, 1999)—despite the mostly male organizational committee—was underlined and reinforced. Women produced tradition, which municipal officials (mostly educated men) then commodified as a consumable product for outsiders.

The discussion lingered longest on what counted as traditional food and drink. The mothers' clubs and other women's organizations would be responsible for preparing the food, and there was an enthusiastic discussion of what kinds of dishes should be prepared for sale at the event. In the following transcript from the meeting, Maribel and Dina discussed a traditional food, the cooked skin of a pig, known to Spanish speakers throughout Bolivia as *khara* or *k'ara* (from Quechua *q'ara* 'skin'). In this segment, as in many other instances in the recording, some speakers feigned ignorance of Quechua-influenced names and foods, despite the fact that it was their job to put on a festival showcasing traditional foods and dances of Saipina.

Transcript 18: M (Maribel), L (Lucho), D (Dina)

1. M: Pero eso le preparan con ese del chancho.	1. M: But they prepare that with the thingy of the pig.

2. L: Ahí también hacemos.	2. L: Over there we do it too.
3. M: ¿Cómo se llama eso?	3. M: What do you call that thing?
4. D: De esa **khara** de chancho.	4. D: With the pork **skin**.
5. M: Hm.	5. M: Mm-hm.
6. D: **Khara** de chancho, ¿no ve?	6. D: Pork **skin**, right?
7. M: Un **khara** de chancho.	7. M: A pork **skin**.
8. D: Hm, lo preparan ahí.	8. D: Mm-hm, they make it there.

The game seemed to be to show that one was enthusiastic about but at the same time removed from the traditional, which is to say, "lower-class," aspects of life in Saipina. In turn 2, Lucho agreed that "we make that" but used the deictic "over there," placing himself in some other place, while in turn 8 Dina said that "they," not "we," make this dish. Maribel, who came from another region of Bolivia, searched for the Quechua word for pork skin. Dina supplied her with the word she was looking for, *esa khara* 'that pork rind (fem.)', but Maribel mistook the gender, calling it *un khara de chancho* 'a pork rind (masc.)' rather than following Dina's lead in giving it the feminine gender marking. I wondered whether, when faced with a typical restaurant menu advertising *<u>khara</u> de chancho* 'pork rind' and *<u>ch'anka</u> de gallina* 'chicken drumstick soup', with *<u>mocochinchi</u>* 'peach-seed nectar' (Quechua borrowings underlined), these individuals would display as much confusion as they were able to summon up at this meeting.

In orienting toward tradition, the participants in this meeting characterized tradition as something that was imagined, a performance. Indeed, it was the most self-consciously "modern" people from the town who invented these performances; the widely traveled mayor, college-educated workers at the town hall, teachers at the local high school. Those who were furthest from living rural agricultural practices were most anxious to cast them as "traditions" (as described by Hill and Hill 1986 for Mexicano speakers).

Women were a key component of this. In the following transcript, Eduardo, the official in charge of tourism and culture, specifically singled out producers of food, drinks, and the mothers' clubs as people who had to be interested and on board before the event could begin to be advertised.

Transcript 19: E (Eduardo)

E: ¿De qué no, nos va a servir invitar a mucha gente que venga a ver y si no va a haber participantes, no sé, no va a haber, e, productos que ofertar, si no va a haber comida, si no va a haber e, refresco? Noo, o sea es, o sea lo primero que hay que hacer es organizarnos entre nosotros y que estemos de acuerdo en que todos participamos con un, con un estan, no sé, con una, con un producto, club de madres, no sé, gente aficionada al final y que puedan promocionar algo y [presentar] algo de, de aquí de la region.	E: What use, what use is it to invite a lot of people to come and see if there won't be any participants, I dunno, there won't be any, um, products to offer, if there won't be food, if there won't be, um, drinks? Noo, I mean, I mean the first thing we have to do is get organized among ourselves and get in agreement that we will all participate with an, with a stand, I dunno, with a, with a product, mothers' club, I dunno, people who are interested in the end and who can promote something and [present] something from, from here from our region.

The women present at the meeting embraced this role, participating enthusiastically in a fierce and often contentious discussion of what was and was not typical of Saipina. This discussion was often explicitly linguistic. People tussled over whether particular foods were "from here" or not. A breakfast dish made of cooked corn and sweetened milk was acceptable if it was called *tujuré* (the lowland pronunciation) but not *tojorí* (the highland pronunciation), but the typical lowland dish *masaco*, made of fried plantains or yucca with bits of pork, was also challenged as "not from here." Another dish, *arepas* 'flatbread', was likewise challenged as "from Vallegrande," that is, not authentically Saipineño. There was another discussion over *ají de trigo*, a dish of cooked wheat, which one person asserted "isn't made here." These discussions were not just about food but about how to define Saipina and how far the "traditional Saipina" could be imagined to extend toward highland or lowland centers.

Transcript 20: E (Eduardo), L (Lucho), R (Reynalda), N (Nina), AM (audience member)

1. E: Jugo de caña.	1. E: Cane juice.
2. AM: De caña.	2. AM: From sugarcane.
3. L: Mocochinchi.	3. L: Peach nectar.
4. R: ¿Mocochinchi? No hay.	4. R: Peach nectar? There isn't any.

5. AM: No hay mocochinchi. Aquí es caldo de caña, el guarapo de caña.	5. AM: There isn't any peach nectar. Here it's cane juice, the *guarapo* from the cane.
6. N: Ah ha.	6. N: Uh-huh.
7. AM: La chicha, colla que le decimos aquí, y la . . . chicha camba.	7. AM: Chicha, *colla* that we call it here, and the . . . chicha camba.
8. L: Chicha de maní tambien.	8. L: Peanut chicha too.

In this transcript, several participants at the meeting debated which drinks were most traditional and how they should be named. Eduardo's suggestion of cane juice was accepted, although a female audience member corrected his use of *jugo* 'juice' to *caldo* 'broth' and then *guarapo,* a word used specifically for the sweet liquid expressed from fresh sugarcane. However, his suggestion of *mocochinchi* 'peach nectar' was rejected. There was a quick discussion of highland chicha (chicha colla), an alcoholic corn beverage, and lowland chicha (chicha camba), which is also corn based but is unfermented and nonalcoholic. The version that was quickly accepted as the ideal and most authentically local was chicha made from peanuts, a sweet nonalcoholic drink. All four drinks—chicha camba, chicha colla, mocochinchi, and chicha de maní—were commonly available for sale in the plaza and served with meals in the homes that I was familiar with in Saipina, with no apparent distinction between their level of authenticity.

While most of the meeting was controlled by the organizers, this discussion of what "counted" as traditional food went on between the women in the audience. Though one of the organizers tried to intervene, saying, "Everyone can participate with whatever they like," it was clear that not only the type of food but also the way it was named was under control and surveillance by the women who would be the primary parties responsible for producing the content of the festival. These women rejected not only highland products as foreign but also lowland products and even dishes from as close as Vallegrande as being not "local" enough to represent Saipina. Through these discussions, they explicitly produced and referenced Saipina's position within and outside the highland/lowland binary while negotiating what it meant to be represented as "traditional Saipina."

What kind of a "showcase" was this production? While it was organized and funded by town leaders, they relied on the expertise and labor of individual women and women's groups to make the event into a success, the kind of success that would justify publicizing the event on regional radio and television. The explicit rationale for this publicity was to draw urban migrants home, as well as to attract people from other parts of Bolivia in the hopes of drawing investment from nongovernmental "organizations." The production of the "traditional" for outside consumption involved legitimizing women as experts in the production of traditional products, even as the educated male organizers positioned themselves even more firmly as "modern," outward oriented, and ignorant of the "traditional" practices that they were trying to promote (on gender, modernity, and language, see Inoue 2006; on gender and development in the Andes, see Radcliffe et al. 2004).

The same inward-outward point of view could be found in a municipal document that I obtained in 2008, part of the town's "municipal plan" (FORTEMU 2004). The tourism assessment characterized Saipina as a *pueblo típico* (typical town), describing its colonial architecture, typical dishes, music, and an array of traditional festival dates. In a later passage, the authors picked out speech style as one of a cluster of unique characteristics of Saipina that set it apart from other towns in the Santa Cruz valleys: "La forma de hablar, ó acento, la típica vestimenta, el tipo de música a través de las coplas, el tradicional guarapo de miel de caña al estilo de Dña. María y Constancio y la deliciosas comidas típicas son tradiciones que distinguen al Saipineño de otras culturas de los valles mesotérmicos de Santa Cruz" (The style of speech, or accent, typical styles of dress, the type of music through coplas, traditional guarapo of cane syrup in the style of Doña María y Constancio, and the delicious typical foods are traditions that distinguish the Saipineño from other cultures of the mesothermic valleys of Santa Cruz) (FORTEMU 2004:25). In this quote, the authors point to a "style of speech, or accent" that is presented side by side with traditional dress, music, and foods. Language, performance, food, and many other factors joined together to form a depiction of what constituted "typical" Saipina. Through these documents and discussions, physical and historical properties of the Saipina valley—agriculture, archaeological sites, flora and fauna—merged with personal and cultural characteristics, including linguistic features, that were constructed as "typical" or "traditional."

The meeting regarding Tradition Day and the municipal tourism document were examples of positioning by individuals who represented traditional Saipina with the goal of attracting profits and investment. The question "What is traditional Saipina?" was also about "What makes traditional Saipina *marketable*?" (on language ideologies, marketing, and tourism, see Jaffe 1999; Jaffe and Oliva 2013). While marketing Saipina was the domain of the highly educated workers at the town hall, it was women who were called upon to play the part of experts in producing "traditional Saipina, and it was women's labor that produced the spectacles and pageants that represented this idea (Fabricant 2009; Goldstein 2000; Rockefeller 1998). Where tradition was female, artisanal, local, and performative, modernity was cast by contrast as male, large-scale or mechanized, national or global, and unmarked (see, e.g., Cody 2013).

INSTITUTIONAL PAGEANTRY

Institutional spaces in Saipina provided a place for narratives of tradition and modernity. In this section, I focus on the role of institutional pageantry (Goldstein 2004; Gustafson 2006), particularly in the schools (Stephenson 1999:111–157), in presenting a narrative of "progress" that cast tradition as anchored in the past through a certain set of practices and images. Modernity, on the other hand, was often unmarked, erased, assumed, but it could be read through contrasting sets of signs.

Schoolchildren were socialized into performing participation in the Bolivian state from an early age (Luykx 1996, 1999). These performances often juxtaposed elements of tradition and modernity. The local kindergarten, founded by nuns who used a Montessori-like method through the Fé y Alegría (Faith and Joy) program, educated children aged three to six. One of the first things the children learned was to assemble at the beginning of the school day in lines arranged by grade, gender, and height and to sing the national anthem and other patriotic songs (Howard 2010; Rodriguez 2016). These gatherings were strictly monitored by the teachers, and children were lectured for wiggling and speaking out of turn. The kindergarten students wore light-blue smocks (girls) and light-blue collared button-down shirts (boys). The morning assembly continued throughout students' education, until they graduated from high school, becoming so naturalized and ingrained that they hardly noticed it. This time was used as an opportunity to teach students not only the national anthem but also other "traditional" Bolivian songs and often to practice "traditional" dances for performances in public spaces during ceremonial events such as the town's anniversary (Howard 2010).

Mothers carefully washed their children's hands and faces and brushed their hair before sending them off to school in the morning. My mother-in-law often despaired of getting her youngest daughter's hair brushed and braided in the morning. I heard her refer to her daughter's hair using the word *chʰampa,*

FIGURE 11. Uniformed schoolchildren assemble to sing the national anthem and other patriotic songs at the beginning of the school day.

a Quechua loanword meaning a clod of turf with roots dangling off it, and *chaska* or *chaskosa*, a star shape, meaning "frizzy" or "tangled." She also lovingly called her a *bruja* 'witch' or referred to her children jokingly as *salvajes* 'savages', words that use discourses of civilization and savagery to oppose orderly, domestic modernity to the untamed, wild, and perhaps threatening life outside the bounds of civilization. Sending a child to school with her hair unbrushed or with a dirty smock was completely out of the question for the mothers I knew; while they might send their children late or with homework half-finished, I never saw a child appear at school without carefully brushed hair and clean clothing. The colonial, modernist history of the white smock and carefully braided hair has been shown in many other contexts (e.g., Archibald 2011; Dawson 2012; Stephenson 1999; Stepputat 2004). In this small-scale, intimate performance of modernity in the form of a frustrated mother trying to rush her daughter out the door to school, there is an undercurrent of colonial racism in referring to wild children as "savages" or "witches." At the same time, the child learned that in moments of frustration, Quechua words come to her mother's tongue, and she learned classificatory systems that were rooted in native Andean ways of structuring the world.

In institutional pageants, indigeneity was framed as part of the past, a performance of Bolivian national identity, but not one closely connected to conceptions of what it meant to be a local Saipineño. One day, I observed the festivities around the Día del Campesino at a small rural school just down the road from Saipina. The Día del Campesino (Day of the Peasant) was the newly renamed version of the holiday once known as the Día del indio (Day of the indian). The program included a performance of the national anthem, a speech by the director of the school, and a speech by the superintendent of the district. The students performed a song called "Himno al indio" (Hymn to the indian), and individual students presented original poems titled "Al indio" (To the indian), "Motivos del indio" (Motifs of the indian), and "Indiecito boliviano" (Little Bolivian indian). There were a variety of dances from different regions of Bolivia, including one to the tune of "La pícara" (see chapter 7), a lip-synch performance, and a comic sketch called *Los trabajadores* (The workers) by students in the eighth grade. The school band played, and each grade paraded from one line drawn in the dirt in front of the school to another line at the end of the block, carrying flags and banners that represented their country, their department, their state, and their school.

There was a printed flyer announcing the program for the day, and the first page included a photograph of a young indigenous woman and child wearing hand-woven highland clothes and leading two llamas. This representation of stereotypically highland "indianness" was framed and controlled by the official stamp of the school, which was identified as a Núcleo Escolar Campesino (Peasant School District) on the cover.[15] The stamp, in official-looking purple ink, was repeated inside under the numbered acts on the program, and there was another stamp with the director's official title, crowned with his signature.

The identification of the school as a *núcleo rural* (rural district) was both aligned with and in opposition to the representations of *indianness* in the program. Indianness was controlled—indeed, elided—by its identification with campesinos at the same time that it was performed by the students as representative of modernity. This version of indigeneity was specifically associated with highland indigeneity—one that was cast as foreign to this area, though it was "Bolivian" in its character. Through this performance, indigeneity was removed from local traditions at the same time that it was put on display, acted

15. Rural or "peasant" school districts are administered separately from the larger, better-paid, and more prestigious urban districts in Bolivia. Schoolteachers are required to spend time teaching in a *núcleo rural* after finishing their teaching degree.

out (on links between campesino and indigenous identity, see Canessa 2005, 2012; Hertzler 2005).

This pattern continued in larger-scale events, such as a pageant put on by high school students in a performance on Bolivian Independence Day. In figure 12, a group of high school students put on a performance that represented Bolivia's state symbols. The young woman with her back to the camera, wearing the school uniform of a white smock, holds Bolivia's official flower, the kantuta, in the colors of Bolivia, yellow, red, and green. The young man facing the camera represents indigenous Santa Cruz, wearing what can only be described as a leopardskin loincloth and a long cape. Despite these lowland-linked signs, he also wore indigenous symbols related to Quechua and Aymara, the *inti* (sun) symbol on his head and chest. There is a *wara* (scepter, wand) lying on the floor by the two young women crouching on the right side of the photo. Both were symbols of authority and power in the Inca/colonial symbolic system (on constructing indigenous identity through performance, see Conklin 1997; Ramos 1994).

FIGURE 12. High school students put on a pageant showcasing Bolivia's state symbols while using stereotypical indigenous dress that combines highland- and lowland-linked elements.

In this presentation, as in the Día del Campesino celebration, the political units of the state of Bolivia were layered on the symbols of an indigenous past, which in turn synthesized symbols or stereotypes of highland and lowland indigeneity. This performance was part of a progression of figures who represented Bolivia's state symbols. The "barbarism" of the young man's public near nakedness contrasted with the elaborately costumed dances that followed. Indigenous identity, then, was both performed and enshrined, both framed as past and juxtaposed with the young woman's prim white school uniform and dressy sandals.

While the loincloth costume was more easily recognizable as a performance, the children in their school uniforms were also engaging in a costumed performance of a more everyday sort. In the process of producing tradition and modernity, tradition was framed as exotic and unusual, linked with indigeneity, specifically, highland indigeneity. Because it was costumed, it was easy to recognize. Yet this framing was produced and performed, not inherent in the categories of "tradition" and "modernity" themselves (Bauman and Briggs 2003). In particular, indigeneity was presented as linked to the past and to bygone days, while modernity was performed through institutional symbols and practices like the white smock, the national anthem, and the official symbols of Bolivia.

PERFORMANCE: THE "COPLA DEL ZAPALLO"

Profe Simón, a beloved high school teacher and musician, was often present at events that represented traditional Saipina. For performances, Profe Simón dressed in a "traditional" style and played "traditional" music, *vallegrandinas* and *coplas*. Traditional dress included a clean white button-down shirt, a black fedora hat in the style of the Santa Cruz valleys, and a hand-woven alforja.[16] Profe Simón often performed along with his daughter, who wore similar attire, with a knee-length black skirt and rubber tire sandals called abarcas, worn by peasants and agricultural workers. On his album covers, on his Facebook page, and in his YouTube videos, he consistently appeared in the same outfit. In collections of music, his style was identified as "Valluno" or "Vallegrandino," but it also appeared in collections of music that was identified as typical of Sucre and

16. This costume is essentially identical to the enregistered figure of the valley cumpa discussed in chapter 1, and the alforja and sandals are also mentioned in "Las patas kjarkas" (chapter 8).

FIGURE 13. Simón "El Sapo" Flores.

Chuquisaca, regions to the west of Saipina in the highlands (see Faudree 2013, 2015 on musical performance, regionalism, and language).

Profe Simón's music drew from a variety of genres and styles. Many of his songs, particularly on the first album that he released, were romantic, nostalgic odes to his homeland. For example, the ode "Molienda y chancaca" ([Cane] mill and raw sugar) romanticized the sugarcane industry in Saipina. "Molienda y el thaco son la tradición que Saipina guarda en su corazón" (The cane mill and the acacia tree are the traditions that Saipina keeps in its heart), he sang. In the same romantic genre were songs such as "Para enamorar" (In order to fall in love) and "Amor ilegal" (Illegal love), dedicated to a woman (or girl) rather than to a place. A few, such as "Paraba frente roja" (Red-crested macaw), had a political agenda. The red-crested macaw, an endangered species endemic to the area, was both a tourist draw and widely considered a pest and a threat to agricultural crops. In his song, Don Simón exhorted his audience, "Even if they eat a few ears of corn, let them live in peace."[17]

17. "Paraba frente roja," https://www.youtube.com/watch?v=nktSrGcHWpY&feature=youtu.be. "Copla del zapallo," https://www.youtube.com/watch?v=AyzVV77JPb4. "Para enamorar," https://www.youtube.

Profe Simón was best known locally, however, for his picaresque *coplas*. Traditionally, these songs, which stretch from Mexico throughout Latin America, are pointed, critical, and sometimes obscene (Solomon 1994). The best-known and best-loved was his "Copla del zapallo" (Copla of the squash), which played on a double entendre between "squash" and lady parts. The "Copla del zapallo" was wildly popular, and Profe Simón performed the song in live appearances for years before he recorded it. The verses regularly changed, with particularly *atrevido* (daring) lines redacted in more formal contexts. Men winked and women giggled and covered their faces when they mentioned the song to me, and a few earnestly inquired whether I understood the double entendre.

The recirculation of tropes linked to "traditional" Saipina through music and performance was an integral component of Profe Simón's prominence in the community. Cane mills, local wildlife, romantic odes, and sly double entendres combined with his visual presentation as a member of the valluno group to give him legitimacy as a representative of Saipina at important civic events. At the same time, Simón's level of education and his status as a well-established resident of the town lent him a degree of respectability. While Profe Simón was well regarded in Saipina, these performances took on a new meaning when they were treated as a representation of "typical Saipina" aimed at outside audiences—visiting dignitaries, public events, audiences on YouTube, or through the circulation of informally produced CDs and DVDs. In these contexts, Simón became a figure representing a type of person—a Saipineño—that performed Saipina's membership in the Santa Cruz valleys and in Bolivia as a whole (as described in chapter 2; on social personae, see Agha 2007a).

The vision that influential Saipineños presented of a distinctively local tradition and modernity could be easily read through pageants put on through local institutions such as the town hall and the schools. These "pageants," literal and figurative, presented certain elements of traditional Saipina as icons that could be contextualized, decontextualized, and circulated (Bauman and Briggs 1990). Individuals participated as figures-cum-archetypes of tradition and modernity—the prim white-frocked schoolgirl, representing "progress" as she held up the national symbols of Bolivia; the local musician, with his black hat and rubber tire sandals, singing suggestive but hilarious songs that incorporated local references and styles of speech.

---

com/watch?v=BJ3T6PUpAIQ. "Amor illegal," https://www.youtube.com/watch?v=TCBl0akYLVU. "Te amo solo a ti," https://www.youtube.com/watch?v=DQLbI393GFo.

The concept of "tradition" was one idea that people appealed to explicitly when they explained in interviews with me what made a person a local Saipineño versus an immigrant or an outsider. In these conversations, my consultants emphasized the importance of living an agricultural lifestyle and upholding local traditions as qualities that were important to being a Saipineño. One example that many people mentioned was *ambrosía* at Carnaval, when people hiked up to their estancias in order to enjoy warm milk fresh from the cow mixed with sugar, cinnamon, and alcoholic *singani*. Ana María, a high school student, told me that people who lived in the city were different from people in Saipina. She said that they were *asquerosos* (squeamish) and explained, grinning, that when her cousins visited from the city for Carnaval they had refused to touch the cow's udder with their own hands.

When I asked my interviewees how the town had changed in recent years, many of them, particularly those who were affiliated with the Green political party, lamented the fact that local traditions were being lost under the influx of Quechua-speaking migrants from the West. "Saipina used to be a town with a lot of traditions," Carlos told me. "Now they're all being lost." When I pressed Carlos and other interviewees to tell me how things had changed exactly, several people mentioned the festival of the Virgin of Urkupiña, a Bolivian saint particularly venerated in the Cochabamba area. Other residents of the town, however, disputed this interpretation, telling me that the procession of the Virgin was a relatively recent tradition and that her chapel had been constructed in recent living memory.

Carlos and other interviewees, distressed that people in Saipina no longer observed the feast of the Virgin of Urkupiña, saw this as an indication that local traditions were quietly falling into disuse as the town filled up with migrants from the western highlands. "They have their own traditions, you see; they're not like ours," Diana told me. Carlos also lay the blame for the declining traditions on the MAS-controlled municipal government, which no longer supported these traditional activities with official resources. The clear implication was that MAS politicians supported outsiders at the expense of local traditions.

Through these conversations, ideas about "tradition" were intertwined with discourses about migration, regional origins, and political affiliations. Yet like other types of social categories, these associations were not always predictable and were open to social negotiation. For example, given Carlos's strong identification with urban Santa Cruz, I found it ironic that he, the son of a legítimo Saipineño and a Quechua-speaking migrant from the West, told me that

Saipina's traditions were being destroyed by western migrants because people in Saipina no longer observed the feast day of a saint that was strongly identified with the Cochabamba area. Through complaints of discontinuity, people who positioned themselves as Saipineños used discourses of "tradition" to cast outsiders—whether urban migrants or rural highlanders—as people who disrupted the naturalized historical essence of Saipina.

CONCLUSION

The visions of tradition that I discuss in this chapter layer references to a temporally and physically continuous local sphere with a complex of signs that encompass practices such as farming, cooking, weaving, and musical performance. This construction of "traditional" practices is part of a production of local identity that relies on a fundamental distinction between insider and outsider and on positioning between West and East, rural and urban, indigenous and nonindigenous identities. The vallegrandino style of music, including coplas; the local style of weaving; styles of dress marked by use of the black vallegrandino fedora; *platos típicos,* or "typical dishes"; and agriculture and the productive economy were all considered quintessential markers of tradition in Saipina. None of these visions of tradition were simply preexisting capital-T Traditions that were universally accepted; rather, they were discussed, negotiated, contested, and produced by different actors within the community with an eye to outside audiences (Graham and Penny 2014; Jaffe 1999; Jaffe and Oliva 2013; Paugh 2005).

The particular versions of tradition and modernity that were projected through these performances were calculated to be attractive to tourists and outsiders, as made explicit in the town hall meeting about Día de la Tradición or in the postcards that Eduardo produced. At the same time, "tradition" was invoked as one of the ways in which Saipineños could be distinguished from outsiders, in performances such as Don Simón's local odes and coplas. As such, the production of local "tradition" created spatial and temporal continuities and discontinuities (Bakhtin 1937; Blommaert 2015; Cody 2013; Inoue 2004; Silverstein 1998) that served to produce Saipina as a continuous or coherent entity and simultaneously to distinguish it from other spheres.

The performance of indigeneity had a special place in the production of Saipina's participation in the Bolivian nation, yet simultaneously it was a sphere apart. Indigeneity was framed as part of the past, outside of the modern, and foreign to Saipina through performances such as the school pageants that I describe in this chapter. Yet at the same time, practices framed as "authentic" or "traditional" were also areas in which linguistic features related to Quechua contact are most common in affective spheres that were linked to women's work and a rural agricultural lifestyle. These embodied practices were removed from indigeneity through Saipineños' participation in rituals of the Bolivian nation such as school assemblies, pageants, and parades. When indigeneity is controlled by the symbols of the state and framed as past, it becomes symbolic and historicized rather than part of a lived experience. These discourses were carried further when people talked about recent immigrants not keeping the "traditions" of Saipina, when they contested the legitimacy of chicha colla and chicha camba as local types of drinks, and even when they combed their children's hair. All of these practices drew on a particular construction of "tradition" in order to reinforce and legitimize distinctions between contemporary Saipineños and highland-linked indigenous groups, despite their participation in a Bolivian historical and institutional production of indigeneity.

In this book, I characterize highland and lowland, western and eastern, indigenous and nonindigenous, colla and camba, and Quechua and Spanish as conceptual opposites that are related through processes of alignment and opposition in the life of the valleys. Saipineños produced "tradition" at local and national levels through institutional pageantry, performance, and material articles such as postcards and CDs in circulation. In doing so, they placed themselves not only with respect to the binaries mentioned above but also in relation to particular conceptualizations of figures of time and place: the historicized Bolivian "indiecito," the modern tourist, the local musician. Through the production, negotiation, and circulation of these figures, performances, and material artifacts, Saipineños placed themselves within a framework of tradition and modernity, past and future. These practices link geographical, linguistic, and ethnoracial binaries to a temporal positioning somewhere in between the racially unmarked modernity of the urban, national sphere and the historicized past of rural indigeneity.

INTERLUDE

At Home in the Saipina Valley

I HAVE HAD many homes in Saipina and the surrounding area. Most of all, though, I remember the summer I lived with my husband's grandparents Doña Antonia and her husband, Don Francisco. I had known Doña Antonia and Don Francisco for six years at that time and had often made the hour-long trek to their house from my rented room outside Saipina. However, I had never spent more than an afternoon there. That summer, with enormous generosity, they opened their home to me and my husband for an extended stay. During this time, I collected recordings of them and their neighbors and generally spent time "hanging out" (or, in fancier terms, doing participant observation) with the farmers and herders who lived just outside the town of Saipina.

To get to the house on la banda (the riverbank) we walked through lush agricultural fields, forded the Mizque River, and walked along sandy paths edged by cane fields and cactus into the hills around the northeastern side of the valley, some distance from Saipina. As we neared the house, we climbed a steep, rocky path up the side of a small hill, the doorstep to the foothills that rose up toward the high mountains to the west. Once we came in sight of the house, we were engulfed in dogs; the younger ones snarled and snapped at us, but the older ones drove them off, then engulfed us in slobbery affection. The young goats wandered around the house, outside their wood-fenced chiquero (corral), and there were some chickens scratching close to the door. When we arrived, Doña Antonia came out the door and greeted us with a hospitable exclamation of delight. She hustled us into the tiny, soot-stained kitchen, where she heated up some soup and passed us palm-shaped balls of homemade goat cheese.

Doña Antonia's husband, Don Francisco, was an active and intelligent man who worked in agriculture throughout his life, a talented musician, and a carpenter and builder. He built his houses himself. The newer house was made of thick, strong adobes and had a tin roof and a solar panel, which powered two lights and occasionally a black-and-white TV. It was much larger than the old house and had big windows in each room, making it lighter and more pleasant. Still, nobody used it very much; it was a nicer place to sleep than the old house, but family life went on in the kitchen or out in the fields.

The kitchen was in the older house, which was made of mud and sticks and sat low to the ground, with few windows. Apart from the kitchen, another room was dedicated to storage, and in the third room Doña Antonia kept a few pigeons. In the kitchen, most things were stored hanging from the roof to keep the roaches and other insects out. The kitchen was tiny and low and smoky, and everything was stained black from decades of cooking over an open fire in the corner of the room. One corner was almost entirely occupied by five-liter jugs that once held vegetable oil but that Doña Antonia reused to bring water from the rainwater runoff pond behind the house or in the dry season from the irrigation ditch running along the bottom of the hill. She brought twenty liters at a time in four jugs, one in each bag of an alforja and one in each hand. Doña Antonia was a slender woman who stood not much more than four and a half feet tall, tiny even by local standards, but she carried these heavy loads up and down the steep incline between her home and the irrigation ditch throughout her seventies and into her eighties. She also gathered and chopped firewood, carrying heavy bundles of wood back to her house after taking the goats out to pasture, and managed an enormous batán, the crescent-shaped grinding stone, that nearly severed my finger when I tried to use it.

Doña Antonia cooked on firewood that she or Don Francisco brought back from the monte. She produced goat meat and cheese at home, and Don Francisco brought huge sacks of rice, flour, sugar, and noodles every few months in a wheelbarrow from Saipina, more than an hour's walk away. They planted some corn for their own use and also a couple crops of sugarcane and potatoes or tomatoes each year. Many of the everyday items around the house were made by hand: rough woolen cloth that Doña Antonia spun and dyed and wove, leather lassos and ropes that Don Francisco cut and braided.

Many people who have seen my photographs of the banda over the years have made more or less subtle comments on the poverty that they perceived there. While they did not have a great deal of liquid cash or modern conveniences, Doña Antonia and

Don Francisco would never have considered themselves poor. They were respectable farmers and landowners; Doña Antonia, like many other older women, often reckoned her assets in terms of her herd of goats, remembering the days when she had sixty or seventy head rather than the thirty or forty that she could handle in her old age. While many of my contacts in the United States assumed that we sent money back to Bolivia, it was quite the reverse—when we visited them, they always sent us home with fresh eggs or cheese or a leg of goat, and when they had a good harvest they shared the cash among the family after paying off their debts.

When people talked about "the olden days" in Saipina, this was what they referenced—a lifestyle that centered on ties to the land, agricultural production, and animal husbandry rather than a bank account. Hard work and generosity were highly valued in this system, and it would be inconceivable to send visitors away without inviting them to a meal. While younger generations of Saipineños were increasingly oriented toward a cash economy, urban mobility, and modern conveniences, they continued to visit parents, grandparents, and other relatives who stood for these fundamental values even in changing times.

CHAPTER 7

CHOLITA OR SEÑORITA?

Gender Expression and Styles of Dress

BEFORE CELL phones, the radio station was a lifeline that families listened to for all their local communication and for national news. On the Quechua-language radio station, broadcast from Aiquile, Doña Juana told me, the messages went on and on for hours. Sometimes it seemed like there were more messages than programming. Then she added, "Cholita decían" (They said "cholita").

"What?" I asked, confused. "You mean the announcer was a cholita?"

"No," she said. "Cholita decían, si la persona era de pollera, señorita si era de falda" (They would say "cholita" if the person wore a pollera and "señorita" if she wore a skirt). For example, a woman who wore a skirt would be called "la señorita María Eugenia Vargas Pardo," but a woman who wore a pollera would be called "la cholita María Eugenia Vargas Pardo." She smiled at the thought, explaining that she didn't understand Quechua, but she often heard the word *cholita* when she listened to messages on the Aiquile station.

On further questioning, I learned that men had only two possible titles on the radio broadcasts: *señor* for older, married men and *joven* for younger, unmarried men. Women, on the other hand, had three options: *señora* for older, married women, and *señorita* for unmarried women who wore straight skirts. A young woman who wore the pollera, married or unmarried, was referred to as *cholita,* though older women who wore the pollera might be referred to as *señora.* This usage could be heard on both the Spanish-language and the Quechua-language radio stations, though it was more common to hear messages addressed to cholitas on the Quechua-language station.

Being a cholita, then, was a social category of such importance that it was used as a title, overriding marital status. Wearing a pollera was not a fashion choice; it was an identity category that set cholitas apart from señoritas. The pollera was the defining icon of cholita identity, while the skirt was an icon of a señorita. Wearing a pollera and identifying as a cholita, moreover, was linked to the use of Quechua rather than Spanish.

WHAT IS A CHOLITA, AND WHAT IS A POLLERA?

The pollera is a style of dress that is iconic of a modern indigenous identity in Bolivia (Haynes 2013; Stephenson 1997). Women who wear the pollera are generally referred to as cholitas, though they can also be more respectfully identified as *de pollera* (pollera wearing). The word *cholita* is the feminine diminutive form of *cholo*, a term that originally referred to indigenous people who moved to urban areas and adopted European dress and customs (de la Cadena 2000). The meaning of the term has shifted somewhat over the past century, and in Bolivia it no longer necessarily holds the connotation of class movement or of erasure of an indigenous identity. While the masculine word *cholo* is still used in other parts of Latin America, particularly in Peru, in Bolivia (in my experience) the masculine form is seldom used. The term *chola* without the diminutive suffix is rather derogatory; people use it in insults but not as a form of polite address. For example, *su chola* (his chola) refers insultingly to a woman who is in an extramarital relationship with a man; a man who is *cholero* is an inveterate skirt-chaser. Thus, the word *cholita* is linked to sexuality and morality as well as to styles of dress (Weismantel 2001).

The pollera first became fashionable in Spain in the early 20th century (Stephenson 1997) but was soon co-opted by Bolivian notions of style and integrated in a local system of meaning. The pollera as it is worn today is by no means the same garment that was worn a hundred years ago (Dirks 1990; Mendoza 1992). In fact, the pollera is not unitary; it is a class of dress, a style category, that contains many subcategories that reference a plethora of identity categories, socioeconomic status, and social stances (Colanzi 2015; Paredes Candia 1992). Saying that a woman wears the pollera is in some ways like saying a woman wears jeans in the United States: What kind of jeans are they? Are they cutoffs, Daisy Dukes, designer, stonewashed, black, tight, baggy, capri length, rolled up, sagging, insulated, off the rack, or the infamous "mom jeans"? While this analogy is a good one in terms of style, there is a point at which it fails. While it is very common for women who wear jeans to wear skirts or dress pants in other contexts, women who wear the pollera generally (but not always!) wear some version of the pollera all the time (Albro 2010:83; Haynes 2015; Van Vleet 2003).

During my fieldwork, I observed that the pollera existed in conversation not only with internal distinctions but also with other types of dress. There were many subtly distinct categories of dress for women, but the pollera stood in contrast to two major ethnically marked categories of dress: indigenous dress and "modern" dress (see chapter 6). Indigenous dress varied by ethnic group and region, but the most prevalent forms for women were skirts and shirts made of hand-spun yarn, with bright embroidered or woven designs contrasting with solid backgrounds, which were generally dark in color. These designs varied by region in highland indigenous communities and were accompanied by *llikllas* (square in shape, they can be folded and worn over the back) *chuspas* (pouches or purses) and other articles of dress, all of which were hand-worked with great care into artful and significant designs (Barragán Romano 1992; Schevill et al. 1996). The most traditional materials were llama, alpaca, and sheep's wool, but synthetic thread was also very commonly used. Weaving was a major status symbol and sign of family and regional connections in indigenous communities in highland Bolivia, as well as an economic activity (Ariel de Vidas 2002; Femenías 2005; Zorn 1997, 2004).

The señorita style of dress, on the other hand, was more familiar and less exotic to people outside the Bolivian context. Women wore straight skirts or pants with *poleras* (T-shirts) or button-down blouses. This style of dress was known as *de falda* (skirt wearing) in Saipina, as opposed to de pollera (Stephenson 1997). In the Santa Cruz valleys, traditional dress for señoritas included a knee-length straight skirt, usually in a dark color; a button-down white or light-colored blouse; a black fedora-style hat, which was worn by both men and women; and abarcas (see chapters 1 and 6). However, in more relaxed moments, the women who wore this style of dress might also wear *buzos* (sweatpants) and poleras. Women who wore the pollera, on the other hand, never (or almost never) wore pants, except as leggings to keep their legs warm underneath the pollera in cold weather (see also Weismantel 2001:106–130).

FIGURE 14. Polleras for sale in La Paz, 2014.

In representations of the pollera outside Bolivia, it was often linked to indigeneity, as in this quotation from the *New York Times*: "The clothing of highland Indian women—the pollera, the 19th-century European hat and the silky shawl known as a manta—have long been a curious sight in Bolivia and Peru. Tourists trekking through the Andes are as charmed by the colorful skirts and brightly colored hats as by colonial towns and the rugged mountains where ancient Indian civilizations thrived" (Forero 2004). This passage forms an image of cholitas as anachronistic, indian, colorful, charming, curious, and probably isolated and rural. In this description, the pollera is linked to Incan civilization, the highlands, indigenousness, "colorful" local culture in Bolivia and Peru, and 19th-century clothing and is framed as a "curiosity." The photos that accompany these descriptions reinforce this impression, depicting cheerful women in bright costumes and in rural highland settings. This conflation of the Andes, indigeneity, highland life, women, and a denial of contemporaneity has been extensively critiqued in the anthropological literature (e.g., Canessa 2005; Haynes 2013; Stephenson 1999). In fact, the pollera has a complex relationship with colonialism (Howard 2010). Wearing the pollera during the late 19th and early 20th centuries was exactly the opposite of a sign of indigeneity; rather, it was a sign of integration in mestizo culture and a rejection of indigenous values, an orientation toward European fashion and morality (de la Cadena 2000).

It is not only foreign venues that use the pollera as a symbol of Bolivia. Bolivian art, both popular and international, incorporates themes that reference the pollera. For example, Bolivia's most famous artist, Mamani Mamani, is an indigenous Aymara artist whose work references the altiplano and frequently includes variations on themes that include pollera-wearing women and references to the Pachamama, the deity associated with the earth in Andean spirituality.[18]

These images join others that circulate in high-profile international publications such as the *New York Times* and the *National Geographic* that position women in polleras as icons of indigeneity, tradition, rural life, and links to the premodern indigenous life. While the meaning that is attached to the use of the pollera in Bolivia contains elements of these themes, it also contains a wealth of other information that is not immediately obvious to the outside gaze.

Within the category of cholitas or pollera wearers, there were a myriad of other distinctions, some of which mirrored other types of binaries within the semiotic field. Older women from the countryside who wore flat-paneled polleras and might not speak Quechua were different from women who wore more modern, fashionable, commercially produced polleras. Women from Cochabamba had a different style of dress from that of Santa Cruz or La Paz. The many accoutrements that were involved in the use and wearing of the pollera communicated subtle signals about the wearer's social class, regional origin, and stylishness or taste. The portfolio of signs that made up the use of the pollera or the character of the cholita conveyed subtle messages about the wearer and her place in the broader social system.

POLLERA AS A PORTFOLIO OF SIGNS

The entire wardrobe of a cholita, including not only the pollera but also every other article of clothing, hairstyle, and accessories that she wore, signaled information about her place in the social system to observers. For this reason, the pollera and its accoutrements formed a coherent portfolio of signs. The body of the cholita represented not only a personal fashion choice; the use of the pollera

18. For examples of Mamani Mamani's art, see http://www.mamani.com.

participated in the construction of Bolivian national identity (Stephenson 1997, 1999) and also played an essential part in gender expression, as I demonstrate in this chapter. In this section, I describe the many different elements of cholita dress that carried social meaning, although this catalog is by no means exhaustive.

While wearing the pollera may seem to be a categorical choice, fashion and style were available to encode subtle signals that oriented its wearer in the larger semiotic field. Within the spectrum of the pollera there was a wealth of information about place of origin, socioeconomic standing, even taste and refinement. Wearing pollera might be a performance for a young woman for whose mother it was an everyday practice. One could be accused of misrepresenting oneself by wearing or not wearing a pollera or by using the wrong style of pollera.

In the first months that I lived in Saipina I was blind to the trends in pollera fashion. I assumed that the velvety polleras in jewel tones that I saw women wearing were just the way polleras were and always had been. Then I noticed a few fashionable women wearing polleras with very thin gold-stitched embroidery. After that I saw polleras made of a thin, crepey material with very thin pleats in a lighter palette. Later, there was a trend of polleras made of a matte, almost rubbery-looking material in very dark tones. After that followed a palette of bright pastel colors with large or small floral decorations. At the time of this writing, polleras in light jewel tones and a velvety fabric with a very short nap and a pronounced sheen were in style. Every year when I returned to Saipina, I saw a new fashion in polleras, and I learned to distinguish people who wore last year's styles from those who wore the most up-to-date and fashionable models (see Weismantel 2001:104–106).

These trendy polleras, the newest and most expensive, would be used by my consultants only on special occasions—holidays, parades, trips, school or municipal ceremonies. For everyday use, most women had a pollera made of a rough, durable fabric in a solid color that would hide stains well—a light olive green, a dark tan. These polleras were for everyday wear, and they were worn hard, often covered by an apron, and then scrubbed at the end of the week. Polleras were distinguished not just by region, social class, style, age, and urban/rural residence but also by function.

The pollera was accompanied by a portfolio of signs that coordinated with the pollera as centerpiece and that had their own stories to tell about their wearers. Perhaps the best known were the hats, which also had distinct regional variants: the *sombrero borsalino* or bowler hat in the highlands, the white straw hat tied with a colorful ribbon in the Cochabamba valleys, the black fedora (worn by both women who wear pollera and those who wear skirts) in the Santa Cruz region (García Recoaro 2014; Guaygua Ch 2003).

Women who wore pollera also wore their hair in long braids. Most women augmented their hair with extensions in matching shades of black or brown; I was told that even blonde hair could be found in the markets, though I never saw anyone wearing this color. The extensions were fastened with laces and braided into the woman's long natural hair. The laces also attached to black, beaded tassels that hung off the end of the braids. These tassels added to the illusion of length and lushness of a wearer's hair. Yet the use of hair extensions, while exceedingly common, was considered to be "cheating" in some way; in 2007 Mariela Molinedo was stripped of her Miss Cholita crown because she was shown to have used hair extensions.[19]

An absolutely essential item of a cholita's wardrobe was her sweater. I saw mostly thin cardigan sweaters in Saipina. These were used to keep warm and protect skin from burning in the sun, but also to tie the skirt modestly around the thighs if the woman thought someone might be able to peek up it—for example, while she was climbing into the back of a truck.

Finally, cholita shoes were a fashion category of their own. Women in La Paz wore dainty flat slippers. Women from the countryside wore plain tire sandals, but these were widely considered ugly and unfeminine. Most women in Saipina disdained these plain abarcas, instead wearing strappy, feminine styles, often ornamented with shiny bits and fake jewels.

Every part of this extensive wardrobe was attached to some kind of social meaning and identification. Everything about the body of a cholita, from her hat to her shoes and everything in between, communicated information about her regional origin, socioeconomic status, personal style, and even occupation. Indeed, a cholita's body defined her whole family; since men did not have dramatically differing styles of dress, their social status was defined by what their wives wore (Barragán Romano 1992; de la Cadena 2000; Stephenson 1999).

Two distinct styles of pollera were used in Saipina during my fieldwork. One was the plain pollera with wide, flat pleats that was worn by older women who came from the rural valleys surrounding the town—the migration wave of the

19. See "False Plaits Cost Beauty Queen Her title," Reuters, July 14, 2007, http://uk.reuters.com/article/oukoe-uk-bolivia-beauty-plaits-idUKN1430133920070714.

1960s and 1970s. These older women from the valleys around Saipina sewed their own modest polleras from flour sacks and lengths of sensible, long-wearing material in drab colors. At the time of my fieldwork, nobody under the age of seventy wore this style of pollera; even women who wore this style of pollera themselves never dressed their daughters in the pollera. Instead, the younger generation wore the straight valluna skirt hemmed at the knee.

Recent migrants from the Cochabamba valleys, on the other hand, bought fancy factory-produced polleras in the latest styles, often in bright colors and patterns with shiny designs in sequins and glitter. It was a terrible shame for these trendsetters to be caught wearing last year's fashions. These were the women whom my consultants referred to when they complained about immigrants and outsiders, MASistas and cholitas. This style was worn by women both young and old, and these migrants were generally assumed to be Quechua speakers.

One day I saw Doña Antonia, who belonged to the first category of pollera wearers, trying on a new pollera her daughter had brought her. It was sewed in the coquettish Cochabamba style, with the fabric gathered and sewed together into a series of horizontal ridged seams around the hips to accentuate the wearer's curves. Doña Antonia giggled as she tried it on and immediately set about pulling the stitches out so that the gathered fabric fell flat against her body. She and her daughter joked about the "hippy" pollera as they reworked it into a more modest style.

The length of a woman's pollera and the style of her hat indexed regional identities: Cochabambinas wore round white straw hats and polleras just above the knee, Paceñas (women from La Paz) wore black bowlers and shin-length polleras, women from the Santa Cruz valleys wore polleras just below the knee with a black fedora. Pollera length also correlated with climate; the shortest, raciest polleras of the thinnest material were found in tropical Santa Cruz. The region/hemline correlation was often commented on; people said that the length of the pollera reflected the temperature of the area where it was worn—cold in the highlands and warm in the lowlands. Yet women generally did not change the style of their polleras even when they moved to a different region of the country, maintaining their distinct regional style of dress regardless of the climate where they lived. The highland merchants that I knew in Saipina returned to their cities of origin year after year to get new polleras in the correct style.

The pollera and all its accessories were much, much more expensive than traditional valley dress and more relaxed styles of dress such as T-shirts and sweatpants. A woman who wore *la falda* (the straight skirt) often had her skirt made by a tailor, but there was little fabric and little sewing involved, and the cost was minimal. Other types of dresses, button-down shirts, T-shirts, and pants could often be obtained from merchants who sold secondhand clothing (usually of North American origin). Because the vast majority of this clothing arrived as donations, which were then sold in batches at auction, the cost of the secondhand clothing was very low—generally no more than a dollar or two for any given item.

The pollera, on the other hand, was made of yards and yards of fabric and also required a host of accessories: blouse, slip, petticoats, apron, cardigan, shoes, hat, jewelry, and hair extensions. Polleras were not manufactured outside Bolivia, and they required specialized tailoring (though they were adjustable, so they were forgiving of bodily changes, and women could usually wear them throughout a pregnancy). It is ironic that tourists often perceive the pollera as a sign of indigeneity and poverty. A middle-of-the-road pollera might run upward of $200, the equivalent of a decent monthly wage. If it was made of good material and in fashion, it could cost significantly more. And nobody could get along with just one pollera—three or four were about the minimum, and some women had dozens of polleras. They were also labor-intensive because they were a pain to wash, the heavy fabric and yards of gathered material making a heavy, sodden mass that had to be painstakingly hand-scrubbed and then hung out to dry.

The use of the pollera created a field of gender expression that contrasted identity as a cholita with identity as a señorita. For women, cholita dress involved wearing not just a gathered skirt but an entire portfolio of signs that communicated information about urban/rural orientation, social class, region of origin, and personal taste. However, all these signs stood in opposition to "modern" dress or the use of straight skirts. The semiotic field was once again divided into a binary, with cholitas standing on one side and señoritas on the other. This positioning had far-reaching implications for what was considered acceptable behavior and acceptable roles for these women, as I describe in the following section.

The link between wearing pollera and speaking Quechua was especially strong. This association erased the fact that some cholitas—notably, the older women who wore the more modest, flat-paneled polleras—did not in fact speak Quechua. Younger women often found it necessary to make this distinction when talking about their mothers and grandmothers; Eva told me, "My mother wears pollera, but she doesn't speak Quechua." Likewise, neighbors sometimes assumed that Doña Antonia was a native Quechua speaker because of her pollera; they were surprised to learn that she did not identify as a native Quechua speaker.

GENDER EXPRESSION: WORK AND SEXUALITY

Cholitas were under intense scrutiny for the way they dressed and the way they talked, the types of technology that they used, and their desires, behavior, and sexual practices (Canessa 2008a). Cultural expectations of women who wore the pollera were different from those for women who wore a skirt or pants. Most cholitas worked, for one thing, and in the rural Bolivian economic system, women often handled the household finances and controlled the money that they and their husbands or children earned. Cholitas also traveled widely, with or without their husbands and children. Cholita women controlled Bolivian markets all over the country, acting not only as streetside vendors but also as powerful and wealthy *mayoristas* (wholesalers) who mediated between farmers and *minoristas* (vendors). While women who wore skirts also worked outside the home, including in the markets, people often commented that it was necessary to know Quechua in order to negotiate with cholita market vendors (see Weismantel 2001:104–130).

Cholitas also worked in the fields. For women from Saipina, women's work in the fields generally centered around cooking, though women also helped with labor-intensive tasks like planting and harvest. Indeed, sowing was preeminently a woman's job, while men plowed, a symbolic division of labor dating back to Inca cosmology (Silverblatt 1987). In the fields, cholita women were preferred for some jobs, such as sowing potatoes and onion seedlings. Cholita women from the town of Mizque, across the border with Cochabamba, had a reputation for being the best transplanters of onion seedlings in the country, and they were widely sought out to perform this difficult and backbreaking labor.

The use of the pollera was seen by many as a symbol of sexuality. While riding along in the car with Nelson, a local agronomist, on a workday, I was shocked to see him lean out the window to yell lewd comments at cholitas working in a field. Other male agronomists told me repeatedly that cholitas don't wear any underwear (the men suggested that this was a concern when spraying toxic pesticides in the fields where cholitas might be working on a regular basis). Whether or not this comment was true or the concern was justified, the topic of what cholitas did or did not wear under their skirts surfaced with great frequency.

Cholitas did seem to enjoy more freedom than the more conventional morality of skirt-wearing señoritas. *Chicherías*, bars where corn beer was made and sold, were generally run by cholitas and were also often well attended by them (on chicha, see Jennings and Bowser 2009). I saw cholita women openly drunk, and I also saw them dancing with, embracing, and kissing men and other women. These activities by a woman who was not a cholita might be used to viciously condemn her; when a cholita did them, though, the response was merely eye rolling about "the way cholitas are." One friend told me that when he lived next door to a chichería, "Las cholitas venían a tener relaciones ahí" (Cholitas came there to have [sexual] relations). He described the whispered conversations that he had overheard on his darkened doorstep, imitating a woman's high-pitched voice with a highland accent and giggling at the memory.

Pollera wearers might be, indeed were expected to be, combative, sexual, and independent, in particular, financially independent (Haynes 2013; Weismantel 2001). However, great social control was exercised over what counted as a "sincere" use of the pollera and who was licensed to be a cholita—or a skirt wearer. Cholitas had free access to roles in which they are often seen, such as working in commerce or in the markets, practicing traditional medicine, working in agriculture or with livestock, and doing child care or domestic work (Seligmann 1989, 1993). However, anxieties and curiosities arose when women who used the pollera moved into other fields—as university graduates, political leaders, truck drivers, athletes. These attitudes could shift rapidly; when cell phones first appeared in rural Bolivia, people found it funny to see a cholita using one of these emblems of modernity. A few years later, only foreigners found anything remarkable about the sight of a cholita with a cell phone glued to her ear, speaking rapidly in Quechua.

POLLERA IN PUBLIC SPACE AND AS PERFORMANCE

The pollera and the female body as embodied in the figure of the cholita act as symbols of the "authentic" Bolivia both inside and outside the country (Stephenson 1997, 1999). As I discussed in the introduction to this chapter, Bolivian national identity was often performed through the figure of the cholita (Droguett 2013). This was visible in promotional materials for tourism in Bolivia, which often prominently featured indigenous women's bodies. Cholita dress was depicted on postcards that were marketed to tourists. As Stephenson details, Bolivian literature often turned on the figure of the pollera, as in Antonio Díaz Villamil's *La niña de sus ojos* (The apple of their eye, 1946) and Carlos Medinaceli's *La Chaskañawi* (Starry eyes, 1957). Though men's clothing certainly communicated information about social class, there was no male equivalent of the pollera. Rather, a man was marked socially by the dress of the woman he married. Cholita dolls were sold at airports; at Alasitas, a festival of miniatures in La Paz, cholita Barbies could be purchased (see Canessa 2008a on the sexual and economic politics of dolls). These images originated from a Bolivian point of view, but they were taken up by an international audience, reinforcing and reifying the image of the picturesque peasant woman.

Popular songs also enshrined the figure of the cholita. In "La pícara," the narrator tells the story of a flirtatious girl (a rough translation of the title). In the opening lines of the song, he says he is "crazy about her, tied to her pollera," and relates how he follows her as she walks down to the river and lifts her pollera to bathe her "lovely brown thighs." The *pícara* knows she is being followed and watched, and she comes back smiling; the singer calls her "daring and coquettish" and compares her to ripe fruit ready to be bitten into, using the Quechua loanword *k'achir* 'to chomp'.

"La pícara"[20]

Era morena y muy bella	She was dark and very beautiful.
Andaba loco por ella	I was crazy about her,
Atado a su pollera.	Tied to her pollera.
Bajando por la quebrada	Walking down the ravine
Por el camino del río	By the river trail,
Esperaba y la seguía.	I waited and I followed her.
Subiéndose la pollera	Lifting up her pollera,
La pícara se bañaba	The pícara bathed
Sus lindos muslos morenos.	Her lovely brown thighs.
Mi corazón galopaba,	My heart galloped.
Sabiendo que le espiaba	Knowing I was spying on her,
Veniaba sonriendo.	She came back smiling.
Tan bonita la imilla,	Such a beautiful girl,
Tan bandida y coqueta,	So daring and coquettish,
Como fruta madura	Like ripe fruit
Lista para k'achirla.	Ready to be bitten into.

20. Sung by the group Los Kjarkas; https://www.youtube.com/watch?v=GS3cIXkTN1M.

In the YouTube video that accompanies this song, both men and women wear bright satin garments. The men wear black fedoras, vests, and short pants, while the women wear cholita costume, with the knee-length skirts and white straw hats of the Cochabamba area. The musicians are pictured playing traditional highland Andean instruments like flutes and panpipes, as well as the ukulele-like *charango*. At the end of the song, the pícara regards a young man who bites suggestively into a large red apple; in the last few frames of the video, she is pulled forcefully into high grass by a man.

These images reinforce the image of frank sexuality that is associated with cholitas. The pícara is perfectly aware that she is being pursued by the young man; she is portrayed as complicit in his pursuit and probably not averse to sexual overtures. Yet despite the lighthearted tone, the image of the young girl being yanked into the high grass at the end of the video is profoundly unsettling.

In contrast to the frank sexuality of "La pícara," a song that is classified within the eastern lowland music genre relates the romantic story of a man who falls in love with an innocent young woman herding sheep. She is described as having blonde hair and green eyes—from which we might presume she is of European descent, unlike the "lovely, dark" pícara—and the chorus states that she has never been accustomed to love, dance, or go courting. Her innocence is reflected in the chaste desires of the singer to "lose himself" with the little shepherdess. The YouTube images for this song are of women wearing the typical lowland garment, the tipoi, or long, loose dress (see Fabricant 2009; Gustafson 2006), and the singers are from the Santa Cruz valleys or eastern lowlands, with a marked "*s*-eating" dialect. Herding sheep in the countryside is typically a job for young children, and this background knowledge adds to the depiction of the little shepherdess as innocent, unlike the knowing and complicit pícara.

"La ovejerita"[21]

Cuando salí de casa en busca de un querer,	When I left home looking for a love,
Encontré una ovejera y de ella me enamoré.	I found a shepherdess, and I fell in love with her.
Esa ovejerita no sabía querer, no sabía bailar, tampoco enamorar.	This little shepherdess didn't go around falling in love, dancing, or courting.
Era de cabellos rubios como los rayos del sol,	She had blonde hair like the rays of the sun,

21. Sung by the group Los Cuatro del Valle, https://www.youtube.com/watch?v=B7YiqdhiwVw.

Era de ojitos verdes que me roba el corazón.	And green eyes that stole my heart.
Esa ovejerita no sabía querer, no sabía bailar, tampoco enamorar.	This little shepherdess didn't go around falling in love, dancing, or courting.
Ahora me la llevo porque es mi querer.	Now I'm carrying her away because she is my love [or "it is my desire"].
Con esa ovejera me voy a perder.	I'm going to lose myself with this little shepherdess.

The chaste, innocent young woman in "La ovejerita" is tied to a stereotypically European appearance and to lowland styles of language and dress, while the knowing and flirtatious young woman wears pollera, uses Spanish mixed with Quechua, and is dark-complexioned. The contrast between different types of sexual morality is embodied through the figures of the innocent little shepherdess and the pícara, the flirt. Both are stories of falling in love, perhaps even of obsession, but they present the women's willingness and availability very differently.

The fact that these figures were differentiated based on region, language, and European or indigenous descent did not mean that the audiences for these songs were different. Indeed, in the Santa Cruz valleys both songs were popular throughout my fieldwork, and they were often played at the same events and by the same artists. However, through the visual iconography of the music videos and the language of the songs, different types of feminine sexuality were aligned with the cholita and señorita categories of gender expression. These categories were linked to regional origin and to language use—in particular, the use of Quechua loanwords.

CROSSING

Because the pollera was a conspicuous, marked style of dress, and it represented a feminized and sexualized persona that was saturated with social meaning, it was especially "good" for humorous cross-dressing. This cross-dressing took many forms: foreign women, the embodiment of modernity, wearing pollera; men, the embodiment of masculinity, wearing pollera; and children, the embodiment of the future, performing "traditional" dances dressed up in pollera (see also chapter 6). Each of these types of cross-dressing had different overtones of humorous transgression of social norms, but they all had in common the use of the pollera by figures—bodies—that were considered inconceivably "other," an impossibility and a contradiction to the terms of what a pollera was and who a cholita could be.

Foreign women were perhaps the prime example of this. While there were light-complexioned cholitas, foreign women were considered to be by definition outside the class of pollera wearers. Because of the incongruity of the sight of a foreign woman in the pollera, we foreigners were often encouraged to wear the pollera as a form of cross-dressing. I knew one American woman who, speaking Quechua and chewing coca, was regularly able to "pass" as a cholita. More often, though, white American or European women wore the pollera as Bolivian university students did, during festivals and dances.

When the women's group that I worked with decided to participate in a dance performance with a dance number that involved wearing the pollera, I agreed to go along with the group. I borrowed a pollera and blouse from my neighbor and danced with the rest of the women. Though several of the women in the group were habitual pollera wearers, even the women who regularly wore skirts switched to pollera for this performance. My appearance in the pollera was the source of great amusement and fun for my friends and neighbors, but I found it embarrassing and awkward. The pollera was rather short for me, and I found it hard to manage modestly when I bent down, sat, or kneeled for photos with the other women in the group. My friends assured me later that they thought I "looked better" in pants. However, the wearing of the pollera by white American or European women was always a source of hilarious entertainment.

The pollera was also used by Bolivian men for satirical cross-dressing. This was most common during the Carnaval season, a time of year when social boundaries are transgressed in many forms (Lecount 1999). In the Carnaval parades, men dressed up as cholitas, with long braids, stuffed bras, and wide skirts, and they danced lewdly alongside Carnaval floats and Carnaval queens to the raucous amusement of onlookers. One dinner theater that was widely advertised in Santa Cruz had men dressed as cholitas as one of its central attractions. Bolivian comedians such as David Santalla were known for their representations of cholita characters. Often these representations were accompanied by high-pitched, rapid, Quechua-accented speech. Like drag queens in the United States, the sexualization of the pollera opened the door for satirical, suggestive reformulations of this style of dress (Barrett 1998, 1999).

Children, on the other hand, performed a different aspect of cholita identity. Very few young girls wore the pollera in Saipina; those who did were recent

FIGURE 15. Costumed schoolchildren wait by their mothers before a dance performance. While the girls are wearing pollera only for their performance, their mothers are women who identify as cholitas and wear the pollera customarily.

migrants who quickly changed to pants and straight skirts. Yet schoolchildren often dressed in pollera when they were called on to perform "traditional" dances for important dates and occasions, representing their municipality (see chapter 6). In these dances, the pollera was treated as a costume that represented "traditional" Bolivia, along with the tipoi and other types of performance dress. Implied in this presentation was the implication that the pollera, like the tipoi, represented a historical style of dress that was no longer present as a modern style (see chapter 6). Yet some of the young girls dressed up as cholitas sat side by side with their mothers, who were "real" cholitas, wearing the pollera not just in performance contexts but all the time.

The sexual and the "traditional" performative roles of the pollera combined in Carnaval season, when *comparsas* (fraternities) specializing in particular dances rehearsed all year round for dance competitions during Carnaval season (Carmona 2008; Gustafson 2006; Mendoza 2000). During these competitions, special versions of the pollera were worn both by women who identified as cholitas and by university students who performed wearing a stylized form of pollera in the dances but who used jeans or miniskirts in their daily life. The use of the pollera in Carnaval ranged from ankle-length Paceña skirts with layers of petticoats to tiny ruffled miniskirts worn by women who danced Caporales, where the skirt's main function is to whirl around in time to the music and show glimpses of flesh underneath (see Bigenho 2016:40–43).

As is the case for the other binary categories that I discuss in this book, the practice of wearing a pollera was meaningless without considering the styles of dress that contrasted with the use of the pollera. That is, cholitas were defined in opposition to other categories. Principally and most saliently, they were defined in contrast to proper, skirt-wearing señoritas. However, considered from other angles, they were also defined in opposition to men, to foreigners, and to modern practices as embodied by schoolchildren. You cannot "cross" unless there is an apparently unbridgeable difference. Cholitas stood for a particular kind of feminine sexuality that was marked as quintessentially "traditional" and that represented an essential piece of the Bolivian national imaginary. At the same time, it participated in a larger semiotic field that linked the use of the pollera to highland indigenous practices and to speaking Quechua.

SHIFTS AND TRANSFORMATIONS

Women who wore pollera could shift to the straight skirt. However, these choices were subject to scrutiny and criticism by others in the community. The shift from pollera to straight skirt could happen in the course of an individual woman's life, when she decided to change from the pollera to a skirt, or it could happen across a generation, when a woman who wore pollera decided to dress her daughter in skirts or pants. The change seldom went in the other direction, from skirt to pollera, though this was not unheard of (Albro 2010:83; Haynes 2013; Weismantel 2001:130). Though Mary Weismantel characterizes the use of the pollera as a "choice," in my observations, women who chose to change from pollera to skirt were subject to particularly vicious gossip. My friend Isabel wore pollera when she first came to Saipina as a preteen; she soon switched to pants and straight skirts after being teased at school. Shortly afterward, her family moved back to their hometown in the western highlands, where all the women and girls wore pollera. Now wearing straight skirts, Isabel was once again mercilessly teased by her schoolmates, who told her that she showed "everything" every time she sat down. When my Saipineño friends talked to me about Isabel, they always mentioned how "she was a real little cholita when she first came to town," although, they implied, she tried to pretend she was not one. By identifying Isabel as a cholita, they essentialized her as a pollera-wearing outsider, a bilingual from the western highlands, and also tied her to negative stereotypes of collas.

In the introduction, I discussed Plácida's negative reaction to a neighbor who had changed from the pollera to slacks. Plácida's neighbor Inocencia had moved to Saipina from the western highlands a few years before, renting a storefront on the main avenue. About the time that she moved into her new storefront, Inocencia stopped wearing pollera and started wearing slacks. I hadn't even noticed when Plácida pointed this out to me as part of a string of complaints about the store next door.

In another case, the son of a wealthy landowning couple became romantically involved with a cholita in Saipina. After they had a child together, she moved in with him at his parents' house. When I spoke to his mother, she was still angry about his choice of partner and complained to me about the woman, shaking her head bitterly and expressing her unhappiness with his *concubina* (concubine; this unflattering term was used to describe a woman who is openly in a relationship without being married, often because her partner was already married to someone else). When I stopped by the house a few years later, the woman had changed her pollera to pants and her long braids to a single ponytail down her back, and she had abandoned the white straw hat that marked her as a Cochabambina. While she had been unguarded and open when she wore the pollera, she greeted me with wary reserve when I met her wearing the skirt.

The change away from pollera was not always so fraught, however. One day I came across a very old photo of my landlady, Felipa, a tough older woman who (unusually for Saipina) wore her hair very short and seemed to care very little about her appearance beyond basic propriety. In the picture, she was sixteen or seventeen, very tall for her age, wearing her hair in two long braids, posing awkwardly with her arms pressed to her sides, and wearing a pollera. I was enormously surprised and immediately asked her about her style of dress. "Oh, yes," she told me, "I wore pollera until I got married, and then I changed to a skirt."

"But why?" I asked her.

"It just didn't feel right," she answered. I don't know whether there were any commentaries in the community when she switched away from pollera; by the time I knew her, there were few people who remembered she had ever worn pollera at all. For Felipa, at least from the perspective of several decades later, the transition away from pollera seemed not to have been the controversial issue that it was for many women who were in the process of transitioning from pollera to skirts.

While it could be difficult to shift from one style of dress to another, and many kinds of social control were exercised over women who did so, women could and did change their style of dress. The difficulty rested in the claims that the women seemed to be making not only about their dress but about their social identification and their place in the broader semiotic field. The pollera was not only a style of dress but a claim to a gender identity, positioning with regard to tradition/modernity, language practices, political stances, and regional and class-based affiliation. It is in this context that women who changed from the pollera to pants or skirts were interrogated for their right to claim different types of identifications.

SHIFTING ACROSS GENERATIONS: "WE WERE BORN TO SKIRTS"

Just as Doña Felipa said that wearing the pollera didn't "feel right," I also heard the "it just feels right" answer from women who chose to wear the pollera. When I spoke to Doña Raquel, Isabel's mother, who had worn the pollera all her life and whose older daughter also wore the pollera, she told me that pants and skirts were uncomfortable and that she found the undergarments that women wore with them confining. A friend of hers, also an older woman who wore pollera, was present with her for the conversation, which took place mostly in Quechua, and she agreed that the pollera was more comfortable and less confining than pants or skirts. I heard this from other women, too; wearing the pollera was a bodily habit and practice and an outgrowth of a larger identity. This framing of pollera use links directly to practice theory approaches that characterize identification—in this case, gender expression—as an outgrowth of bodily practices and day-to-day routines (Bourdieu 1972; Mahmood 2005; Ortner 1996, 2006).

When I talked to older women from the valleys surrounding Saipina about their choice to wear pollera or straight skirts, they downplayed their own agency (Ahearn 2001), characterizing the use of the pollera less as a decision or a choice than as an inevitability. Doña Antonia said that she wore pollera because "mi mamita era de pollera" (my mother wore pollera). Yet she never dressed her own daughters in pollera, saying, "Ya no era de moda" (It wasn't the style anymore). Immediately afterward, she mentioned bringing her daughters to the town of Saipina in order to study and get an education. We talked about Doña Felipa, whom she had known as a young woman, and she said that everyone "allá en esos altos" (out there in those highlands) wore pollera. According to her recollection, Doña Felipa had changed her style of dress around the time she moved to the Saipina area.

Doña Antonia told me that when she was a child, there were groups of people who wore hand-spun black embroidered clothes in indigenous styles but no women who wore straight skirts. In the old days, young women who wore pollera had greater freedom to travel, work, and manage money than indigenous women. They were also often independent at a relatively young age, managing their own families when today's young women might be in high school or college. Yet as women moved from the rural valleys to more urban areas like Saipina, they changed their own style of dress or dressed their daughters in straight skirts. While cholitas had greater personal freedom than señoritas or indigenous women, they were shut out of opportunities for education and social mobility. Later, I asked Doña Juana, Antonia's daughter, about the pollera and why she never wore it. She said she'd tried on her mother's pollera for fun—dressing up—but she never wore one seriously. "Hemos nacido a la falda o al pantalón" (We were born to skirts or pants), she said.

I asked Doña Eustaquia, another older woman from the local valleys, about wearing pollera. She said she didn't know why she wore the pollera, she had just always worn it. She said her daughters had pressured her to switch to a skirt, but she didn't want to. Rather, she joked, "me he acostumbrado al pantalon" (I've gotten used to wearing pants), pointing to the knitted leggings she wore under her pollera. She said her oldest daughter wore pollera for a while when they lived in Pasorapa, a highland town across the border in Cochabamba, but she soon switched to a skirt after they moved to Saipina.

Doña Lorenza, a highland migrant and a *mujer de pollera* (pollera-wearing woman), said that she wore pollera because she had always worn pollera and had never worn anything else. She emphasized that everyone in the town where she came from wore pollera. Yet she, too, dressed her daughter in skirts and pants. Her daughter moved to Saipina at the age of three or four and had always worn pants or skirts. I asked Doña Lorenza about people who changed from pollera to skirts, and she speculated that perhaps they did it because the pollera was so expensive. But she expressed disgust for women who changed their style of dress and mentioned scornfully, "Some of them don't even know how to read, but they wear a skirt."

Young women in Saipina generally did not want to be cholitas (for another examination of this attitude, see O'Connell 2013). When I took my sister-in-law to the city, where she wanted to buy herself a pair of shoes to wear at her high school graduation, she lingered for a long time over a pair of strappy silver sandals before deciding that they looked "like something a cholita would wear" and rejecting them. Being a cholita was a mark of being an immigrant and an outsider. During my fieldwork there were no girls attending the local high school who wore pollera.

CONCLUSION

Despite the inevitability with which women characterized their decision to wear the pollera or skirts—to be a señorita or a cholita—there were clear associations with each category. Women who wore skirts were educated and grew up in urban areas, while women who wore polleras were less educated and came from the rural highlands. Moving to the larger town of Saipina generally meant wearing a skirt, obtaining an education, and becoming a señorita. While women presented this change to me as something inevitable—"We were born to skirts"—it was a change that not only daughters but also their mothers saw as symbolizing an aspiration to a different kind of identity, a different kind of future, from the roles that were available to a cholita. The reasons why particular practices of dress and bodily practice "felt right" shaped and responded to the ways that these women saw themselves as part of a broader social field.

In the example that I used to open this book, Doña Plácida questioned, "How can she wear a straight skirt when everyone knows she speaks Quechua and is a member of MAS?" Cholitas participated in a cluster of signs within the semiotic field that also included being from the western highlands, speaking Quechua, and being recent migrants. Wearing the pollera indexed a cluster of ideas that were intimately related. Cholitas, through their portfolio of signs related to their style of dress, stood in for a host of social identifications: region, class, sexuality. More than anything else, the assumption that cholitas were Quechua speakers was so pervasive that it underlay nearly every reference to either category. To be a Quechua speaker was to be a mujer de pollera or to be close to one; to be a cholita was to speak Quechua. The two were tightly connected both within the social system of Saipina and in the Bolivian national imagination more generally (Stephenson 1999; Weismantel 2001).

The oppositions between categories were ideologically constructed as firm and impermeable. However, despite these ideologies, people could and did change from one category to the other. These changes and transformations were not free of anxieties. In discourses surrounding cholitas and discussing the use of the pollera, it was never dress alone that determined the way that these categories were framed but also language, socioeconomic status, morality, sexuality, and a host of other overlapping identifications. The structure of the semiotic field played a powerful role in placing cholitas within a web of concepts that went beyond dress, style, and history to concepts of race, language, geography, morality, and sexuality.

INTERLUDE

It's as If One Were Blind: Education and Literacy

DOÑA ANTONIA was unusual among the older women that I knew because she knew how to read. Even more remarkably, she had learned to read as a small child; her father was a profesor (schoolteacher), she told me, and he taught her and her brother to read and write from the time they were very young. By the time he died, when she was eight years old, she already knew how to read, how to write letters and numbers, and how to sign her name. After he died, she went to school for another year or two—first and second grades—but she told me that she learned little. "It wasn't like having my father teach me," she said. "Besides, I already knew how to read and write."

Her sister-in-law Braulia was more typical of older women. Doña Braulia had gone to school for only one year, learning little, and she felt her illiteracy keenly. Her father had not believed going to school would do any good, especially for a woman. In contrast, her brother Don Francisco had picked up reading and writing in his travels as a young man, and he did both slowly but serviceably. "And it's so necessary. It's as if one were blind," Braulia told me. "It makes me so sad, and it makes me angry that there was so much I never learned. I was good at it." She insisted that she was too old and short-sighted to learn as an adult, but she helped to support her granddaughter while she attended college as a young mother. "I don't care so much about the boys," she told me. "It's us women who suffer, isn't it?"

As Braulia suggested to me, uneducated women had an especially hard time in Saipina. Men could always work in agriculture or get a technical degree in agronomy, veterinary science, health, or other applied fields. There were some opportunities for educated women, who could work as teachers in the local schools, as cashiers at the local credit union, or as nurses at the local hospital, all jobs that paid decent salaries and allowed for self-sufficiency. Uneducated women, though, ended up caring for children (their own or others'), cooking, cleaning, and working in the fields. These backbreaking jobs were poorly compensated or uncompensated, and they were exactly the life that families hoped their daughters would escape by sending them to college.

Moving to the city was no guarantee of educational success, however. After finishing high school, my sister-in-law Inés moved from Saipina to the city of Santa Cruz. She hoped to study pharmacy at the public university, which was more prestigious and less expensive than private universities or institutos. However, she scored low on the entrance exams and was unable to gain admittance. With the help of a relative, she found a job working as a waitress, then at a supermarket, and then for a distributor that operated within the supermarket chain. She enrolled in classes at an instituto in order to try again for the university entrance exams, but she worked long hours at the supermarket and was often too tired to go to class. "Maybe it's an excuse, that I was working, but I couldn't seem to do well in my classes at the institute, so I stopped going," she told me.

When she first moved to the city, Inés lived with an aunt who owned a bakery. She was tired when she came home and interacted little with her aunt's family. The aunt accused her of laziness and made her home life miserable. "I don't know what she wanted. I guess I was supposed to take care of her and clean the house," Inés told me with a grimace. In addition, the constant noise and pollution of the city bothered her. She felt exhausted and depressed, crying herself to sleep at night.

Using her earnings from her job, Inés soon moved to her own rented room, a tiny space in a peripheral urban neighborhood that had a reputation for being dangerous. She split her time between her work hours and her own room, seldom going out to clubs and visiting friends only occasionally. A few years later, her younger brother Ramón graduated from high school and joined her in the city, moving into her rented room with her. Unlike Inés, he was able to pass—barely—the entrance exam at the public university, and he enrolled in classes. Inés continued to pay the rent as a way of supporting her brother during his studies. Other relatives chipped in from time to time as well. However, Ramón had a hard time in his classes, failing most of them during his first semester.

When I asked her what she liked best about Santa Cruz, Inés shrugged wordlessly. She told me that she didn't like it at first because of the noise and the alienation of big-city life. While other migrants I spoke with emphasized the economic opportunities available in the city and the active social life they led, Inés felt that she was stuck in a dead-end job and had few friends. She was most animated when she talked about a kitten she had adopted, telling me about its explorations, expanding the perimeter of its territory around the neighborhood. Inés seemed to be staying in the city largely because it was not Saipina.

Over the course of three generations, access to education became steadily more widespread and easily available. While Doña Antonia's father was unusual in seeking to educate his daughter at even a basic level, most of her granddaughter's classmates moved to the city to continue their education after high school. Older farmers often did not know how to sign their name or read the instructions on a bottle of pesticide; younger people typically finished high school, and many even studied at a university in the city. However, educational inequalities persisted as young people in the city struggled with alienation, depression, poverty, the temptations of wild living, and the lack of a social safety net.

CHAPTER 8

THE ROUGH HEELS

Urban Migrants, Rural Roots

THE SONG "Las patas kjarkas," performed by the popular group México Chico, was played incessantly on the radio and at parties during my years in Bolivia. Sung from the point of view of a young man, the song describes a young woman who moves from the countryside to the city. The singer laments the transformation from a modest girl from the country to a woman from the city. But the singer claims that the young woman, despite her attempts at modernization, is always given away by her *patas kjarkas*, the rough, cracked calluses that afflict many country people from repeated wetting and drying of their feet in alkaline waters and walking over dusty trails.

In the following song lyrics, Quechua loanwords are bolded.

"Las patas kjarkas"[22]

Cuando salen de su pueblo,	When they leave their hometown,
Inocentes las **imillas**,	The innocent **girls**,
De aquí se van con alforjas,	They leave here with woven bags,
De allá vuelven con mochilas.	They return with backpacks.
Amarraban sus cabellos	They tied up their hair
Con **k'aytu** de tres colores,	With tricolored homespun **wool**,

22. As sung by México Chico, https://www.youtube.com/watch?v=UMTajWXXpQE.

Vuelven **chheras** y otras chocas,
Como león de un circo pobre
Ay yay yay vidita mía,
¿Porque diablos sos así?
Si aquí vos comías **thaco**.
Aura diz que cupesí.
Usaban sus largas faldas
Que tapaban las rodillas.
Aura visten minifalda,
Se les ve la rabadilla.
Por zapatotas agujas
Lo cambiaron sus abarcas
Se ponen sus medias nailon
Pa tapar sus patas **kjarkas**.
Ay yay yay vidita mia,
¿Porque diablos sos así?
Si aquí vos comías **thaco**
Aura diz que cupesí.
(¡Wheee las patas kjarkas!)

They come back **frizzed**, and some bleached,
Like the lion at a two-bit circus.
Ay yay yay my darling,
Why the heck are you like this?
Here, you ate **thaco**.
Now you say it's cupesí.
They wore long skirts
That covered their knees.
Now they wear miniskirts,
You can see their tailbone.
For spike-heeled shoes
They exchanged their rubber-tire sandals.
They wear nylons
To cover their **cracked** heels.
Ay yay yay my darling,
Why the heck are you like this?
Here, you ate **thaco**.
Now you say it's cupesí.
(Whee! The cracked heels!)

"Las patas kjarkas" draws together multiple signs into a single cluster of ideas that contrast the urban migrant to the down-home country girl through a binary organization that contrasts signs of rural orientation to signs of urban orientation. The migrant wears high heels; the country girl wears tire sandals. The migrant carries a backpack; the country girl an alforja. The migrant dyes and perms her hair; the country girl ties it up with homespun wool. The migrant uses vocabulary that is associated with the lowlands; the country girl uses Quechua loanwords. All of these signs participate in the construction of an urban-rural binary that can be "read" in the body of the female migrant (Brettell 2000, 2003; Pedraza 1991; Silvey 2005).

The use of contact features and Quechua loanwords plays an important part in establishing the setting, and the opposition, that is enacted through the song. The title "Las patas kjarkas" is marked by the Quechua loanword *k*^{h}*arka* 'dry, cracked' and by the Quechua-influenced use of *patas* 'paws, legs' instead of the standard Spanish *pies* 'feet' or *talones* 'heels'. Along with changing her alforja for a backpack and her long braids for dyed and artificially curled hair,[23] the young woman changes the Quechua loanword *t'aco* 'acacia tree' for the lowland version,

23. The word for curly, *ch*^{h}*era,* is a Quechua loanword that is specific to the Santa Cruz valleys; in Cochabamba people say *churka* instead.

cupesí. Homespun wool is *k'aytu*, a Quechua loanword, as is *imilla* 'young girl or woman'. The word that the singer uses to refer impertinently to the woman's backside is the word used for the tailbone of a chicken. These loanwords, along with countrified Spanish such as the exaggerated reduction of words like *aura* for *ahora* 'now', the syllable-final /s/ lenition, and the use of the very familiar *vos* person, set a social frame that is specific to rural people in the Santa Cruz valleys, especially those whose Spanish is marked by a great deal of contact with Quechua (Babel 2012, 2014a, 2014b, 2016d). The song echoed many of the themes that I heard from my consultants about the differences between urban and rural groups. Language, dress, and sexuality were prime sites for the production of difference, and it was particularly in the bodies of young women that these differences were performed and criticized (see Bigenho 2005 on women, music, and the Bolivian national imaginary).

One reason why the song was so popular was because it described an experience that many people in the Saipina valley could relate to. Migration from Saipina to the city of Santa Cruz was overwhelmingly common (see Bergholdt 1999; Hasbún 2003; Kirshner 2010; Mura 2016; Rojas 1998; Stearman 1987). Virtually every family I knew in Saipina had some members living in the urban area. After young people finished high school, it was a rite of passage for them to leave and do something different. Both men and women went to Santa Cruz to work or to pursue a university education, and some men left for their yearlong military service. Often people returned to Saipina in their midthirties when they had families, saying that the pace of life was slower and the town was safer than urban neighborhoods (on Bolivian internal migration, see Andersen 2002; Evia et al. 1999; Fabricant 2012).

People who moved to the city often maintained links with their extended family and friends. Many if not most Saipina migrants lived in a neighborhood in Santa Cruz that was populated largely by Saipineños, and young people got together for soccer games and parties. Many urban migrants participated in Carnaval fraternities, comparsas, and returned to Saipina to dance during Carnaval (on the role of festivals in a migrant neighborhood of Cochabamba, see Goldstein 2004). Saipineños in the city returned home for major holidays, especially Carnaval in February and Todos Santos, a holiday in remembrance of the dead, in early November. Others returned for the town anniversary in August and for smaller holidays such as Christmas and New Year or the town's patron saint day. Conversely, middle and high school students often spent school vacations with relatives in the city or traveled to the city to work as maids or manual laborers during school breaks in order to save up money. Though the trip averaged seven hours in each direction, many people I knew treated it as a jaunt, making day trips between the city and Saipina. This ease of movement was facilitated by the constant availability of passenger buses, which traveled up to four times a day between the two locations.

Because of the psychological if not spatiotemporal proximity of Santa Cruz, the continuing migration of young people in extended family networks, and the active social life of Saipineños in the city, many urban migrants continued to identify strongly with Saipina and to maintain relationships with people in the rural area, even years after they left (on migratory continuity across space, see Rockefeller 2010). Of all the urban migrants I spoke with, some of whom had lived for decades in the city, all said that they identified as Saipineños.

The reception that rural migrants to the city received from their urban classmates was less than welcoming. Despite their own perception of their in-between status, migrants from Saipina to the city of Cochabamba in the West were considered cambas (eastern lowlanders), while migrants from Saipina to the city of Santa Cruz in the East were labeled collas (western highlanders). The latter was the more negative term. Eduardo, who studied in Cochabamba, told me, "In Cochabamba I didn't experience any racism. They called us cambas, but it was affectionate, 'Hey, why don't you invite the cambas to the party?' And in Santa Cruz when they call you a colla they mean it as an insult." This was confirmed by Noemí when she told me that her teachers and classmates would make fun of her and call her names for the way she dressed and talked. "What did they call you?" I asked. She shrugged. "They call us collas," she said simply.

When I spoke to young people who had lived in the city, their comments revolved around a set of common themes that echoed the social commentary of "Las patas kjarkas." Women felt pressure to dress in less modest and more revealing fashions than they wore in the countryside. Sofía told me, "The girls who live in the city wear pants that are tighter here," indicating her thighs and butt. Her sister Elsa, who worked in a professional position in Santa Cruz, talked about showing her chest, saying, "Girls in the city wear spaghetti straps, and we [girls from the rural areas] feel self-conscious showing our shoulders and our chests." Elsa also talked about the embarrassment of having a farmer's tan, clearly visible tan lines from T-shirts, which were revealed when she wore skimpy tops.

In the following interview transcript, Noemí discusses differences in standards of dress that affected her as a young female migrant to the city.

Transcript 21: N (Noemí), A (Anna)

1. A: ¿O sea, qué clase de ropa se ponían allá?	1. A: So, what kind of clothes did they wear over there?
2. N: Por ejemplo las señoritas, siempre el chor, la mayoría, arriba de la rodilla. Si es la falda, lo mismo. Apreta, arriba de la rodilla. Tampoco no, no exagerada, ¿no? Que sea bien corta. Pero apreta y arriba de la rodilla. Y yo aquí usaba al revés abajo de la rodilla. Y la mayoría usaba buzo.	2. N: For example, the young ladies, always with shorts, mostly above the knee. If it's a skirt, the same. Tight, above the knee. Not too much, exaggerated, either, right? If it's too short. But tight and above the knee. And here I used the reverse, below the knee. And most of us used sweatpants (leggings).
3. Y en cambio allá, "¿Qué? ¿Dónde estás?" O como dicen, ¿no? "¿Estás en el alto?" Que allá, ¿no? hace frío. "¿Por qué te pones buzo aquí?"	3. And there, on the other hand, "What? Where do you think you are?" Or as they say, right? "Are you in the highlands?" Because there, right, it's cold. "Why do you wear sweatpants (leggings) here?"
4. Yo he tenido que cambiar, no el hecho porque me sentía cómoda, sino para sentirme bien, o sentirme que estoy con ellas. Porque si no, uno hasta en eso, hasta en la forma de vestir a uno le hacen a un lado.	4. I had to change, not because I felt comfortable, just to feel good, or feel that I was with the other women. Because if not, even in that, even in the way you dress they put you to one side.

Noemí attended college in the city for several years after graduating from high school in Saipina. When I interviewed her, she had recently graduated and was working in another region of Bolivia. In her interview with me, Noemí emphasized her discomfort with city norms of dress but at the same time her desire to fit in with other women her age in the university setting. Although she said repeatedly that she never felt comfortable wearing city clothes—tight skirts above the knee—she wore them in order to feel like one of the group and to avoid negative commentaries like the one she quotes in the interview: "Where do you think you are? . . . Are you in the highlands?" In this comment, wearing unfashionable clothing is linked to rural origins, and being from the rural highlands is equated with a lack of sophistication in a clustering of ideas that oppose frumpy rural highlanders to fashionable urban lowlanders—the same binary that is presented in "Las patas kjarkas," but with the opposite value assignment. While the narrator of "Las patas kjarkas" positively values country language, styles of dress, and modesty, these things are a liability in the eyes of Noemí's urban classmates.

Like Noemí, other interviewees consistently mentioned clothing as an important difference between the country and the city. City people were characterized as wearing clothing that was more fashionable, more expensive, and more revealing than country clothing. During the cold *surazos* of the winter months,[24] Eva told me, "I would go to class in two or three layers of sweaters, and I would be freezing cold, and I saw my classmates wearing fashionable jackets and boots." The ability of her classmates to afford just the right kind of clothes was something that made her notice her own dowdiness and physical discomfort.

These physical signs acted as indices of impoverished migrants from the rural countryside, and young women students felt intense pressure to conform to a more urban style of dress. However, they were caught in a double bind when they returned to the countryside and were judged by conservative local standards of dress. They might be accused of being above themselves, out of touch, or citified when they returned to their hometown. Changes in dress and language were not only questions of personal style; they were also tightly linked to questions of morality, modesty, and sexuality through the lens of rural-to-urban migration.

The semiotic field surrounding urban migrants from the rural valleys centered on binaries involving language, socioeconomic class, and contrasting styles of dress and sexuality. However, the values that were placed on opposing sides of the binary depended on perspective: while people from urban Santa Cruz ridiculed young women from the countryside for their unsophisticated behavior, their friends back home criticized their urban orientation when they returned to Saipina from the city.

THE URBAN MIGRANT SPEAKS BACK: "EL DESACTUALIZAU"

I had always heard "Las patas kjarkas" on the radio in Saipina. It wasn't until I was back in the United States several years later, searching for the lyrics to the song, that I realized that a sequel had been made and was posted on YouTube. Later, I heard it on the radio in both Saipina and urban Santa Cruz, though not

24. A *surazo* is comparable to a nor'easter in the northern United States: icy cold winds sweeping off the southern glaciers. Surazos affect much of eastern Bolivia but are less severe in the valleys, including Saipina, than in the lowland plains.

as often as the original. The sequel, titled “El desactualizau” (The outdated one), was styled as a response to “Las patas kjarkas.” Sung from the point of view of the young female migrant, the video established an explicit dialogue between the songs by starting with the words, “So it’s the cracked heels, is it? Now listen to this one!” Onscreen, the young woman from the video for “Las patas kjarkas” flicks a remote control to turn off the last strains of that song’s video on a large TV and steps out of bed. Throughout the rest of the video, she taunts a male migrant addressee, apparently the narrator of the first “Las patas kjarkas” song, as she tries on miniskirts and parades around the city of Santa Cruz in high heels and revealing shirts on the arm of a suave, upper-class young man who drives a red sports car. Meanwhile, the countrified migrant is shown following her around and making a fool of himself, selling cheap drinks on the streets as an ambulatory vendor, serving her at an expensive club, and ultimately toppling into a swimming pool as he cranes his head to get a look at her.

“El desactualizau”[25]

Con que las patas kjarkas, ¿no?	So it’s the cracked heels, is it?
Escuchá estita!	Listen to this one!
Fuerza, México Chico [pause]!	Strength, México Chico [pause]!
Alegría, alegría!	Joy, joy!
Si me ves de minifalda	If you see me in a miniskirt
Ya no me llamas la **imilla**	Don’t call me **baby** anymore
Se te están chorreando ya tus babas	Your drool is running down your chin
Mirándome mi rabadilla.	Looking at my tailbone.
Con agüita y jabón	With water and soap
Cualquier **kjarka** se me quita.	I can get rid of any **cracked** skin.
Lo [unintelligible] de vos se queda	[unintelligible] What you have will stay.
No lo quitas nunquita.	You’ll never get rid of it, ever.
Si me pongo taco aguja	If I wear high heels
Todo lo que está de moda	And everything that is in style
No es pa conquistarte a vos.	It’s not to win *you* over.
Esto es lo que te incomoda.	That’s what’s bothering you.
El burro aunque sea mañudó,	The donkey, even if it’s clever,
No pasa por la **p’inkina**.	Doesn’t cross over the **stile**.
Y vos que me estás siguiendo,	And you, when you follow me,
Estás cayendo como gallina.	Are staggering around like a hen.
[repeat]	[repeat]

25. Performed by México Chico; https://www.youtube.com/watch?v=JJByMr7H45o.

Ya lo tengo listo el **pjullu**	I've got my **woven blanket** all ready
Con **k'ayto** de tres colores	With **homespun wool** in three colors
Pa taparme en estos sures	To cover me in these chilly days
Minifalda pa estos calores.	Miniskirt for these warm days.
Actualízate, más vale	It's better to get up to date
Al mundo y su evolución	With the world and its evolution
Sin olvidar nuestras costumbres,	Without forgetting our customs,
La música y la tradición.	Music and tradition.
Para seguirte enseñando	To continue showing you
Entráte a esta dirección	Go to this address
Triple doble ve y punto	Triple double u and dot
México Chico punto com.	México Chico dot com.
El burro aunque sea mañudó,	The donkey, even if it's clever,
No pasa por la **p'inkina**.	Doesn't cross over the **stile**.
Yo vos que me estás siguiendo	And you, when you follow me,
Estás cayendo como gallina.	Are staggering around like a hen.
[repeat]	[repeat]

In this video, the female migrant sings in first person and is in control of her own sexuality. Far from being ridiculous, she accuses her interlocutor of jealousy. The singer argues, "With water and soap, I can get rid of any cracked skin. . . . What you are will stay. You'll never get rid of it, ever." Along with the images in the video, this discussion foregrounds the greater class mobility of women and the limitations of the migrant experience: while women can change their clothes and perhaps the way they talk, using their physical attractiveness to move up the social ladder, uneducated male migrants often find themselves stuck in low-paying manual labor and service jobs (Bastia 2011; Bastia and Busse 2011; Gal 1978, 1988). The singer rubs this in at the end of the song, calling her migrant suitor a *burro* 'ass, donkey': "The donkey, even if it's clever, never crosses over the stile." Using down-home vocabulary that includes Quechua loanwords, the singer demonstrates that she can cross class boundaries that her male suitor never can. At the same time, the singer uses a strong urban Santa Cruz accent, marked especially by syllable-final aspiration of *s*, as she sings the lyrics of the song.[26] This linguistic positioning plays into her characterization of herself as a person who can live between two worlds.

In the visual language of the video as well, the singer disputes the notion that she cannot be true to her migrant identity while embracing signs of a rural

26. Thanks to Fernando Unzueta for making this point to me.

identity. She unfolds a hand-woven blanket, observing that she keeps her *pjullu* for cold days and her miniskirt for warm days. She claims that she can go back and forth between her rural and urban identities, in effect, positioning herself "in between" the binary distinction of the rural/urban dichotomy. In the next stanza, she chides her suitor for being out of date but argues that migrants should never forget their customs from back home, which she identifies as "music and tradition" (Bigenho 2016). She disputes the claim that leaving the rural area means selling out and becoming a stranger, someone foreign to her rural roots.

The singer also breaks the narrative frame of the song by placing an apparent plug for the musical group that performs the song, México Chico, in the penultimate stanza, suggesting that the listener/addressee visit the website www.mexicochico.com. As far as I have been able to ascertain, this website has never existed. At the time of this writing, the group was best represented online on YouTube and on an official Facebook page. Therefore, the use of this phrase acts as a kind of invocation of modernity, a positioning of the singer and through her the migrant as a sophisticated urban insider.

Like the narrator of "El desactualizau," many urban migrants found opportunities in the city that they wouldn't have found in the countryside. Carlos, who came from a wealthy family in Saipina and had extensive family networks in the city, told me, "I like it here. It's a place where you can grow. And I think if I'd stayed in Saipina or in Comarapa [a neighboring town], I never would have gone anywhere." He repeated the metaphor of "growth" several times in our conversation, detailing his plans to start his own business. "There's more movement," Pamela, who worked in a bank in Santa Cruz, told me. "There are opportunities there [in Santa Cruz] that I couldn't find here [in Saipina]," her friend Elsa, a college student, agreed.

Other migrants told me that they found the city fun and interesting and cosmopolitan in a way that rural Saipina was not. Carlos said that he started to feel at home in the city when his classmates started inviting him out to parties and social events, and his world expanded. He described feeling bored and out of touch in Saipina. Elsa agreed. "Now when I come home [to Saipina] I feel like there's nothing to do here," Elsa told me. "I go down to the plaza, I don't see anyone I know. I get bored. Mostly I stay at home. Sometimes I don't even leave my yard except to go to the bus station and back." Urban migrants complained about the lack of nightlife and especially Internet in Saipina and eagerly posted on social media when they were back in the city.

For other migrants, though, the city brought into glaring focus the economic disparities between the country and the city—more the experience of the out-of-place rural bumpkin in "El desactualizau" than that of the sophisticated female narrator. Iván, who lived in the city briefly as a child, told me that he walked for three hours to visit a friend who lived across town because he couldn't afford bus fare—just fifty cents of a Bolivian peso for schoolchildren, less than ten American cents, about the cost of a gumball. "And how did you get back?" I asked him. "My friend's parents lent me money," he admitted. The topic of buses came up frequently, given that most people from Saipina lived in outer neighborhoods where the cost of living was lower than in the center and could not afford taxis, much less their own vehicle (on geographical marginality in the Andes, see Goldstein 2004; Haynes 2016; Salcedo 2013). "Everything is *gasto* [expenses] in the city," Silvio told me. "Even to take a *micro* [bus], you have to spend money to go and to come back. If I went to my classes, I had to take two buses each way—one, two, three, four bus fares day after day. It adds up."

"My mom would send me money," Eva told me, "but sometimes it was just fifty pesos, and you know that doesn't go far in the city." She added, "I know how hard she worked for that money, but it just didn't last." While many of the rural-to-urban migrants I spoke to reported similar experiences, this was not the general rule for urban students at the public university in Santa Cruz. "Most of my classmates just studied. They didn't have to work like I did," Eva told me. She worried about having money for bus fare, class materials, and food while living in the city. In contrast, she told me that in Saipina "nobody starves": "Here you can always go help someone out in the fields, and they'll send you home with food; there, you have to buy everything."

Beyond economic disparities, many migrants felt alienated because the environment of the city was different from that of a rural town. "People from the city don't say hello in the street," Efraím told me. "I know people, guys I went to high school with, who now ride past me on the street on their motorcycles and don't even say hi," Noemí said. "I recognize them, but they don't talk to me." Even Carlos, whose attitude toward the city was generally positive, told me, "At first I found it hard to get used to the city, the noise, the crime, going straight from home to school and from school to home."

Violence—more specifically, the fear of violence—was a constant stressor for rural migrants to the city, especially given that they tended to live in dangerous *barrios marginales* (marginal neighborhoods) (Kirshner 2010). When I asked how the city was different from Saipina, everyone mentioned crime. "I never stay out past eight o'clock,"Teo told me. Glover said he had been mugged in broad daylight. "Everyone says to be careful at night," he said, "but I was assaulted in the middle of the day." Women who worked in the markets or who handled large sums of money as part of their job were particular targets. Both Damiana and Reina, who sold products in the large markets in the city, told me about having been watched, studied, before being mugged when they were carrying large sums of money.

"El desactualizau" questions the urban/rural binary set forth in "Las patas kjarkas," but it sets up a different contrast, between the successful urban migrant, who is able to translate her geographical mobility into class mobility, and the unsuccessful country bumpkin, who is relegated to low-paying service positions (and never gets the girl). It is no accident that it is the female migrant who is portrayed as successful in "Las patas kjarkas." Women had greater class mobility in the city but fewer economic and professional opportunities in the countryside than men did (Bastia 2011; Bastia and Busse 2011). Conversely, men could and often did fall back on a comfortable life in agriculture or transportation back home if they failed to get a college education. For this reason, I found that female migrants were more motivated to succeed academically and professionally and to "fit in" in the city. Rural parents, too, observed that young women were *más agudas* (sharper, more intelligent) than young men; this was undoubtedly related to the greater costs of failure for female migrants. The urban/rural binary was bisected by a gender binary that could shape and affect the motivations for moving to the city, as well as the experience that migrants underwent once they were there.

SEX AND MORALITY: "EL REFINAU"

The third and final response to "Las patas kjarkas," a song called "El refinau" (The dude), takes the point of view of a woman who has stayed in the countryside while her boyfriend or lover migrates to the city. This song accuses the male migrant of becoming urbanized and effeminate. Both the lyrics and the images in the video depict a group of young men wearing urban-style clothing: wide calf-length pants worn low on the hips in the style of a Mexican American cholo, sleeveless shirts or bare chests, earrings and face piercings, long hair, dreads, eyeglasses, sunglasses, and bandannas.[27] Along with these signs, the male urban migrants are also pictured as pudgy—a state that is difficult to achieve as a rural agricultural worker.

"El refinau"[28]

De allá de mis valles, hasta por aquí	From back home in the valleys, up to around here
Vine preguntando qué será de ti.	I came asking what happened to you.
Cuando te encontré no supe qué hacer	When I found you I didn't know what to do.
Esta **churiquita** ya nada que ver.	This ***churiquita*** has nothing to do with you.
Te seguí mirando, qué mechas tenías.	I kept staring at you, what locks you had.
Ese tu arito ya me confundía.	Your little earring confused me.
Pantalones anchos como empollerado.	Wide pants like a pollera.
Será por los aros, que te has cambiado.	Maybe because of the earrings, you sure have changed.
Ay negrito lindo, te habías refinau.	Oh dark and handsome, you have become refined.
Que el **ch'arque** con **k'ara**, le llamás majau.	**Jerky** with **pork skin** you now call *majau.*
Y con pañueleto dicen que te ven	And apparently they see you around with a head rag
Como con pollera pero sin sostén.	As if wearing pollera but with no brassiere.
Hasta de tu nombre te quieres cambiar.	Even your name you want to change.
Cambiate de todo, sentate a orinar.	Go ahead and change everything, sit down to pee.
Ay negrito lindo [unintelligible], te fue	Oh dark and handsome [unintelligible],
No sé si sos hombre o sos al revés.	I don't know if you're a man or the reverse.

While I heard the other two songs on the radio and saw them posted online, I only found this song on YouTube. It was not widely circulated and had fewer views than the other two songs. However, it echoed themes that I heard in interviews, contrasting dangerous, sexualized, and immoral urban spheres with wholesome, homely, and moral rural spheres.

In the lyrics of the song, the singer marvels at the young man's long hair, earrings, and wide pants "as if wearing pollera." She also points to the male migrant's bandanna, which he wears around his head, as a sign associated with cholitas; she says, "As if wearing pollera but with no brassiere." In the closing words of the song, the woman insults the male migrant by questioning his

27. The cholo in Mexican American culture shares a common origin with the Bolivian cholita but has undergone a much different history and development. See Mendoza-Denton (2008).
28. Performed by México Chico; https://www.youtube.com/watch?v=awo2jQs_2ig.

masculinity: "Sit down to pee" and "I don't know if you're a man or the reverse." The video shows the man shaking off a bevy of attractive urban women to go off with an exaggeratedly mincing male friend. Even the term *refinau* 'refined' is an insult that is commonly aimed at people who act like they're too good for their rural roots. At the same time, the singer positions herself as a person from the valleys (see chapters 1 and 4) through linguistic signs like the use of Quechua loanwords (in boldface) and the reduction of intervocalic /d/.

This social commentary underlined comments that I heard about differences in men's dress in the city. Teo, who lived in Santa Cruz and Cochabamba before returning to start a family in Saipina, told me, "In the city, you always have to buy *ropa de marca* [brand-name clothing]." Specifically, rural-to-urban male migrants tended to wear North American styles that indexed North American urban and street-influenced contexts. Sofía, a high school student in Saipina, told me that "the men [in Santa Cruz] wear wide pants and baseball caps." Several young men who had lived in the city told me about returning to rural Saipina with long hair or cornrows and being mocked as effeminate and dandified.

Like the female migrant in "Las patas kjarkas," the male migrant in this video changes the way that he talks. In this case, too, the lexical item under scrutiny is a food item that is known by a Quechua name: *Ch'arki con k'ara* 'jerky with fried pork rind', which the singer pronounces with exaggerated ejectives. It is transformed in *majau*, a stereotypically eastern dish of soupy rice with bits of fried jerky and diced vegetables.

In contrast to the male urban migrant, the women in this video have long, braided hair. They wear ankle-length skirts and the black fedora hat of the valleys. Many of them carry baskets covered in cloth, perhaps signifying bread or agricultural products. While "El desactualizau" questions the urban/rural dichotomy, this video reifies it through these clear contrasts between markers of rural and urban identity.

In particular, the video questions the male migrant's masculinity, suggesting that he has become effeminate and perhaps even attracted to men. These accusations are scandalous in the context of rural Bolivia, where open same-sex relationships are highly taboo.[29] Like the hypersexualized female migrant in "Las patas kjarkas," the subject of "El refinau" has drifted into dangerously immoral sexual territory through his association with the urban sphere.

29. While negative attitudes toward same-sex relationships are slowly changing in major urban areas in Bolivia, particularly among the upper classes, homophobia continues to be a violent reality throughout the country.

Both male and female migrants' exposure to the urban sphere was considered to have dangerous effects on their morality and, in particular, their sexuality, as the discussions of women's clothing earlier in this chapter illustrate. The use of revealing clothing acted as an index of greater promiscuity. Eva told me, "The young people are more *atrevidos* [daring] in the city. There are things I didn't know, I never talked about; even the technology, they were things girls don't know about here in the countryside." I understood this to be a veiled reference to contraception, which was widely used by women in the city but not easily available to girls in the countryside. Eva added that this was one reason why naive girls from the countryside were easily "fooled" by predatory city men.[30]

Urban migrants could go astray in other ways as well. Several people talked to me about high school and college classmates who "se echan a perder" (waste themselves). These boys—primarily boys—pretended to study but in reality dedicated themselves to drinking, doing drugs, and partying while taking money from their parents. Consultants whispered to me about Facebook posts that revealed that urban migrants who posed as "students" in reality spent most of their nights out at clubs and in bars. Several consultants emphasized to me that in most cases, the parents were hardworking farmers who might themselves be illiterate and who didn't know to ask about grades or other signs of progress. "My mom wasn't like some others," Diana, the daughter of a high school teacher, said. "She asked every semester for my grades, and I had to show them to her." Referring to young men who lost their way, Eva said, "They never think of the sacrifices that their parents make for them." Carlos told me about a classmate who lived for years in the city and never finished his degree, eventually returning to Saipina to live with his parents and work in agriculture. "I wonder what it must be like for his father," he said. "I can only imagine that he must be disappointed." Betraying one's parents and taking advantage of their hard-earned money while wasting it on drugs and partying was another way that urban migrants violated the moral code of the rural sphere.

Some urban migrants even criticized themselves for becoming soft and lazy in the city, in contrast to the matter-of-fact work ethic of the countryside. When I asked her how she had changed since living in the city, Noemí told me, "Now I'm reluctant to go look for firewood. The noise from the

30. The word *engañada* (fooled) is used to mean being tricked into having sexual relations with and sometimes getting pregnant by a man who has no intention of committing to a relationship.

street bothers me, and sometimes I get annoyed even by the dust on my feet." Noemí was strongly oriented toward life in Saipina; she did not enjoy her life in the city, she married a young man from Saipina, and she earnestly hoped to return there as soon as a job opened up. "I hope I'm never too good for my mother," she told me. She said that she got annoyed at herself for having gotten lazy, that these things were part of her life, and she was frustrated to find herself changing in these ways—becoming *refinada* (refined), as people from the countryside mockingly put it.

Acting lazy and soft, becoming sexualized in dangerous ways, and being of dubious moral character were linked with the urban sphere in these songs and through the comments that I heard from my consultants. In contrast, people from the countryside were constructed as modest, hardworking, and honest. Through these discourses, urban migrants were cast as sexualized, arrogant, and morally suspect, categories that aligned with their migration history within the broader semiotic field.

THE REAL GIVEAWAY: LANGUAGE

In "Las patas kjarkas," the cracked heels of the urban migrant give away her country roots. However, the marker that was most salient, most subject to social commentary, and most difficult to erase was language. For virtually everyone who had experienced urban migration, language was a key index of regional origin and urban versus rural orientation (de los Heros 2001; Escobar 2000; Godenzzi 2008; Howard 2007; Klee and Caravedo 2006).

I spoke to my consultants at length about language, and they all said they had noticed differences between Saipina and Santa Cruz. In particular, people mentioned the use of Quechua loanwords as setting Saipina speech apart from Santa Cruz, telling me that they spoke Spanish that was *mezclado* (mixed) with Quechua. In addition to Quechua loanwords, there were several other features that were closely associated with people who came from the rural valleys. Several people commented on the intervocalic reduction of *d*, as in the titles "El desactualizau" (normatively *desactualizado*) and "El refinau" (normatively *refinado*). Likewise, Elsa told a story about a coworker whose use of *iw* for the perfective *ido* 'to [have] gone' was made fun of by other office workers. Diminutives and augmentatives were another source of variation that people commented on; while people in the city used *-ingo* and *-ango*, people in the countryside used *-ito* and *-ote*, the more common Spanish variants. Consultants explicitly evoked the fact that *-ito* is the more standard form when evaluating their speech compared to urban varieties. Nevertheless, the use of *-ito* was negatively evaluated by urbanites because of its links to the countryside and to Quechua speakers. "My boss used to make fun of me when I said things like *ahoritita* [right away]," Eva told me, using a double diminutive suffix (*-it-it-a*). "He said he could tell right away that I was from the [Santa Cruz] valleys."

Transcript 22: Eva

Y todo el tiempo él se hacía la burla de, de, de algunas palabras que yo hablaba, por ejemplo a veces me, me, me decía que se lo haga algo, yo le decía "¡Ahoritita!" "¡Ahoritita voy!" O "¡Un ratito!" Y todo el tiempo él, él, lo disfrutaba escuchar esas palabras, aunque yo trataba de de, de algunas cosas, como mezcla—, nosotros hablamos me—, mezclado con el Quechua, algunas palabras yo trataba de corregirme, porque [se ríe] . . . aunque nunca me dio vergüenza. A mí no me da vergüenza hablarle algunas cosas que nosotros hablamos aquí, no me da vergüenza.	And all the time he would make fun of, of, of some words that I spoke, for example, sometimes he, he, he told me to do something for him, and I said to him, "I'm coming right away!" Or "Just a sec!" And all the time, he, he, he enjoyed hearing those words, though I tried to, to, to, some things, like mix—, we speak mi—, mixed with Quechua, some words I would try to correct myself, because [she laughs] . . . though I was never ashamed. I have never been ashamed to say some things that we say here, it does not make me ashamed.

While Eva emphasized that she was "never ashamed" to speak like someone from the countryside, her boss's teasing drew attention to the fact that her use of diminutives like *un ratito* 'just a sec' and *ahoritita* 'right away' were not considered standard Spanish in urban contexts. Other consultants described being criticized by their professors at the university, who were sometimes vicious in their comments about rural styles of speech. The power dynamics between employer and employee, professor and student made these observations particularly salient to the young people whose speech was being negatively evaluated.

Transcript 23: Noemí

O sea, incluso nos ponían apodo, las profesoras ahí. Toda, no sé, nos cuesta dialogar en su lengua de ellos, bien fluido, siempre han estado en un ambiente no sé, no, cómo le puedo decir, ummm, más adelantado en la cuidad. Siempre, no, todo, siempre llega allá más antes que acá. Y uno hasta el hecho de emitir, emitir una palabra nos cuesta, ¿no? El hecho de equivocarnos. ¡¡¡Y se rían!!!	Or even they would call us names, the teachers there. Everything, I don't know, it's hard for us to dialogue in their language, fluently, they've always been in an environment that I don't know, how can I say, ummm, more advanced in the city. Always, everything always arrives there before it comes here. And even getting a word out is hard for us, right? The fact of messing up. And [that] they laugh!!!

Even though she had lived in the city for years, Noemí was visibly agitated as she described the discomfort and linguistic discrimination that she suffered in urban Santa Cruz. And though Eva claimed not to be ashamed of talking like a valluna, she said later in our interview that she sometimes corrected her mother when she used Quechua loanwords like *chhichi*, meaning "dirty." Pamela, another urban migrant, told me that she didn't correct her mother directly but that she asked her not to use words like *quemante* 'burning' instead of *caliente* 'hot' around her son, whom her mother was bringing up while Pamela finished her studies. While this word is not of Quechua origin, it is linked to rural ways of speaking. Shortly afterward, Pamela chuckled when she heard her son remark that a soccer ball he was playing with was *chhusu* 'flat', a Quechua loanword. Noemí, on the other hand, told me, "I would never change the way I speak, because I'm proud of my mother. I'm wouldn't ever do anything to hurt her. I'm not trying to be better than my family." Migrants balanced delicately between not being ashamed of their rural roots and their uneducated parents and living up to the standards of dress and language that were enforced in the city.

As evidenced by Pamela's and Eva's comments about correcting their mothers' speech, these ideologies made their way to Saipina through family relationships. Older siblings who had migrated to the city commented on the way their younger siblings talked. "My younger brother, he talks really funny," Diana told me. "I really hear the Saipina accent when he talks." Carlos, her older brother, agreed. "I want to bring my brother here [to Santa Cruz]," he told me, "so he can start learning how things are here." Elsa also poked fun at her sister Ana María while Ana María was sitting within earshot. "She talks *chistoso* [funny]," she said. "It must be because she was born here [in Saipina] and grew up here."

While many consultants were ambivalent about using their rural home variety, others saw style shifting as a necessity for communicating with people around them. Serena and Lucho, a professional couple living in Saipina, said that they were corrected by their professors at the university and told to use a more formal register of speech. "The example that comes to mind is 'suture,'" said Serena. "One of my classmates said *coser* [sew], and the professor came down on them hard, saying, 'Are we in the market? The word is *suture*, not *sew*.' But," she continued, "when I'm working with people here in the countryside, I have to speak their language. If I use those technical terms, nobody will understand me." Lucho agreed, saying that unless it was a question of accuracy, he tried to translate scientific terms for common veterinary illnesses into local names.

Though the great majority of urban migrants told me that their use of countrified speech alienated them from their urban peers, men seemed to be less affected than women. Glover, a young university student, told me that he had formed a social group among friends who all came from different parts of rural Bolivia. "We all talk the same," he said. "Sometimes there are differences, but you know, since my mom speaks Quechua, I usually understand them." Glover found that using Quechua-influenced Spanish gave him something in common with other rural-to-urban migrants. Men like Glover and Carlos, who studied in the same majors as the women I spoke to, reported that they had experienced few or no overt comments on their speech, though they did notice a difference between urban and rural ways of speaking. At the other end of the socioeconomic scale, men who worked in blue-collar jobs in the city were either less receptive or less sensitive to linguistic criticism. "Yes, people talk differently, but I never have," Teo said to me. "I wonder why that is? I never have changed the way that I talk." Given the fact that Teo, though economically successful, had never attended college, it seemed likely that he never experienced the discrimination and the mocking that young women professionals in the city described and that undoubtedly influenced their understanding of the way that they spoke. Likewise, Angel, a blue-collar worker in the city, told me that his employees and coworkers were all migrants from different parts of Bolivia and that they enjoyed comparing their different accents and joking about them. The pressure to learn how to speak in a more educated register seemed to be most intense for professional young women like Elsa, Noemí, and Eva, all of whom were highly conscious of linguistic differences between the countryside and the city and told me that they had been explicitly corrected and rebuked for their manner of speaking (see, e.g., Gal 1978 on women, language, and political economy).

It is no accident that all three of the songs that I describe in this chapter used Quechua loanwords and wordplay to distinguish between urban and rural orientations. Ways of speaking were one of the principal ways in which differences between native urbanites and migrants from the rural valleys were constructed. Because of power differentials between urban employers and professors and their rural migrant employees and students, the costs of using countrified Spanish could be high. Like discourses about clothing, these forms of linguistic discrimination seem to be especially intense for female migrants. Language was a key field in which the binary between urban and rural orientations was acted out, but urban migrants' experiences were also affected by their gender and social mobility.

CONCLUSION

The songs and interviews that I describe in this chapter enmesh migration with gender, sexual relationships, sexual orientation, and sexual jealousy, as well as class markers, styles of dress, food, and language. These ideas cluster around two binary poles: modest but unsophisticated rural people and sophisticated but dangerously sexualized urban migrants. Language was an especially sensitive index of urban versus rural orientation, and my consultants were acutely aware of the contrast between rural, Quechua-influenced Spanish and urban lowland varieties. The goals of migration varied somewhat among migrants, but they were largely connected to a desire for social mobility through work and education. At the same time, the music videos demonstrate that migration is not just migration but a framework that acts as an umbrella for a complex system of signs.

The experience of migration was different for men and for women (Bastia 2011; Bastia and Busse 2011). The recurring themes of sexuality and sexual jealousy in the cracked-heels songs may be just a way of making them entertaining, of giving them a storyline. However, behind this storyline, there is a real story about a change in orientation from rural to urban life and the changes in social class that go along with it. The transformation from the innocent girl in the countryside to the street-wise city girl who uses her sexuality to move up in the world is one way of expressing anxieties about rapid changes in local culture, particularly as experienced through the bodies, sexuality, and education of women. It was for women that the experience, and the risks, of migration seemed to be most acute; because men had a comfortable lifestyle in the countryside to fall back on, while uneducated women faced a life of difficult domestic labor, female migrants had more at stake when they tried to fit in to urban contexts (Gal 1978, 1988).

The alignment of binary contrasts that I have discussed throughout this book shifts when we consider urban migrants from Saipina to Santa Cruz. While Saipineños on their home territory considered themselves to be ni camba ni colla (chapter 1), in the lowland capital they were cast as rural western collas (Bergholdt 1999; Hurtado 2005; Stearman 1987). In conversations between urban migrants and their families back home, on the other hand, a contrast emerged between the unsophisticated but moral country bumpkin and the immoral urban sophisticate. As in chapter 4, where migrants from the highlands were characterized as antisocial, the homeland retained a positive moral character in contrast to the dangerous outside (in this case, urban) sphere.

The contrast between urban and rural spheres is another example of a binary that is set up within a larger semiotic system that contrasts West and East, colla and camba, highland and lowland. While Saipineños situated themselves in the middle of these binaries when they were on their own turf, they were cast as immigrants and outsiders when they traveled to urban Santa Cruz. Because migrants from the rural valleys were placed in a less powerful position when they stepped outside of their home sphere into the fast-paced world of urban Santa Cruz, they had less room to negotiate their own social position. Urban migrants, in particular, female migrants, found themselves caught between their hopes for social mobility in the city and their loyalty to their families back home. Negative attitudes toward language varieties perceived as Andean or rural had a strong effect on language use among urban migrants (de los Heros 2001; Escobar 2000; Godenzzi 2008; Howard 2007; Mick 2011; Salcedo 2013).

Urban migrants navigated two worlds—an urban sphere in which they were themselves outsiders, perhaps undesirable ones; and their connection to their rural hometown, where they were closely scrutinized for changes that they had undergone due to the experience of migration. The "here" and "there" of rural-to-urban migration (Mick 2011) is one more example of a set of binary categories that participants crossed and complicated through their discourses and their actions—pulling out their pjullus for cold days and their miniskirts for warm days, changing back into comfortable clothes when they returned home to the countryside.

INTERLUDE

From Saipina to Santa Cruz

DOÑA ANTONIA'S youngest daughter, Leticia, was born in Doña Antonia's house in the banda. She grew up traveling between the family's home on the riverbank and their house in Saipina, where she could attend school. Like many young women, she became pregnant in her late teens, before finishing high school. Her partner was a serious, steady young man who was already a successful farmer, and people thought her lucky to join a hardworking agricultural family.

Doña Leticia thought differently. "I just couldn't see myself staying there, carrying his lunch out to the fields every day," she told me. Instead, she left home to finish high school in the neighboring town of Comarapa, leaving her young son with his father and paternal grandmother. Soon afterward, she traveled to Santa Cruz, where she stayed with her brother and his family, to study at the university. "They were my family, they were like my mother and father," she told me. She lived in their large house in a small, separate room that was designed to be a maid's quarters.

I heard from other relatives that once Leticia moved to Santa Cruz, she became estranged from her husband's family. When Leticia visited, infrequently, they would not let her meet with her son. Leticia retreated, visiting less and less often and practically never communicating with her son. At most, she sent him small gifts through visiting relatives. "I wasn't able to go home," she told me. "It was too expensive, and there was never any time."

Meanwhile, Leticia finished college and found a job with the Bolivian police force investigating crimes against minors—rapes, murders, child abuse. She sometimes spoke to me about her cases, clearly disturbed by the cruelty that people could unleash on smaller, weaker children. She studied for a law degree, and when she earned it, she was promoted within the police department. With her increased salary, she was able to move out of her brother's house after having lived there for many years.

She told me that it had been hard to get used to the city when she first moved there. "Where we came from, it was entirely different," she said. "We had never even seen a bus, and here there was so much movement, so much noise. It was disorienting. My first boss, he helped me a lot," she said. "He came from Cochabamba, from the countryside, and he understood what it was like. To be a person without a lot of resources."

In her late thirties, Doña Leticia had another son and began raising him as a single mother. As he grew, it became clear that he suffered from developmental disabilities. He was a big, strong boy, tall and heavy for his age, and public schools were unable to handle him. Determined not to abandon her son, Doña Leticia relied on a patchwork of friends and paid caretakers to look after him while she worked long hours, leaving early in the morning and coming home after dark. She doted on her son, taking him out on excursions and buying him treats on the weekends. When he was still quite young, she was suddenly promoted from within the police department to the role of fiscal, a public prosecutor and an important position in the Bolivian legal and judicial system.

"It's hard," she told me. "They expect me to work all the time, weekends and everything. Sometimes I have to say no, and they censure me. I've already got two marks against me. If I get three, I'm going to be in big trouble. But I can't leave my son—I have to see him sometimes. Even if it's just on the weekends."

Leticia emphasized to me that she had cut practically all her ties with Saipina. While most of the urban migrants whom I interviewed returned home to Saipina several times a year and maintained close relationships with people from their hometown, she told me that she knew nobody from Saipina and that she never spent time with Saipineños in the city. She returned to Saipina once or twice a year, generally staying for only a day or two. At the time that I interviewed her, she had lived in the city for twenty-five years, more than half of her life.

I was surprised, then, when I asked whether she would ever consider returning to Saipina and she replied in the affirmative. "I'd like to go back," she told me. "Maybe start up a little store, do something where I could spend more time with my son." She repeated what she had told me before about the demands of her job and the choices she was forced to make. "If I could move back to

Saipina, maybe I could keep him with me," she said. "I could take care of him. I would do it for him."

Born on a tiny farm on the outskirts of Saipina, Leticia was in the first generation of women in Saipina who were torn between their own future and that of their children, and she was forced to make terrible choices in order to pursue an education and a career. "I've had to give up everything," she told me toward the end of our interview, stone-faced. "I even had to abandon my son." She seemed determined not to have to repeat that choice again. I admired her for her tenacity in the face of impossible circumstances; as I learned from other urban migrants, even decades later it was not easy for children who studied at rural schools in the countryside to achieve success at the university. Leticia overcame great barriers to gain her professional status and independence, drawing on remarkable tenacity, drive, and dedication to her career.

CONCLUSION

Semiotic Fields

"Saipina has become full of all those women in pollerita, those Quechua speakers."

"How can she wear pants when everyone knows she's a Quechua speaker, one of those people from MAS?"

"All the indios will go, and all the autonomistas will stay."

"We may be MAS, but we don't speak Quechua."

"We're the kind of MASistas you can talk to."

"I think a real, true Saipineño will never speak Quechua. They might learn it, but they will never speak it well."

"We speak neither camba nor colla."

I BEGAN THIS book by discussing two comments that stood out to me from all of the many things that I heard during my fieldwork: "All the indios will go, and all the autonomistas will stay" and "How can she wear pants when everyone knows she's a Quechua speaker, one of those people from MAS?" These comments simply do not make sense unless we consider the semiotic field in which they are deployed. Once we consider them within the context of the semiotic field, however, they open a door to considering how social categorization crosses categories. In the material I have discussed in this book, ethnicity, regional identification, gender, migration status, and political positioning all work together as part of a coherent semiotic field through their organization in a series of binary oppositions. Opposing binary poles are aligned into clusters of related concepts, each of which contrasts with any member of the opposite cluster.

Comments like those above weave together disparate categories: the regional identity categories camba and colla, legitimacy and social recognition, styles of dress, migration status, race, ethnicity, physical appearance, politics, and, above all, language. Through these comments, the categories of pollera-wearing, Quechua-speaking, indigenous, rural, colla highlanders are implicitly and explicitly contrasted with white or mestizo, autonomista-supporting, monolingual, urban lowlanders. Saipineños positioned themselves in the middle of these binaries—people who wore neither pollera nor miniskirts but modest knee-length straight skirts; people who spoke Spanish but with Quechua influence; people whose cultural identity was defined by being neither camba nor colla; MAS supporters, perhaps, but in a moderate vein. In positioning themselves as "in between," however, they reified and reproduced the opposing structures that they used to locate themselves.

The key insight of structuralism as influenced by the discipline of linguistics is that signs take on meaning through participation in systems of contrast (Jakobson 1957, 1960, 1990; Lévi-Strauss 1962, 1966, 1980). However, as poststructuralist critiques have pointed out, these systems are fundamentally social objects, and they are created in practice and through constant negotiation between actors (Bourdieu 1972; Certeau 1984; Giddens 1984; Mahmood 2005; Ortner 1996, 2006; Sahlins 1985). The binaries that I describe in this book are produced, not found natural objects in the world. For this reason, they are not simple oppositions but interpretations of a complex, hierarchical, and often shifting network of signs within multiple spheres of interaction.

Through processes of alignment and opposition, people link categories that range from linguistic to geographical to racial to political to temporal to gender expression to sexuality into a coherent system of signification. Semiotic alignment, the process that creates clusters of signs, becomes visible when people make comments that cross categories, treating them as if they were equivalent. These comments are anything but rare, but it takes a whole book to examine what they mean and how they work together. Indeed, after a while they become so commonplace that we don't even notice them; we just laugh when a lunch patron teases a waitress for pretending not to know what runtuphiri, or egg porridge, is, accusing her of having become "refined" and rejecting her local valley identity (chapter 1).

The semiotic field has a coherent internal structure that is produced through these processes of alignment and opposition. As I have shown throughout this book, we can identify binaries such as highland versus lowland, West versus East, legitimate versus desconocido, cholita versus señorita, urban versus rural, and the MAS political party versus the Green autonomy movement. Elements on one side of the dichotomy (e.g., highland, western, migrant, cholita, MAS) are treated as functional equivalents—grouped together in clusters through processes of *iconization*—and each element is treated as if it were equally contrastive to any element on the other side of the dichotomy. Language plays an important part in this system: Quechua bilingualism is linked to the cluster that also includes being a highland western migrant who wears pollera and belongs to MAS, while Spanish monolingualism is linked to eastern lowlanders who support the Green Party. Through this process, language dominance is linked to styles of dress, gender, and political orientation.

TABLE 2

Western	Eastern
Highland	Lowland
Quechua speaker	Spanish monolingual
MAS	Greens
Indigenous	Nonindigenous

The prototypical Quechua speaker is an indigenous woman who wears pollera, comes from the western highlands, supports the MAS political party, and is identified as a colla. Each of these signs becomes an icon of the others through its place within the structure of the semiotic field. In Saipina, she would be characterized as a *desconocida* (stranger) by long-term residents, and she can be assumed to be a migrant (on stereotypes and prototypes, see Agha 1998; Gelman 1999; Gelman and Hirschfeld 1999; McConnell-Ginet 1979). As I discuss in chapter 2, the way that people identify themselves—and are identified—along these scales can affect the way that their language use is understood and interpreted. While western highlanders are characterized as less capable speakers because of their use of Quechua contact features, local vallunos can use Quechua contact features in order to mark their local identity. On the other hand, the use of Quechua contact features by highly able, highly educated speakers can be socially costly if they are not evaluated as having an authentic claim to group identity.

There is a tendency for one side of the binary—in this case, the Quechua, migrant, pollera, MAS side—to be treated as "marked," while the other side is treated as unmarked. This is perhaps clearest when we look at race, in which there is a clearly articulated category for indigenous identity but no clearly equivalent category for mestizo identity, which I have labeled as "nonindigenous" in Table 2. However, markedness can shift; when people identify themselves as standing in between two sides of the binary, as Saipineños consistently do, the unmarked categories become those that stand between two poles: people who maintain "traditions" linked to indigenous practices and indigenous spheres while performing separateness from contemporary indigeneity for urban outsiders (chapter 6).

These binaries are in no sense absolute or removed from practice. As practice theorists have argued, social structures are developed through repeated actions and discourses that have the power to produce, reify, and even transform social structures (for linguistic anthropological approaches, see Ahearn 2001; Eckert 2000; Eckert and McConnell-Ginet 1992; Mendoza-Denton 2008). The social structures that I describe in this book are rooted in practice and interaction, and they are reproduced through particular instances of language use and social evaluation. Nor are these structures exempt from contestation. Indeed, the production of the identity category valluno to describe a local person is a discursive step that explicitly challenges the camba/colla dichotomy: "We are neither one nor the other." Clusters of categories do not fit together perfectly; poles can shift. When Saipineños travel to the city as urban migrants, they find themselves navigating a new place in the binary: they may be characterized as colla outsiders by contacts in the city but at the same time viewed by people in the rural countryside as having been transformed by their urban experience (chapter 8). Insiders and outsiders can be described through a system that distinguishes western migrants from "legitimate" insiders, but when Saipineños perform "traditional" Saipina, they also orient toward a different group of outsiders, political or development groups that may have the power to transfer resources to local actors (chapter 6).

People use conceptual oppositions to navigate their own identity; to police or control others' claims to identity categories, stances, or practices; and to reify or question categories that are in circulation. I do not think that binaries are the only possible way to configure a social system (groups of categories based on three or four clusters are certainly possible), but the binary structure provides a powerful tool for the creation of social meaning at multiple levels (Irvine and Gal 2000; Lévi-Strauss 1966).

The meaning of linguistic features, like other social signs, is not fixed. Rather, it is accomplished through comparison to, and in contrast with, patterns of speech that are linked to ideas about speech contexts, groups of speakers, and even individual speakers. In chapter 2 I describe how the particular linguistic features are evaluated differently based on the social categorization of their speakers. Similarly, particular linguistic variables have different kinds of meanings, ranging from momentary social stances to stable personae, depending on the context in which they are used (Campbell-Kibler 2008; Carmichael 2016; Eckert 2008; Hay et al. 2006; McGowan 2016; Sumner et al. 2013). Here I describe the overarching social structures that organize these kinds of contextual meanings. The pollera-wearing Quechua speaker is a particular type of figure within a semiotic field that generates personae who are linked to particular linguistic patterns or ways of speaking (Agha 2005, 2007a). It is through the lens of these patterns that particular linguistic features are deployed or recognized (or misrecognized, or rejected). For example, as I describe in the case of Esteban, the mayor's brother (chapter 2), the use of a particular linguistic feature can be seen as a claim to an identity that can then be evaluated as authentic or inauthentic.

The relationships between signs and people are seldom clear-cut, and the links between different types of signs are multiple and context dependent (Eckert 2008). Yet people do organize social structure through sign relationships and position themselves with respect to these categories. When Doña Mónica says that her neighbor is "almost" a Saipineño after living in Saipina for more than thirty years (chapter 4), she is managing a complex set of social relationships: her own status as a "legitimate" Saipineña with the right to evaluate others; her generally positive stance toward their personal relationship at the time we spoke; his nonmembership in the class of *real* Saipineños due to his western origins and his use of Quechua; but his closeness to being a Saipineño due to her recognition of his long-term productive membership in the community.

SIGNS AND SIGN SYSTEMS

My approach to the material that I analyze in this book draws on a long tradition in linguistic anthropology that connects large-scale social structures to the details of language use and the ways that people understand language. People produce semiotic systems—systems of meaning—through sign relationships. These relationships link particular individuals and their practices to social groups and structures through processes that make linkages appear "natural" to participants in the social system (Agha 2007; Irvine and Gal 2000; Peirce

1955). The way that individuals position themselves with respect to social practices produces identity categories that locate them with respect to a particular configuration of a social world (Bucholtz 2010; Bucholtz and Hall 2004, 2005; Eckert 2000; Kiesling 1998). These systems are interconnected through the use of styles that draw together disparate types of linguistic and social practices into bundles or clusters of ideas that can be "read" as parts of a coherent whole (Bucholtz 2010; Eckert and McConnell-Ginet 1992; Eckert and Rickford 2001; Irvine 2001; Johnstone 2005). Sign systems work together in relationships that cohere or contrast with other styles within the system (Abbott 1995; Irvine 2001). In turn, clusters of ideas, including ideas about language, are linked to political formations and power differentials in society through ideological processes (Irvine and Gal 2000; Silverstein 1979; Woolard 1998). The meaning of linguistic features is not stable; it draws on context and can shift or hold multiple, sometimes contradictory meanings (Eckert 2008).

Language participates in a system of social categorization that is articulated through structural and semiotic relationships (Clifford 2001; Grossberg 1986; Hall 1996). When people position themselves through language, dress, and political positioning—when they paint their houses in MAS blue or cruceño green, when they wear knee-length straight skirts or polleras—they are drawing on a system of signs that can be expressed through their associations with a cluster of signs aligned through binary relationships. These sign relationships form the structure that people refer to when they position themselves as cambas, collas, or vallunos—ethnic categories, identity stances, stylistic claims that can be expressed through the use of a valluno sombrero or the juxtaposition of lowland-indexed *s* aspiration and highland-indexed Quechua loanwords.

The fact that the camba/colla divide exists as a stable system of reference even as individuals position themselves as moderate MASistas or legitimate autonomistas reveals the extent to which the social system itself exists as a resource for individuals who manage their stylistic and identity practices. This is the reason why people can be challenged for their style of dress, or why children can perform the use of the pollera that their mothers wear on a regular basis; it is why urban migrants understand the way they are positioned as colla outsiders even as they contest that label through their claim to a valluno identity.

When Saipineños say they are neither cambas nor collas, it serves to reinforce the relevance of this binary system of distinction even as they position themselves as "in between." We can see the same process in the stance of the moderate MASistas or in the emergence of the valluno figure, with his tire sandals, black fedora, and hand-woven bags over his shoulder, in popular culture and performance. Negotiating one's place in the space between a binary does not erase the binary or the power of the discourses that maintain it as a space of negotiation.

When I call this system of social categorization "relatively" stable, this does not mean that it is inflexible. Rather, it is reproduced only through practice, and every new instantiation provides the potential for transformation or sedimentation (Bourdieu 1972; Mahmood 2005; Ortner 1984, 2006; Sahlins 1985). When people are angry with their neighbors or express fear and shock at a crime committed by young people (chapter 2), they understand and process these events and emotions by drawing them into a frame of interpretation that aligns amoral or unsociable behavior with status as an outsider and immigrant, a colla. The colla outsider becomes a figure that contrasts with the safe moral and ethical ground of the insider, or conocido. It is through this same opposition that the mayor is able to reassure me that I am not in danger despite the political tensions of the country by casting me as a conocida rather than as a (morally and ethically suspect) foreigner (chapter 4).

The relationships that I have described in this book are by no means innocent of power, hegemony, and class distinctions (Hall 1986; Laclau 2006; Voloshinov 1986; Williams 1977). When Spanish-speaking vallunos express antipathy toward Quechua-speaking indigenous people, when urban migrants are criticized for speaking like hicks, and when rural Bolivians align themselves with the autonomista elites, they participate in discourses that reflect and generate power differentials. These attitudes and ideologies control segments of the population that have been historically subjugated—in particular, indigenous people, poor people, rural people, and women, who "speak back" to power through alternative forms of discourse and systems of value (Pratt 1991).

One of the ways that power and hegemony infiltrate the social system that I have described is through the interpretation of categories as marked and unmarked (Barrett 1998; Bucholtz 2001; Haspelmath 2006). The fact that mestizo identity is interpreted as unmarked while indigenous identity is marked, or that women's bodies and dress styles are explicitly marked while men's are often treated as neutral, is a sign of the power structures that govern and infuse the social system that I describe. Likewise, urban migrants' efforts to assert a distinctive valluno identity in the face of the widespread, virulent discrimination against rural highland migrants can be understood as a struggle for a claim to higher socioeconomic status, a struggle that is explicitly gendered and classed in the "patas kjarkas" videos (chapter 8). As linguistic anthropologists have long argued, language and, indeed, semiotic systems in general are not neutral objects (Duranti 2001). When we see signs as deeply embedded in context, we engage with relationships of power and privilege that are intrinsic to the process of meaning making.

IS THIS REALLY A BOOK ABOUT LANGUAGE? AND WHY DOES IT MATTER?

This is a book that is about a social system. There will be parts of this book that linguists, particularly those who consider themselves formal or cognitive linguists, will not have the faintest interest in. Yet I believe that linguistic anthropologists urgently need to engage with work in cognitive linguistics, sociophonetics, and psycholinguistics. As linguistics engages more deeply with social categorization, we must theorize social identities in increasingly complex and socially realistic ways.

The discipline of linguistics now finds itself in a moment of profound transformation due to the increasing influence of statistically based models of language learning and use (see, e.g., Ortega 2009). These models allow for and in some cases necessitate an understanding of social context in the study of language acquisition, linguistic structure, and language perception and production. The idea that human beings perceive linguistic structure together with social categorization is increasingly well supported. In cognitive linguistics, exemplar models, and Bayesian models, linguistic patterns emerge through the accrual of experience with correlations between different types of signs (Drager and Kirtley 2016; Johnson 2006; Pierrehumbert 2001). Crucially, however, we must ask ourselves *how* signs emerge as meaningful and how relations between signs—not just correlations but oppositions—are formed. As such, we are beginning to recognize that linguistics—cognitive and structural linguistics—is deeply social at its core (Coetzee and Pater 2011; Croft 2009; Queen 2012). When my consultants perceive linguistic material like syllable-final *s* or the discourse marker *pues*, they do so with reference to categories like camba and colla that are complex and difficult to unravel (Babel 2014a). These questions of social meaning in language are unanswerable without deep engagement with social theory.

There is a natural bridge between practice theory and models that hold that linguistic information is stored along with rich social context (Drager and

Kirtley 2016; Johnson 2006; Pierrehumbert 2001). Scholarship in the field of sociophonetics in particular has developed detailed models of cognitive storage, models that would be enriched by drawing on ethnographic understandings of interaction and the structure of the larger social context (Mendoza-Denton 2008; Zimman 2016).

Our awareness of social categories is complex and multilayered. We process social information at many levels, some more or less conscious or more or less explicit (Babel 2016b). Social categorization has effects not only at the interactional level but at the level of language processing (McGowan 2011, 2015; Sumner and Kataoka 2013; Sumner et al. 2013). However, experimental and quantitative understandings of social group formation are not always in step with social theory, and vice versa.

As a researcher who works in the "border" fields of sociolinguistics and linguistic anthropology, I feel it is important to emphasize the relevance of ethnographic work not only to the further reaches of cultural studies and anthropology but also to formal linguistics. In this book, I use ethnographic methods and cultural analysis in order to place language within a larger system of signs. This larger system of meaning gives the context through which category formation occurs.

BETWEEN HIGHLAND AND LOWLAND

Of all the binaries that I discuss in this book, perhaps the greatest binary of all is the Andes/Amazonia binary as it has been produced in the academic literature. Contrasts between highland and lowland have so thoroughly seeped in and penetrated academic thinking that the Andes and Amazonia are often considered to be separate fields of inquiry—despite the fact that this dichotomy has been critiqued both in the field of linguistics (Adelaar et al. 2006; Camino 1977; Valenzuela 2015; Van Gijn 2014) and in ethnographic and historical accounts (Emlen 2014, 2016; Gade 1972; Greene 2007; Renard Casevitz et al. 1988; Santos-Granero 2002). Like the other binaries that I discuss in this book, it is discourse that produces the Andes and Amazonia as separate, discrete regions. Scholars may then use these poles in order to position themselves as Andeanists, Amazonianists, or a little bit of both, but the opposition between Andes and Amazonia forms its own powerful historically and disciplinarily rooted binary. Of course, it is not only in scholarly accounts that these regions are discursively produced;

throughout this book, I have closely examined the *production* of highland and lowland as contrasting categories through an examination of a town that positions itself as neither highland nor lowland, neither Andean nor Amazonian, but something in between.

When I read ethnographies of Bolivia, there is often a feeling of disconnect—elements that seem intimately familiar, and others that are entirely strange. My experience of Bolivia has been fundamentally one that is connected to personal relationships and interactions in a part of Bolivia that some might characterize as peripheral and disconnected from centers of power (Goldstein 2004; Haynes 2016). Nevertheless, the Santa Cruz valleys play an important role in national politics as a "swing" region, precisely because people's social identifications are so malleable and complex. A close understanding of how people negotiate political, regional, and ethnic identification is essential to understanding how national politics are enacted in the contemporary Bolivian context (Albro 2010; Fabricant and Postero 2013; Gustafson 2008, 2011; Postero 2010). The choice to identify with national political groups is both socially controlled and shaped by personal experiences and relationships. This personal level is one that I have tried to illustrate through the use of ethnographic description and fine-grained perspectives on social categories throughout this book.

Because I describe the social system in Saipina from a distance and at a general scale, I worry that this social system can seem abstract. It is not. The characteristics of the semiotic field are created in and through the lived experiences of individuals and in interactions between people in a particular place at a particular time. In order to demonstrate this reality even through the "screen" of ethnography, I have made an effort to let my own personal positioning and point of view shine through in the interludes and to tell some of the stories of my consultants, close friends, and relatives who live the system that I describe.

Language is an important nexus of social categorization in Bolivia. Even as the country proudly claims a high degree of linguistic diversity and is home to one of the most secure and best-established indigenous language communities in Latin America, it has been suggested that processes of rural-to-urban migration and the influence of higher education threaten the bi- and multilingualism of a younger generation of speakers (Howard 2007; Kalt 2012). Understanding how people use and identify with Quechua and other indigenous languages—even when they claim a Spanish-speaking identity—can help to broaden our understanding of what it means to be an indigenous language speaker. In addition, I call attention to the experience of rural speakers of a variety of Spanish that has extensive Quechua contact influence. As I have shown in this book, the use of Quechua contact features is an important aspect of local identity in Saipina specifically and in the Santa Cruz valleys region more broadly. This is a type of experience that cannot be found either in elite urban political circles or in rural indigenous contexts, and this book is unique in discussing the broader social context of being "ni camba ni colla" in Bolivia today.

CONCLUSION

When my consultants talk about being neither camba nor colla, they are situating themselves not only geographically but also in terms of language, styles of dress, political stances, and orientation toward modernity. While they negotiate and in some ways reject this binary, it remains a powerful framing device for the production of identity claims in their discourses and consequently in my data.

The meaning of language in use is produced through systems of contrast and is rooted in particular communities, speakers, and utterances. Linguistic signs are linked to other social characteristics through iconic relationships. Both linguistic and nonlinguistic material participates in a broader system of social meaning that constitutes the semiotic field, an overarching structure that organizes social and linguistic practices into a coherent system of meaning. I have described a community located in central Bolivia in which speakers use Quechua contact features in Spanish to situate themselves with relation to dialectics of tradition and modernity, East and West, highland and lowland, and Spanish and Quechua. These patterns of variation must be understood as one part of the construction of social meaning in this community, which also encompasses related categories such as dress styles, migration patterns, ethnicity, and political affiliation.

Can a Quechua speaker wear pants rather than the pollera? The fact that she *does* gives us all the answer that we need. I can almost hear Doña Inocencia saying, as my husband said when he was teased about dating a gringa, "¿No puedo?" (Can't I?) with a subtext of "Do I need your permission?" or, as children used to say at my elementary school, "It's a free country." Yet people are free only to the extent to which their actions can be incorporated into a more or less coherent, structured, if perhaps contested frame of reference. Ultimately, it is the ways that these choices are framed, challenged, and defended through multiple interacting systems of interpretation that give us insight into the ways that people organize their world, social categories, and experiences.

POSTSCRIPT

Leaving

SOME THINGS have changed in the years since I first arrived in Saipina. While the town once felt remote and sleepy, it is now bustling and busy, full of life and ambition. There are now sprawling new neighborhoods where ten years ago there was nothing but cactus. Motorcycles roar along the streets from early in the morning until late at night. Chicherías blare loud music at all hours. Hand-lettered signs on doors advertise things for sale and positions available—maids, day laborers for agricultural work. There are huge tractors and earth-moving machines parked around the corner from my house. Few people use the public phones anymore now that everyone has cell phones, and the beautiful view of the valley from my living room window is sandwiched between two huge cell phone towers.

The bus stop in Santa Cruz is still on the same huge avenue, but a few doors down in a larger office. The buses, too, are bigger—much bigger. They still claim to be like airplanes flying, but on land. This is still aspirational. The road is, if anything, worse than before, but there is more equipment working, and tractors are often available to straighten out things that go wrong. More people have private vehicles, but the buses are even more packed than ever. The ayudantes have changed over to a new generation, although many of the drivers remain the same. Martín immigrated to Stockholm, and I see smiling photos of his son, who followed him some years later, captioned in Swedish on Facebook.

When I'm in town, I still travel that road from Santa Cruz to Saipina. I enjoy stopping in Samaipata, but once I've had my spaetzle, I'm ready to move on. When I get to Saipina, there are people waiting for me. I even think the cactus are beautiful sometimes.

In 2002 houses were mostly single-story adobe structures built around a central courtyard with tile roofs. As of 2015 there are many two- and three-story buildings throughout town. These new houses were built out of cement and brick, with fashionable decorative touches, ground-floor garages, and large plate-glass windows. When I was a volunteer, like most of my neighbors, I used a bicycle or my feet as my primary means of transportation. In those days, only a few lucky neighbors had *vagonetas* (station wagons), which they used as taxis, or old trucks for transporting sugarcane that seemed in danger of falling apart at any moment as they rattled up and down the dusty, unpaved road. Now there is a line of taxis waiting at the plaza at all hours of the day. When my husband was a child, he played soccer under the street lights at night until the generator was cut off at ten p.m. Now the entire town is connected to an electrical grid, and instead of buying tanks of cooking fuel, most houses are connected to a much cheaper direct gas distribution network. The water system has been expanded many times to accommodate the growing population of the town.

When we bought a lot far up on the east flank of town in 2005, we had no neighbors, and people laughed at us for building a home where people kept their free-range pigs. Ten years later, all the surrounding land has been divided into lots and sold to homeowners. As of this writing, we live close to a large industrial sugar-processing plant. There are neighbors on all sides, including a well-established evangelical church across the street.

As the years have passed, my role in the community has changed. As a young single woman, I was essentially free to go where I wanted and do what I wished. I often spent long periods of time as a visitor in people's houses, helping them with their work, eating their food, playing with their children. As a young married woman, a daughter-in-law, I grew closer to my husband's family, especially my mother-in-law and her parents and children. They continue to be my closest friends and contacts in Saipina.

Over the years, there have been changes around me. Young people whom I met as babies and kindergarteners went to college, moved to the city, or started their own families. People aged. Men and women I knew as strong, healthy adults grew sick with diabetes, heart trouble, Chagas disease, strokes. Older people's health deteriorated. Don Francisco suffered a stroke that left him bedridden in increasingly poor condition for four years before his death in November 2014. Doña Antonia, as of this writing, is in relatively good condition physically but sometimes wanders mentally. After Don Francisco's decline, she moved away from the banda and now lives with her daughter, Doña Juana, and a granddaughter in the new house near the hospital.

Saipina is a vital and energetic town. People are drawn to its strong agricultural economy and to the comfortable standard of living that it is possible to achieve with hard work and a little luck. In the midst of all this change, the social system has changed and shifted as well, though not as drastically as the physical and economic surroundings of the town. The material in this book is written from my own partial perspective and is drawn largely from the first decade of the 2000s, though I have updated much of the material through my latest visit in 2015. The written word stays constant; people and places change. I cannot claim to have written a book that is about the Andes or even about Bolivia; rather, this is a book about one particular place at one particular time, through my own eyes and with the perspective and guidance of my friends and family, to whom I extend my great and sincere thanks for the stories they have given me to tell.

REFERENCES

Abbott, Andrew. 1995. Things of Boundaries. Social Research 62(4): 857–882.

Abu-Lughod, Lila. 1996. Writing against Culture. *In* Recapturing Anthropology: Working in the Present. R. G. Fox, ed. Pp. 137–162. Santa Fe, NM: School for Advanced Research Press.

Adelaar, Willem. 1977. Tarma Quechua: Grammar, Texts, Dictionary. Lisse: Peter de Ridder Press.

Adelaar, Willem F. H., Alexandra Y. Aikhenvald, and Robert M. W. Dixon. 2006. The Quechua Impact in Amuesha, an Arawak Language of the Peruvian Amazon. *In* Grammars in Contact: A Cross-Linguistic Typology. A. Aikhenvald, ed. Pp. 290–312. Oxford: Oxford University Press.

Adelaar, Willem, and Peter Muysken. 2004. The Languages of the Andes. Cambridge: Cambridge University Press.

Agha, Asif. 1998. Stereotypes and Registers of Honorific Language. Language in Society 27(2): 151–194.

———. 2005. Voice, Footing, Enregisterment. Journal of Linguistic Anthropology 15(1): 38–59.

———. 2007a. Language and Social Relations. New York: Cambridge University Press.

———. 2007b. Recombinant Selves in Mass Mediated Spacetime. Language & Communication 27(3): 320–335.

Ahearn, Laura M. 2001. Language and Agency. Annual Review of Anthropology 30(1): 109–137.

Ahmad, Rizwan. 2011. Urdu in Devanagari: Shifting Orthographic Practices and Muslim Identity in Delhi. Language in Society 40(3): 259–284.

Albó, Xavier. 1970. Social Constraints on Cochabamba Quechua. Ithaca, NY: Cornell University Press.

———. 1979. The Future of the Oppressed Languages in the Andes. *In* Language and Society: Anthropological Issues. W. C. McCormack and S. A. Wurm, eds. Pp. 309–330. The Hague: Mouton.

———. 2004. El futuro del Quechua visto desde una perspectiva Boliviana. International Journal of the Sociology of Language 167:119–130.

Albro, Robert. 2010. Roosters at Midnight: Indigenous Signs and Stigma in Local Bolivian Politics. Santa Fe, NM: School for Advanced Research.

Allen, Catherine J. 1988. The Hold Life Has: Coca and Cultural Identity in an Andean Community. Washington, DC: Smithsonian Institution.

———. 1998. When Utensils Revolt: Mind, Matter, and Modes of Being in the Pre-Columbian Andes. RES: Anthropology and Aesthetics 33:18–27.

———. 2011. Foxboy: Intimacy and Aesthetics in Andean Stories. Austin: University of Texas Press.

Andersen, Lykke E. 2002. Rural-Urban Migration in Bolivia: Advantages and Disadvantages. Documento de trabajo, Instituto de Investigaciones Socio-económicas, Universidad Católica Boliviana.

Andrien, Kenneth J. 2001. Andean Worlds: Indigenous History, Culture, and Consciousness under Spanish rule, 1532–1825. Albuquerque: University of New Mexico Press.

Archibald, Priscilla. 2011. Imagining Modernity in the Andes. Lewisburg, PA: Bucknell University Press.

Ariel de Vidas, Anath. 2002. Memoria textil e industria del recuerdo en los Andes: Identidades a prueba del turismo en Perú, Bolivia y Ecuador. Quito, Ecuador: Editorial Abya Yala.

Artaraz, Kepa. 2012. Bolivia: Refounding the Nation. London: Pluto Press.

Assies, Willem. 2006. La "media luna" sobre Bolivia: Nación, región, etnia y clase social (The "half moon" over Bolivia: Nation, region, ethnicity and class). América latina hoy 43:87–105.

Babel, Anna M. 2011. Why Don't All Contact Features Act Alike? Contact Features as Enregistered Features. Journal of Language Contact 4(1): 56–91.

———. 2012. Uso de rasgos de contacto en el español andino: La influencia de la identidad. Neue Romania 41:5–26.

———. 2014a. Highlanders Whistle When They Talk—or Do They? *Pues* Variation as an Index of Regional Identity in the Santa Cruz Valleys of Bolivia. Journal of Sociolinguistics 18(5): 604–633.

———. 2014b. The Role of Context in Interpreting Linguistic Variables. Boletín de filología de la Universidad de Chile 49(2): 49–85.

———. 2014c. Time and Reminiscence in Contact: Dynamism and Stasis in Contact-Induced Change. Spanish in Context 11(3): 311–344.

———. 2016a. Affective Motivations for Borrowing: Performing Local Identity through Loan Phonology. Language and Communication 49:70–83.

———, ed. 2016b. Awareness and Control in Sociolinguistic Research. New York: Cambridge University Press.

———. 2016c. Preface. *In* Awareness and Control in Sociolinguistic Research. Anna M. Babel, ed. Pp. xix–xxii. New York: Cambridge University Press.

———. 2016d. Silence as Control: Shame and Self-Consciousness in Sociolinguistic Positioning. *In* Awareness and Control in Sociolinguistic Research. Anna M. Babel, ed. Pp. 200–228. New York: Cambridge University Press.

———. 2017. Aspirates and Ejectives in Quechua-Influenced Spanish. Spanish in Context 14(2): 159–185.

Babel, Anna M., and Stefan Pfänder. 2013. Doing Copying: Why Typology Doesn't Matter to Language Speakers. *In* Congruence in Contact-Induced Language Change: Language Families, Typological Resemblance, and Perceived Similarity. J. Besters-Dilger, C. Dermarkar, S. Pfänder, and A. Rabus, eds. Pp. 239–257. Berlin: De Gruyter.

Bakhtin, Mikhail M. 1937. Forms of Time and of the Chronotope in the Novel: Notes toward a Historical Poetics. *In* Narrative Dynamics: Essays on Time, Plot, Closure, and Frames. B. Richardson, ed. Pp. 15–24. Columbus: Ohio State University Press.

Bakker, Peter. 1997. A Language of Our Own: The Genesis of Michif, the Mixed Cree-French Language of the Canadian Métis. New York: Oxford University Press.

Bakker, Peter, and Maarten Mous. 1994. Introduction. *In* Mixed Languages: 15 Case Studies in Language Intertwining. Pp. 1–11. Amsterdam: IFOTT.

Barbieri, Chiara, Paul Heggarty, Daniele Yang Yao, Gianmarco Ferri, Sara De Fanti, Stefania Sarno, Graziella Ciani, Alessio Boattini, Donata Luiselli, and Davide Pettener. 2014. Between Andes and Amazon: The Genetic Profile of the Arawak-Speaking Yanesha. American Journal of Physical Anthropology 155(4): 600–609.

Barragán Romano, Rossana. 1997. Entre polleras, ñañacas y lliqllas: Los mestizos y cholas en la conformación de la "Tercera República." *In* Tradición y modernidad en los Andes: Estudios y debates regionales andinos. H. Urbano, ed. Pp. 43–73. Cuzco, Peru: Instituto Bartolomé de las Casas. Barrett, Rusty. 1998. Markedness and Styleswitching in Performances by African American Drag Queens. *In* Codes and Consequences: Choosing Linguistic Varieties. C. Myers-Scotton, ed. Pp. 139–161. Oxford: Oxford University Press.

———. 1999. Indexing Polyphonous Identity in the Speech of African American Drag Queens. *In* Reinventing Identities: The Gendered Self in Discourse. M. Bucholtz, A. C. Liang, and L. A. Sutton, eds. Pp. 313–331. Oxford: Oxford University Press.

Bastia, Tanja. 2011. Migration as Protest? Negotiating Gender, Class, and Ethnicity in Urban Bolivia. Environment and Planning A 43(7): 1514–1529.

Bastia, Tanja, and Erika Busse. 2011. Transnational Migration and Changing Gender Relations in Peruvian and Bolivian Cities. Diversities 13(1): 19–33.

Bauman, Richard, and Charles Briggs. 1990. Poetics and Performance as Critical Perspectives on Language and Social Life. Annual Review of Anthropology 19(1): 59–88.

———. 2003. Voices of Modernity: Language Ideologies and the Politics of Inequality. New York: Cambridge University Press.

Bergholdt, A. 1999. Cambas y collas: Un estudio sobre identidad cultural en Santa Cruz de la Sierra, Bolivia. Aarhus, Denmark: Centro de Estudios Latinoamericanos, Universidad de Aarhus.

Beyersdorff, Margot. 1998. The Meeting of Two Imperial Languages in the Quechua-Spanish Vocabulary of Diego de Gonzalez Holguín. *In* Andean Oral Traditions: Discourse and Literature. M. Beyersdorff and S. Dedenbach-Salazar Saenz, eds. Pp. 257–283. Bonn: Bonn Americanist Studies.

Bigenho, Michelle. 2005. Making Music Safe for the Nation. *In* Natives Making Nation: Gender, Indigeneity, and the State in the Andes. A. Canessa, ed. Pp. 60–80. Tucson: University of Arizona Press.

———. 2016. Sounding Indigenous: Authenticity in Bolivian Music Performance. Berlin: Springer.

Blommaert, Jan. 2015. Chronotopes, Scales, and Complexity in the Study of Language in Society. Annual Review of Anthropology 44:105–116.

Bourdieu, Pierre. 1972. Outline of a Theory of Practice. Cambridge: Cambridge University Press.

———. 1991. Language and Symbolic Power. Cambridge, MA: Harvard University Press.

Boynton, Sylvia. 1981. A Phonemic Analysis of Monolingual Andean (Bolivian) Spanish. *In* The Aymara Language in Its Social and Cultural Context. M. J. Hardman, ed. Pp. 199–204. Gainesville: University Press of Florida.

Brettell, Caroline B. 2000. Theorizing Migration in Anthropology. *In* Migration Theory: Talking across Disciplines. C. B. Brettell and J. F. Hollifield, eds. Pp. 97–137. New York: Routledge.

———. 2003. Anthropology of Migration: Essays on Transnationalism, Ethnicity, and Identity. Walnut Creek: Altamira Press.

Browman, David L. 1978. Toward the Development of the Tiahuanaco (Tiwanaku) State. *In* Advances in Andean Archaeology. D. Bowman, ed. Pp. 327–349. The Hague: De Gruyter.

Brown, Esther L., and Rena Torres Cacoullos. 2003. Spanish [s]. *In* A Romance Perspective on Language Knowledge and Use: Selected Papers from the 31st Linguistic Symposium on Romance Languages. L. Lopez and R. Cameron, eds. Pp. 21–38. Philadelphia: John Benjamins.

Brown, Roger, and Albert Gilman. 1960. The Pronouns of Power and Solidarity. *In* Style in Language. T. Seboek, ed. Pp. 253–276. Cambridge, MA: MIT Press.

Bucholtz, Mary. 2001. The Whiteness of Nerds: Superstandard English and Racial Markedness. Journal of Linguistic Anthropology 11(1): 84–100.

———. 2010. White Kids: Language, Race, and Styles of Youth Identity. New York: Cambridge University Press.

Bucholtz, Mary, and Kira Hall. 2004. Language and Identity. *In* The Blackwell Companion to Linguistic Anthropology. A. Duranti, ed. Pp. 369–395. Malden, MA: Blackwell.

———. 2005. Identity and Interaction: A Sociocultural Linguistic Approach. Discourse Studies 7:585–614.

———. 2016. Embodied Sociolinguistics. *In* Sociolinguistics: Theoretical Debates. N. Coupland, ed. Pp. 173–200. New York: Cambridge University Press.

Bustamante-López, Isabel, and Mercedes Niño-Murcia. 1995. Impositive Speech Acts in Northern Andean Spanish: A Pragmatic Description. Hispania 78:885–897.

Calvo Pérez, Julio. 2000. Partículas en el castellano andino. *In* Teoría y práctica del contacto: El Español en América en el candelero. J. Calvo Pérez, ed. Pp. 73–112. Madrid: Iberoamericana/Vervuert.

———. 2008. Perú. *In* El Español en América: Contactos lingüísticos en Hispanoamérica. A. Palacios, ed. Pp. 189–210. Barcelona: Ariel.

Camacho, José, Liliana Paredes, and Liliana Sánchez. 1995. The Genitive Clitic and the Genitive Construction in Andean Spanish. Probus 7(2): 133–146.

Camino, Alejandro. 1977. Trueque, correrias e intercambios entre los Quechuas andinos y los Piro y Machiguenga de la montana peruana. Amazonia Peruana Lima 1(2): 123–140.

Campbell-Kibler, Kathryn. 2008. I'll Be the Judge of That: Diversity in Social Perceptions of (ING). Language in Society 37(5): 637–659.

Canagarajah, Suresh. 2011. Codemeshing in Academic Writing: Identifying Teachable Strategies of Translanguaging. Modern Language Journal 95(3): 401–417.

Canessa, Andrew. 2005. Natives Making Nation: Gender, Indigeneity, and the State in the Andes. Tucson: University of Arizona Press.

———. 2007. Who Is Indigenous? Self-Identification, Indigeneity, and Claims to Justice in Contemporary Bolivia. Urban Anthropology and Studies of Cultural Systems and World Economic Development 36:195–237.

———. 2008a. The Past Is Not Another Country: Exploring Indigenous Histories in Bolivia. History and Anthropology 19:353–369.

———. 2008b. Sex and the Citizen: Barbies and Beauty Queens in the Age of Evo Morales 1. Journal of Latin American Cultural Studies 17(1): 41–64.

———. 2012. Intimate Indigeneities: Race, Sex, and History in the Small Spaces of Andean Life. Durham, NC: Duke University Press.

Carmichael, Katie. 2016. Place-Linked Expectations and Listener Awareness of Regional Accents. *In* Awareness and Control in Sociolinguistic Research. A. M. Babel, ed. New York: Cambridge University Press.

Carmona, Alicia. 2008. Bailaremos: Participation in Morenada Dance Fraternities among Bolivian Immigrants in Argentina. New York: New York University Press.

Carr, Summerson, and Michael Lempert. 2016. Scale: Discourse and Dimensions of Social Life. Oakland: University of California Press.

Cerrón-Palomino, Rodolfo. 2003. Castellano andino: Aspectos sociolingüísticos, pedagógicos y gramaticales. Lima: Pontificia Universidad Católica del Perú.

———. 1994. Quechumara: Estructuras paralelas del quechua y del aimara. Vol. 42. La Paz: Centro de Investigación y Promoción del Campesinado.

Certeau, Michel de. 1984. The Practice of Everyday Life. Berkeley: University of California Press.

Chumacero, R., J. P. Colque, G. Sanjinés, E. Sotomayor, C. Costas, P. Cameron, J. Salgado, J. Plata, and A. W. Vadillo. 2010. Reconfigurando territorios: Reforma agraria, control territorial y gobiernos indígenas en Bolivia (Informe 2009). Fundación Tierra 9995477017.

Clifford, James. 1983. On Ethnographic Authority. Representations 2:118–146.

———. 1986. On Ethnographic Allegory. *In* Writing Culture: The Poetics and Politics of Ethnography. Pp. 98–121. Berkeley: University of California Press.

———. 2001. Indigenous Articulations. Contemporary Pacific 13(2): 467–490.

Cody, Francis. 2013. The Light of Knowledge: Literacy Activism and the Politics of Writing in South India. Ithaca, NY: Cornell University Press.

Coetzee, Andries W., and Joe Pater. 2011. The Place of Variation in Phonological Theory. *In* The Handbook of Phonological Theory. Pp. 401–434. Hoboken, NJ: John Wiley & Sons.

Colanzi, Liliana. 2015. La rebelión de las cholas. *In* El País. April 17. https://elpais.com/elpais/2015/04/10/eps/1428661748_198900.html.

Comboni Salinas, Sonia, and José Manuel Juárez Nuñez. 2001. Educación, cultura y derechos indigenas: El caso de la reforma educativa boliviana. Revista iberoamericana de educación 27:125–152.

Conklin, Beth A. 1997. Body Paint, Feathers, and VCRs: Aesthetics and Authenticity in Amazonian Activism. American Ethnologist 24(4): 711–737.

Coronel-Molina, Serafin M., and Linda L. Grabner-Coronel. 2005. Lenguas e identidades en los Andes: Perspectivas ideolólogicas y culturales. Quito, Ecuador: Editorial Abya Yala.

Covey, R. Alan. 2006. How the Incas Built Their Heartland: State Formation and the Innovation of Imperial Strategies in the Sacred Valley, Peru. Ann Arbor: University of Michigan Press.

Crapanzano, Vincent. 1996. "Self"-Centering Narratives. *In* Natural Histories of Discourse. M. Silverstein and G. Urban, eds. Pp. 106–127. Chicago: University of Chicago Press.

Croft, William. 2009. Towards a Social Cognitive Linguistics. *In* New Directions in Cognitive Linguistics. V. Evans, and S. Poucel, eds. Amsterdam: John Benjamins.

Cusihuaman, Antonio. 1976. Gramática quechua: Cuzco–Collao. Lima, Peru: Ministerio de educación.

Dawson, Alexander S. 2012. Histories and Memories of the Indian Boarding Schools in Mexico, Canada, and the United States. Latin American Perspectives 39(5): 80–99.

de Granda, Germán. 2001. Estudios de lingüística andina Lima. Lima: Pontificia Universidad Católica del Peru, Fondo Editorial.

de la Cadena, Marisol. 2000. Indigenous Mestizos: The Politics of Race and Culture in Cuzco, Peru, 1919–1991. Durham, NC: Duke University Press.

Delforge, Ann Marie. 2012. "Nobody Wants to Sound Like a Provinciano": The Recession of Unstressed Vowel Devoicing in the Spanish of Cusco, Perú. Journal of Sociolinguistics 16:311–335.

de los Heros, Susana. 2001. Discurso, identidad y género en el castellano peruano. Lima: Pontificia Universidad Católica del Peru.

Derrida, Jacques. 1978. Writing and Difference. Chicago: University of Chicago Press.

Díaz Villamil, Antonio. 1946. La niña de sus ojos. La Paz: Editorial Juventud.

Dingemanse, Mark. 2012. Advances in the Cross-Linguistic Study of Ideophones. Language and Linguistics Compass 6(10): 654–672.

Dirks, Nicholas. 1990. History as a Sign of the Modern. Public Culture 2(2): 25–33.

Drager, Katie, and Joelle Kirtley. 2016. Awareness, Salience, and Stereotypes in Exemplar-Based Models of Speech Production and Perception. *In* Awareness and Control in Sociolinguistic Research. A. M. Babel, ed. Pp. 1–24. Cambridge: Cambridge University Press.

Droguett, Francisca María Fernández. 2013. Género y mestizaje en América Latina: Las figuras de la chola y la china en Los Andes. Revista Estudios Cotidianos 1(3): 376–386.

Duranti, Alessandro. 1994. Politics and Grammar: Agency in Samoan Political Discourse. American Ethnologist 17:646–666.

———. 2001. Linguistic Anthropology: History, Ideas, and Issues. *In* Linguistic Anthropology: A Reader. A. Duranti, ed. Pp. 1–38. Hoboken, NJ: John Wiley and Sons.

Durston, Alan. 2007. Pastoral Quechua: The History of Christian Translation in Colonial Peru. Notre Dame, IN: University of Notre Dame Press.

Eaton, Kent. 2007. Backlash in Bolivia: Regional Autonomy as a Reaction against Indigenous Mobilization. Politics & Society 35(1): 71–102.

———. 2011. Conservative Autonomy Movements: Territorial Dimensions of Ideological Conflict in Bolivia and Ecuador. Comparative Politics 43(3): 291–310.

Eckert, Penelope. 2000. Linguistic Variation as Social Practice: The Linguistic Construction of Identity in Belten High. Oxford: Blackwell.

———. 2008. Variation and the Indexical Field. Journal of Sociolinguistics 12(4): 453–476.

Eckert, Penelope, and Sally McConnell-Ginet. 1992. Think Practically and Look Locally: Language and Gender as Community-Based Practice. Annual Review of Anthropology 21:461–490.

Eckert, Penelope, and John R. Rickford. 2001. Style and Sociolinguistic Variation. Cambridge: Cambridge University Press.

Emlen, Nicholas Q. 2014. Language and Coffee in a Trilingual Matsigenka-Quechua-Spanish Frontier Community on the Andean-Amazonian Borderland of Southern Peru. Ph.D. dissertation, University of Michigan.

———. 2015. Public Discourse and Community Formation in a Trilingual Matsigenka-Quechua-Spanish Frontier Community of Southern Peru. Language in Society 44:679–703.

———. 2016. Multilingualism in the Andes and Amazonia: A View from In-Between. Journal of Latin American and Caribbean Anthropology. DOI: doi:10.1111/jlca.12250.

Escandell, Xavier, and Maria Tapias. 2010. Transnational Lives, Travelling Emotions and Idioms of Distress among Bolivian Migrants in Spain. Journal of Ethnic and Migration Studies 36(3): 407–423.

Escobar, Alberto. 1976. Bilingualism and Dialectology in Peru. International Journal of the Sociology of Language 9:85–96.

Escobar, Anna María. 1988. Hacia una tipología del bilinguísmo en el Perú. Lima: Instituto de Estudios Peruanos.

———. 1994. Andean Spanish and Bilingual Spanish: Linguistic Characteristics. *In* Language in the Andes. P. Cole, G. Hermon, and D. Martin, eds. Pp. 51–71. Newark: Center for Latin American Studies, University of Delaware.

———. 1997. Contrastive and Innovative Uses of the Present Perfect and the Preterite in Spanish in Contact with Quechua. Hispania 80(4): 859–870.

———. 2000. Contacto social y lingüístico: El español en contacto con el quechua en el Perú. Lima: Pontificia Universidad Católica del Perú.

———. 2011. Spanish in Contact with Quechua. Handbook of Hispanic Sociolinguistics. M. Díaz-Campos, ed. Pp. 321–352. Hoboken, NJ: John Wiley and Sons.

Evia, José Luis, Miguel S. Urquiola, Lykke Andersen, Eduardo Antelo, and Osvaldo Nina. 1999. Geography and Development in Bolivia: Migration, Urban and Industrial Concentration, Welfare, and Convergence: 1950–1992. IDB Working Paper No. 115.

Fabricant, Nicole. 2009. Performative Politics: The Camba Countermovement in Eastern Bolivia. American Ethnologist 36(4): 768–783.

———. 2012. Mobilizing Bolivia's Displaced: Indigenous Politics, and the Struggle over Land. Chapel Hill: University of North Carolina Press.

Fabricant, Nicole,, and Bret Gustafson. 2011. Remapping Bolivia: Resources, Territory, and Indigeneity in a Plurinational State. Santa Fe, NM: School for Advanced Research Press.

Fabricant, Nicole,, and Nancy Postero. 2013. Contested Bodies, Contested States: Performance, Emotions, and New Forms of Regional Governance in Santa Cruz, Bolivia. Journal of Latin American and Caribbean Anthropology 18(2): 187–211.

Faller, Martina Theresia. 2002. Semantics and Pragmatics of Evidentials in Cuzco Quechua. Ph.D. dissertation, Stanford University.

Faudree, Paja. 2013. Singing for the Dead: The Politics of Indigenous Revival in Mexico. Durham, NC: Duke University Press.

———. 2015. Singing for the Dead, on and off Line: Diversity, Migration, and Scale in Mexican Muertos Music. Language & Communication 44:31–43.

Femenías, Blenda. 2005. Gender and the Boundaries of Dress in Contemporary Peru. Austin: University of Texas Press.

Fernández, Víctor. 2014. El español de los inmigrantes de los Andes bolivianos en el Norte Grande de Chile: Convergencias y divergencias dialectales en el marco de una situación de contacto. Ph.D. dissertation, Université de Montréal.

Fernández García, Mercedes. 2009. Bolivianos en España. Revista de Indias 69(245): 171–198.

File-Muriel, Richard J., and Earl K. Brown. 2011. The Gradient Nature of S-Lenition in Caleño Spanish. Language Variation and Change 23(2): 223–243.

Finot, Enrique. 1978. Historia de la conquista del oriente boliviano. La Paz: Libreria Editorial Juventud.

Firestone, Amy. 2013. Quechua and Spanish in the Urban Andes: A Study on Language Dynamics and Identity Construction among Peruvian Youth. Ph.D. dissertation, University of Illinois at Urbana-Champaign.

Flesken, Anaïd. 2012. Changing Ethnic Boundaries: Politics and Identity in Bolivia, 2000–2010. Ph.D. dissertation, Exeter University.

———. 2013. The Constructions and Reconstructions of an Identity: An Examination of the Regional Autonomy Movement in Santa Cruz, Bolivia. Ethnopolitics Papers 22: 1–32.

Floyd, Rick. 1999. The Structure of Evidential Categories in Wanka Quechua. Dallas, TX: Summer Institute of Linguistics.

Forero, Juan. 2004. Women Leave Traditional Bolivian Dress in Closet. *New York Times*, October 14, 2004. http://www.nytimes.com/2004/10/14/world/women-leave-traditional-bolivian-dress-in-closet.html.

FORTEMU: Proyecto formulación de planes de ordenamiento territorial municipal. 2004. "Diagnóstico de turismo Municipio de Saipina" and "Estudio socioeconómico Municipio de Saipina." Prefectura de Santa Cruz, gestión 2004. Ejecutivos: Rinaldo Durán Flores, Naya Eid Hurtado; Equipo técnico: Weimar Chávez Cuenca, Israel Arana Claure, Dulfredo Caba Espada. Santa Cruz, Bolivia.

Gade, Daniel W. 1972. Comercio y colonización en la zona de contacto entre la sierra y las tierras bajas del valle del Urubamba en el Perú. Paper presented to the XXXIX Congreso Internacional de Americanistas.

Gal, Susan. 1978. Peasant Men Can't Get Wives: Language Change and Sex Roles in a Bilingual Community. Language in Society 7(1): 1–16.

———. 1988. The Political Economy of Code Choice. *In* Code-Switching: Anthropological and Sociolinguistic Perspectives. M. Heller, ed. Pp. 245–264. Berlin: Mouton de Gruyter.

Gal, Susan, and Judith T. Irvine. 1995. The Boundaries of Languages and Disciplines: How Ideologies Construct Difference. Social Research 62:967–1001.

García Canclini, Néstor. 1995. Culturas híbridas: Estrategias para entrar y salir de la modernidad. Minneapolis: University of Minnesota Press.

García Recoaro, Nicolás. 2014. Las cholas y su mundo de polleras. Cuadernos del Centro de Estudios en Diseño y Comunicación: Ensayos 47:181–186.

García, Ofelia, and Li Wei. 2014. Translanguaging and Education. *In* Translanguaging: Language, Bilingualism and Education, O. García and L. Wei, eds. Pp. 63–77. Berlin: Springer.

García Tesoro, Ana Isabel. 2015. Valores emergentes del pretérito pluscuamperfecto en el español andino hablado en Chinchero (Cuzco). Boletín de Filología 50(2): 51–75.

Geertz, Clifford. 1973. The Interpretation of Cultures. New York: Basic Books.

Gegeo, David Welchman, and Karen Ann Watson-Gegeo. 1999. Adult Education, Language Change, and Issues of Identity and Authenticity in Kwara'ae (Solomon Islands). Anthropology & Education Quarterly 30:22–36.

Gelman, Susan. 1999. Essentialism. *In* MIT Encyclopedia of Cognitive Science. R. A. Wilson and F. Keil, eds. Pp. 281–282. Cambridge, MA: MIT Press.

Gelman, Susan, and Lawrence Hirschfeld. 1999. How Biological Is Essentialism? *In* Folkbiology. D. Medin and S. Atran, eds. Pp. 403–446. Cambridge, MA: MIT Press.

Giddens, Anthony. 1984. The Constitution of Society: Outline of the Theory of Structuration. Berkeley: University of California Press.

Godenzzi, Juan Carlos. 1992. Cambios lingüísticos y modernización en los Andes: El caso de Puno. Tradición y modernidad en los Andes 86:257.

———. 1996. Educación bilingue intercultural en los Andes y la Amazonia. Revista Andina 28 (14[2]): 559–581.

———, ed. 2005. En las redes del lenguaje: Cognición, discurso, y sociedad en los Andes Lima. Lima: Universidad del Pacífico.

———. 2008. Trazas lingüísticas y discursivas de la ciudad: El caso de Lima. Tinkuy: Boletín de investigación y debate 9:47–64.

Goldstein, Daniel M. 2000. Names, Places, and Power: Collective Identity in the Miss Oruro Pageant, Cochabamba, Bolivia. PoLAR: Political and Legal Anthropology Review 23(1): 1–24.

———. 2004. The Spectacular City: Violence and Urban Performance in Bolivia. Durham, NC: Duke University Press.

———. 2012. Outlawed: Between Security and Rights in a Bolivian City. Durham, NC: Duke University Press.

Goodwin, Charles. 2000. Action and Embodiment within Situated Human Interaction. Journal of Pragmatics 32:1489–1522.

Graham, Laura R., and H. Glenn Penny. 2014. Performing Indigeneity: Global Histories and Contemporary Experiences. Lincoln: University of Nebraska Press.

Gray-Molina, George, Ernesto Perez de Rada, and Ernesto Yáñez. 1999. La economía política de reformas institucionales en Bolivia. https://publications.iadb.org/handle/11319/2027. Inter-American Development Bank.

Greene, Shane. 2007. Entre lo indio, lo negro, y lo incaico: The Spatial Hierarchies of Difference in Multicultural Peru. Journal of Latin American and Caribbean Anthropology 12(2): 441–474.

Grossberg, Lawrence. 1986. On Postmodernism and Articulation: An Interview with Stuart Hall. Journal of Communication Inquiry 10(2): 45–60.

Guaygua Ch, Germán. 2003. La fiesta del Gran Poder: El escenario de construcción de identidades urbanas en la ciudad de La Paz, Bolivia. Temas sociales 171.

Gusfield, Joseph R. 1967. Tradition and Modernity: Misplaced Polarities in the Study of Social Change. American Journal of Sociology 72(4): 351–362.

Gustafson, Bret. 2006. Spectacles of Autonomy and Crisis: Or, What Bulls and Beauty Queens Have to Do with Regionalism in Eastern Bolivia. Journal of Latin American Anthropology 11(2): 351–379.

———. 2008. By Means Legal and Otherwise: The Bolivian Right Regroups. NACLA Report on the Americas 41(1): 20–25.

———. 2009a. Manipulating Cartographies: Plurinationalism, Autonomy, and Indigenous Resurgence in Bolivia. Anthropological Quarterly 82(4): 985–1016.

———. 2009b. New Languages of the State: Indigenous Resurgence and the Politics of Knowledge in Bolivia. Durham, NC: Duke University Press.

———. 2010. When States Act Like Movements: Dismantling Local Power and Seating Sovereignty in Post-neoliberal Bolivia. Latin American Perspectives 37(4): 48–66.

———. 2011. O, lo que los toros y la reinas de belleza tienen que ver con el regionalismo en el Oriente Boliviano. Número 7 Año 2011:102.

Hall, Kira, Donna Meryl Goldstein, and Matthew Bruce Ingram. 2016. The Hands of Donald Trump: Entertainment, Gesture, Spectacle. HAU: Journal of Ethnographic Theory 6(2): 71–100.

Hall, Stuart. 1986. Gramsci's Relevance for the Study of Race and Ethnicity. Journal of Communication Inquiry 10(2): 5–27.

Hall, Stuart. 1990. Cultural Identity and Diaspora. *In* Identity: Community, Culture, Difference. J. Rutherford, ed. Pp. 222–237. London: Lawrence & Wishart.

———. 1996. Race, Articulation, and Societies structured in Dominance. *In* Black British Cultural Studies: A Reader. H. A. Baker Jr., M. Diawara, and R. H. Lindeborg, eds. Pp. 16–60. Chicago: University of Chicago Press.

Harkness, Nicholas. 2012. Vowel Harmony Redux: Correct Sounds, English Loan Words, and the Sociocultural Life of a Phonological Structure in Korean. Journal of Sociolinguistics 16(3): 358–381.

———. 2013. Songs of Seoul: An Ethnography of Voice and Voicing in Christian South Korea. Berkeley: University of California Press.

Harris, Olivia. 1980. The Power of Signs: Gender, Culture, and the Wild in the Bolivian Andes. *In* Nature, Culture, and Gender. C. MacCormack and M. Strathern, eds. Pp. 70–94. Cambridge: Cambridge University Press.

———, ed. 2000. To Make the Earth Bear Fruit: Essays on Fertility, Work and Gender in Highland Bolivia. London: Institute of Latin American Studies.

Hasbún, Paula Peña. 2003. La permanente construcción de lo cruceño: Un estudio sobre la identidad en Santa Cruz de la Sierra. La Paz, Bolivia: Centro de Estudios para el Desarrollo Urbano y Regional, Universidad Autónoma Gabriel Rene Moreno.

Haspelmath, Martin. 2006. Against Markedness (and What to Replace It With). Journal of Linguistics 42(1): 25–70.

Haugen, Einar. 1966. Dialect, Language, Nation. American Anthropologist 68:922–935.

Hay, Jennifer, and Katie Drager. 2010. Stuffed Toys and Speech Perception. Linguistics 48(4): 865–892.

Hay, Jennifer, Paul Warren, and Katie Drager. 2006. Factors Influencing Speech Perception in the Context of a Merger-in-Progress. Journal of Phonetics 34(4): 458–484.

Haynes, Nell. 2013. Global Cholas: Reworking Tradition and Modernity in Bolivian Lucha Libre. Journal of Latin American and Caribbean Anthropology 18(3): 432–446.

———. 2015. UnBoliviable Bouts: Gender and Essentialisation of Bolivia's Cholitas Luchadoras. *In* Global Perspectives on Women in Combat Sports. C. R. Matthews and A. Channon, eds. Pp. 267–283. Berlin: Springer.

———. 2016. Social Media in Northern Chile. London: University College of London Press.

Herrero, Joaquín, and Federico Sánchez de Lozada. 1978. Gramática quechua: Estructura del quechua boliviano contemporaneo. Cochabamba, Bolivia: Editorial Universo.

Hertzler, Douglas. 2005. Campesinos and Originarios! Class and Ethnicity in Rural Movements in the Bolivian Lowlands. Journal of Latin American Anthropology 10(1): 45–71.

Hill, Jane. 2001. Mock Spanish, Covert Racism and the (Leaky) Boundary between Public and Private Spheres. *In* Languages and Publics: The Making of Authority. S. Gal and K. Woolard, eds. Pp. 83–102. Manchester, UK: St. Jerome.

Hill, Jane H., and Kenneth C. Hill. 1986. Speaking Mexicano: The Dynamics of Syncretic Language in Central Mexico. Tucson: University of Arizona Press.

Hintz, Diane M. 2007. Past Tense Forms and Their Functions in South Conchucos Quechua: Time, Evidentiality, Discourse Structure, and Affect. Ph.D. dissertation, University of California, Santa Barbara.

Hornberger, Nancy H. 1997. Indigenous Literacies in the Americas: Language Planning from the Bottom Up. Berlin: Walter de Gruyter.

———. 1998. Language Policy, Language Education, Language Rights: Indigenous, Immigrant, and International Perspectives. Language in Society 27(4): 439–458.

Hornberger, Nancy H., and Serafin Coronel-Molina. 2004. Quechua Language Shift, Maintenance, and Revitalization in the Andes. International Journal of the Sociology of Language 167:9–67.

Hornberger, Nancy H., and Holly Link. 2012. Translanguaging and Transnational Literacies in Multilingual Classrooms: A Biliteracy Lens. International Journal of Bilingual Education and Bilingualism 15(3): 261–278.

Hornberger, Nancy H., and Luis Enrique López. 1998. Policy, Possibility and Paradox: Indigenous Multilingualism and Education in Peru and Bolivia. *In* Beyond Bilingualism: Multilingualism and Multilingual Education. J. Cenoz and F. Genesee, eds. Pp. 206–242. Philadelphia: Multilingual Matters

Howard, Rosaleen. 2004. Quechua in Tantamayo (Peru): Towards a "Social Archaeology" of Language. International Journal of the Sociology of Language 167:95–118.

———. 2007. Por los linderos de la lengua: Ideologías lingüísticas en los Andes. Lima: Instituto de Estudios Peruanos.

———. 2010. Language, Signs, and the Performance of Power: The Discursive Struggle over Decolonization in the Bolivia of Evo Morales. Latin American Perspectives 37(3): 176–194.

Howard-Malverde, Rosaleen. 1995. Pachamama Is a Spanish Word: Linguistic Tension between Aymara, Quechua, and Spanish in Northern Potosí (Bolivia). Anthropological Linguistics 37(2): 141–168.

———. 1998. Grasping Awareness: Mother-Tongue Literacy for Quechua Speaking Women in Northern Potosí, Bolivia. International Journal of Educational Development 18(3): 181–196.

Humphreys Bebbington, Denise, and Anthony Bebbington. 2010. Anatomy of a Regional Conflict: Tarija and Resource Grievances in Morales's Bolivia. Latin American Perspectives 37:140–160.

Hurtado, A. R. 2005. Cambas y collas: Los paradigmas de una nueva nación. Santa Cruz, Bolivia: Imprenta Gráfica Sirena.

Hymes, Dell. 1972. Models of the Interaction of Language and Social Setting. *In* Directions in Sociolinguistics: The Ethnography of Communication. J. Gumperz and D. Hymes, eds. Pp. 35–71. New York: Holt, Rinehart and Winston.

Inoue, Miyako. 2004. What Does Language Remember? Indexical Inversion and the Naturalized History of Japanese Women. Journal of Linguistic Anthropology 14(1): 39–56.

———. 2006. Vicarious Language: Gender and Linguistic Modernity in Japan. Berkeley: University of California Press.

Irvine, Judith T. 2001. "Style" as Distinctiveness: The Culture and Ideology of Linguistic Differentiation. *In* Style and Sociolinguistic Variation. P. Eckert and J. R. Rickford, eds. Pp. 21–43. Cambridge: Cambridge University Press.

Irvine, Judith T., and Susan Gal. 2000. Language Ideology and Linguistic Differentiation. *In* Regimes of Language. P. Kroskrity, ed. Pp. 35–83. Santa Fe, NM: School of American Research Press.

Jaffe, Alexandra. 1999. Ideologies in Action: Language Politics on Corsica. Berlin: Mouton de Gruyter.

Jaffe, Alexandra, and Cedric Oliva. 2013. Linguistic Creativity in Corsican Tourist Context. *In* Multilingualism and the Periphery. S. Pietikainen and H. Kelly-Holmes, eds. Pp. 95–117. Oxford: Oxford University Press.

Jakobson, Roman. 1957. Shifters, Verbal Categories, and the Russian Verb. *In* Selected Writings II: Word and Language. Pp. 130–147. The Hague: Mouton.

———. 1960. Linguistics and Poetics. *In* Style in Language. T. Sebeok, ed. Pp. 350–359. Cambridge, MA: MIT Press.

———. 1990. On Language. Cambridge, MA: Harvard University Press.

Jennings, Justin, and Brenda J. Bowser. 2009. Drink, Power, and Society in the Andes. Gainesville: University Press of Florida.

Johnson, Keith. 2006. Resonance in an Exemplar-Based Lexicon: The Emergence of Social Identity and Phonology. Journal of Phonetics 34(4): 485–499.

Johnstone, Barbara. 2005. Style and the Linguistic Individual: A Sociolinguistic Approach to Voice. *In* Stance: Sociolinguistic Perspectives. A. Jaffe, ed. Pp. 29–50. Oxford: Oxford University Press.

Johnstone, Barbara, Jennifer Andrus, and Andrew E. Danielson. 2006. Mobility, Indexicality, and the Enregisterment of "Pittsburghese." Journal of English Linguistics 32(4): 77–104.

Julien, Catherine J. 2008. Desde el Oriente: Documentos para la historia del oriente boliviano y Santa Cruz la vieja (1542–1597). Santa Cruz, Bolivia: Fondo Editorial Municipal.

Kalt, Susan E. 2012. Spanish as a Second Language When L1 Is Quechua: Endangered Languages and the SLA Researcher. Second Language Research 28(2): 265–279.

Kiesling, Scott Fabius. 1998. Men's Identities and Sociolinguistic Variation: The Case of Fraternity Men. Journal of Sociolinguistics 2(1): 69–99.

King, Kendall A., and Nancy H. Hornberger. 2004. Quechua Sociolinguistics. International Journal of the Sociology of Language 167, special issue. K. A. King and N. H. Hornberger, eds.

Kirshner, Joshua. 2010. Migrants' Voices: Negotiating Autonomy in Santa Cruz. Latin American Perspectives 37(4): 108–124.

Klee, Carol A. 1996. The Spanish of the Peruvian Andes: The Influence of Quechua on Spanish Language Structure. *In* Spanish in Contact. A. Roca and J. B. Benson, eds. Pp. 73–91. Somerville, MA: Cascadilla.

———. 2009. Migrations and Globalization: Their Effects on Contact Varieties of Latin American Spanish. *In* Español en los Estados Unidos y otros contextos de contacto. M. Lacorte and J. Leeman, eds. Pp. 39–66. Madrid: Vervuert Iberoamericana.

Klee, Carol A., and Rocío Caravedo. 2006. Andean Spanish and the Spanish of Lima: Linguistic Variation and Change in a Contact Situation. *In* Globalization and Language in the Spanish-Speaking World. C. Mar-Molinero, ed. Pp. 94–113. New York: Palgrave Macmillan.

Klein, Herb. 2003. A Concise History of Bolivia. Cambridge: Cambridge University Press.

Kohl, Benjamin, and Rosalind Bresnahan. 2010. Introduction Bolivia under Morales: National Agenda, Regional Challenges, and the Struggle for Hegemony. Los Angeles: Sage Publications.

Kuipers, Joel. 1998. Language, Identity, and Marginality in Indonesia. Cambridge: Cambridge University Press.

Kusters, Wouter. 2003. Quechua. *In* Linguistic Complexity: The Influence of Social Change on Verbal Inflection, 249–300. Utrecht: Netherlands Graduate School of Linguistics (LOT).

Kuznar, Lawrence A. 1999. The Inca Empire: Detailing the Complexities of Core/Periphery Interactions. *In* World-Systems Theory in Practice: Leadership, Production, and Exchange. P. N. Kardulias, ed. Pp. 223–240. Lanham, MD: Rowman & Littlefield Publishers.

Laclau, Ernesto. 2006. Ideology and Post-Marxism. Journal of Political Ideologies 11(2): 103–114.

Lara, Jesus. 1991. Diccionario qheshwa–castellano, castellano–qheshwa. La Paz / Cochabamba, Bolivia: Los amigos del libro.

Larraín, Felipe, and Jeffrey D. Sachs. 1998. Bolivia 1985–1992: Reforms, Results, and Challenges. *In* Economic Reforms in Latin America. H. Costin and H. Vanolli, eds. Pp. 145–168. Orlando, FL: Dryden Press.

Larson, Brooke. 1988. Colonialism and Agrarian Transformation in Bolivia: Cochabamba, 1550–1900. Princeton, NJ: Princeton University Press.

Larson, Brooke, and Olivia Harris. 1995. Ethnicity, Markets, and Migration in the Andes: At the Crossroads of History and Anthropology. Durham, NC: Duke University Press.

Lathrap, Donald W. 1973. The Antiquity and Importance of Long-Distance Trade Relationships in the Moist Tropics of Pre-Columbian South America. World Archaeology 5(2): 170–186.

Lecount, Cynthia. 1999. Carnival in Bolivia: Devils Dancing for the Virgin. Western Folklore 58(3/4): 231–252.

Lefebvre, Claire. 2006. Creole Genesis and the Acquisition of Grammar: The Case of Haitian Creole. New York: Cambridge University Press.

Lévi-Strauss, Claude. 1962. The Savage Mind. Chicago: University of Chicago Press.

———. 1966. The Elementary Structures of Kinship. Boston: Beacon Press.

———. 1980. Introduction to Roman Jakobson, Six Lectures on Sound and Meaning. Cambridge, MA: MIT Press.

Lipski, John M. 2004. El Español de América. Madrid: Cátedra.

López, Luis Enrique. 2006. Diversidad y ecología del lenguaje en Bolivia. Cochabamba, Bolivia: PROEIB Andes.

Lopez Pila, Esther. 2014. "We Don't Lie and Cheat Like the Collas Do": Highland–Lowland Regionalist Tensions and Indigenous Identity Politics in Amazonian Bolivia. Critique of Anthropology 34(4): 429–449.

Lowrey, Kathleen. 2006. Bolivia multiétnico y pluricultural, Ten Years Later: White Separatism in the Bolivian Lowlands. Latin American and Caribbean Ethnic Studies 1(1): 63–84.

Luykx, Aurolyn. 1996. From Indios to Profesionales: Stereotypes and Student Resistance in Bolivian Teacher Training. The Cultural Production of the Educated Person: Critical Ethnographies of Schooling and Local Practice. B. A. Levinson, D. E. Foley, and D. C. Holland, eds. Pp. 239–272. Albany: State University of New York Press.

———. 1999. The Citizen Factory: Schooling and Cultural Production in Bolivia. New York: SUNY Press.

———. 2003. Whose Language Is It Anyway? Historical Fetishism and the Construction of Expertise in Bolivian Language Planning. Current Issues in Comparative Education 5(2): 92–102.

———. 2004. The Future of Quechua and the Quechua of the Future: Language Ideologies and Language Planning in Bolivia. International Journal of the Sociology of Language 167:147–158.

Mahmood, Saba. 2005. Politics of Piety: The Islamic Revival and the Feminist Subject. Princeton, NJ: Princeton University Press.

Mamani, Pablo. 2003. El rugir de la multitud: Levantamiento de la ciudad aymara de El Alto y caída del gobierno de Sánchez de Lozada. Temas Sociales 4(12): 118–130.

Manley, Marilyn S. 2007. Cross-Linguistic Influence of the Cuzco Epistemic System on Andean Spanish. *In* Spanish in Contact: Policy, Social, and Linguistic Inquiries. K. Potowski and R. Cameron, eds. Pp. 192–209. Amsterdam/Philadelphia: John Benjamin.

Mannheim, Bruce. 1984. Una nación acorralada: Southern Peruvian Quechua Language Planning and Politics in Historical Perspective. Language in Society 13(3): 291–309.

———. 1991. The Language of the Inka since the European Invasion. Austin: University of Texas Press.

Manning, Paul. 2010. The Semiotics of Brand. Annual Review of Anthropology 39:33–49.

Manning, Paul, and Ann Uplisashvili. 2007. "Our Beer": Ethnographic Brands in Postsocialist Georgia. American Anthropologist 109(4): 626–641.

Martínez, Angelita, ed. 2009. El entremado de los lenguajes. Buenos Aires: La Crujía Ediciones.

McConnell-Ginet, Sally. 1979. Prototypes, Pronouns and Persons. *In* Ethnolinguistics: Boas, Sapir, and Whorf Revisited. 63–83.

McGowan, Kevin B. 2011. The Role of Socioindexical Expectation in Speech Perception. Thesis, University of Michigan.

———. 2015. Social Expectation Improves Speech Perception in Noise. Language and Speech 58(4): 502–521.

———. 2016. Sounding Chinese and Listening Chinese: Imitation, Perception, and Awareness of Non-native Phonology. *In* Awareness and Control in Sociolinguistic Research. A. M. Babel, ed. Pp. 25–61. Cambridge: Cambridge University Press.

Meek, Barbra A. 2012. We Are Our Language: An Ethnography of Language Revitalization in a Northern Athabaskan Community. Tucson: University of Arizona Press.

Mendoza, Gunnar. 1992. Hacia la identificación historiográfica de la Chola Boliviana. *In* La chola boliviana: Obra de investigación folklórica. Antonio Paredes Candia, ed. Pp. 7–27. La Paz: Isla.

Mendoza, José G. 2008. Bolivia. *In* El español en América: Contactos lingüísticos en Hispanoamérica. Pp. 213–236. Barcelona: Editorial Ariel.

Mendoza, Zoila S. 2000. Shaping Society through Dance: Mestizo Ritual Performance in the Peruvian Andes. Chicago: University of Chicago Press.

Mendoza-Denton, Norma. 2008. Homegirls: Symbolic Practices in the Making of Latina Youth Styles. Malden, MA: Blackwell.

Mick, Carola. 2011. Discourses of "Border-Crossers": Peruvian Domestic Workers in Lima as Social Actors. Discourse Studies 13:189–209.

Molina, Fernando. 2008. Bolivia: La geografía de un conflicto. Nueva Sociedad 218:4–14.

Molina, Talia. 2012. La interacción castellano-quechua: Hacia una comprensión lingüística, ideológica y cultural del fenómeno de "imposición" del castellano del Perú. Ph.D. dissertation, Concordia University, Montreal, Canada.

Mondada, Lorenza. 2016. Challenges of Multimodality: Language and the Body in Social Interaction. Journal of Sociolinguistics 20(3): 336–366.

Moore, Robert E. 2003. From Genericide to Viral Marketing: On "Brand." Language, and Communication 23(3): 331–357.

Muntendam, Antje. 2011. Focus, Intonation, and Language Contact: A Case Study of Andean Spanish. Paper presented at the conference "Frecuencia, cambio, y contacto lingüístico: El caso del español de los Andes." Freiburg, Germany.

Mura, Julie Michele. 2016. Geographical Conflict in Bolivia: Mobilization of Identity by the Comité Pro Santa Cruz. Ph.D. dissertation, Florida State University, Tallahassee.

Murra, John V. 1985. The Limits and Limitations of the "Vertical Archipelago" in the Andes. *In* Andean Ecology and Civilization: An Interdisciplinary Perspective on Andean Ecological Complementarity. S. Masuda, I. Shimida, and C. Morris, eds. Pp. 15–20. Tokyo: University of Tokyo Press.

Muysken, Pieter. 2002. La categoria del plural en el quechua boliviano. *In* La Romania americana: Procesos lingüísticos en situaciones de contacto. N. Diaz, R. Ludwig, and S. Pfander, eds. Pp. 209–217. Vervuert: Prensa Iberoamericana.

———. 2004. Two Languages in Two Countries: The Use of Spanish and Quechua in Songs and Poems from Peru and Ecuador. *In* Quechua Verbal Artistry: The Inscription of Andean Voices. G. Delgado and J. Schecter, eds. Pp. 35–60. Bonn: Institut für Altamerikanistik und Ethnologie.

Nino-Murcia, M. Mercedes. 1988. Construcciones verbales del español andino: Interacción quechua-española en la frontera colombo-ecuatoriana, Colombia. Ph.D. dissertation, University of Michigan.

———. 1992. El futuro sintético en el español norandino: Caso de mandato atenuado. Hispania 75(3): 705–713.

———. 1997. Linguistic Purism in Cuzco, Peru: A Historical Perspective. Language Problems and Language Planning 21(2): 134–161.

Nuckolls, Janis B. 1996. Sounds Like Life: Sound-Symbolic Grammar, Performance, and Cognition in Pastaza Quechua. New York: Oxford University Press.

Nuckolls, Janis B., Elizabeth Nielsen, Joseph A. Stanley, and Roseanna Hopper. 2016. The Systematic Stretching and Contracting of Ideophonic Phonology in Pastaza Quichua. International Journal of American Linguistics 82:95–116.

Núñez, Rafael E., and Eve Sweetser. 2006. With the Future behind Them: Convergent Evidence from Aymara Language and Gesture in the Crosslinguistic Comparison of Spatial Construals of Time. Cognitive Science 30(3): 401–450.

O'Connell, Kathleen Mary. 2013. No voy a ir a la universidad con pollera: La negociación de la identidad sociocultural desde la perspectiva de los estudiantes rurales andinos y amazónicos de una universidad pública. Thesis, Pontificia Universidad Católica del Perú.

Olbertz, Hella. 2005. Dizque en el español andino ecuatoriano: Conservador e innovador. *In* Encuentros y conflictos: Bilingüismo y contacto de lenguas en el mundo andino. H. Olbertz and P. Muysken, eds. Pp. 77–94. Madrid: Iboamericana/Vervuert.

Ortega, Lourdes. 2009. Understanding Second Language Acquisition. London: Hodder Arnold.

Ortner, Sherry. 1984. Theory in Anthropology since the Sixties. Comparative Studies in Society and History 26(1): 126–166.

———. 1995. Resistance and the Problem of Ethnographic Refusal. Comparative Studies in Society and History 37:173–193.

———. 1996. Making Gender: Towards a Feminist, Minority, Postcolonial, Subaltern, etc. Theory of Practice. *In* Making Gender: The Politics and Erotics of Culture. Pp. 1–20. Boston: Beacon.

———. 2006. Anthropology and Social Theory: Culture, Power, and the Acting Subject. Durham, NC: Duke University Press.

Paredes, Liliana. 1992. Assibilation of (r) in the Andean-Spanish Variety in Lima. Paper presented at the conference "New Ways of Analyzing Variation 21." NWAV, Michigan.

Paredes Candia, Antonio. 1992. La chola boliviana. La Paz: Ediciones ISLA.

Paugh, Amy L. 2005. Multilingual Play: Children's Code-Switching, Role Play, and Agency in Dominica, West Indies. Language in Society 34(1): 63–86.

Pedraza, Silvia. 1991. Women and Migration: The Social Consequences of Gender. Annual Review of Sociology 17(1): 303–325.

Peirce, Charles Sanders. 1955. Logic as Semiotic. *In* Philosophical Writings of Pierce. J. Buchler, ed. Pp. 98–115. New York: Dover.

Perreault, Tom, and Gabriela Valdivia. 2010. Hydrocarbons, Popular Protest and National Imaginaries: Ecuador and Bolivia in Comparative Context. Geoforum 41:689–699.

Pfänder, Stefan. 2002. Contacto y cambio lingüístico en Cochabamba (Bolivia). *In* La Romanía americana: Procesos lingüísticos en situaciones de contacto. N. Díaz, R. Ludwig, and S. Pfänder, eds. Pp. 219–254. Madrid: Iberoamericana/Vervuert.

Pfänder, Stefan, Juan Ennis, Mario Soto, and España Villegas. 2009. Gramática mestiza: Presencia del quechua en el castellano. La Paz: Academia Boliviana de la Lengua & Editorial Signo.

Pierrehumbert, Janet B. 2001. Stochastic Phonology. GLOT 5:157–169.

Pineo, Ronn. 2016. Progress in Bolivia: Declining the United States Influence and the Victories of Evo Morales. Journal of Developing Societies 32(4): 421–453.

Poplack, Shana. 1980. The Notion of the Plural in Puerto Rican Spanish: Competing Constraints on (S) Deletion. Locating Language in Time and Space 1:55–67.

Postero, Nancy Grey. 2007. Now We Are Citizens: Indigenous Politics in Postmulticultural Bolivia. Stanford, CA: Stanford University Press.

———. 2010. Morales's MAS Government: Building Indigenous Popular Hegemony in Bolivia. Latin American Perspectives 37:18–34.

Pratt, Mary Louise. 1991. Arts of the Contact Zone. Profession 33–40.

Price, Marie, and Audrey Singer. 2008. Edge Gateways: Suburbs, Immigrants and the Politics of Reception in Metropolitan Washington. *In* Twenty-First Century Immigrant Gateways. A. Singer, C. Bretell, and S. Hardwick, eds. Pp. 137–168. Washington, DC: Brookings Institute.

Queen, Robin. 2012. Turkish-German Bilinguals and Their Intonation: Triangulating Evidence about Contact-Induced Language Change. Language 88(4): 791–816.

Radcliffe, Sarah A., Nina Laurie, and Robert Andolina. 2004. The Transnationalization of Gender and Reimagining Andean Indigenous Development. Signs: Journal of Women in Culture and Society 29(2): 387–416.

Ramos, Alcida Rita. 1994. The Hyperreal Indian. Critique of Anthropology 14(2): 153–171.

Real Academia Española. 2009. Diccionario de la Real Academia Española. 22nd ed.

Regalsky, Pablo, and Franciso Quisbert. 2008. Bolivia indígena: De gobiernos comunitarios en busca de autonomía a la lucha por la hegemonía. *In* Gobernar [en] la diversidad: Experiencias indígenas desde América Latina. Hacia la investigación de co-labor. X. Leyva, A. Burguete, and S. Speed, eds. Pp. 151–188. Mexico City: Casa Chata Centro de Investigaciones y Estudios Superiores en Antropología Social.

Remlinger, Kathryn. 2009. Everyone Up Here: Enregisterment and Identity in Michigan's Keweenaw Peninsula. American Speech 84(2): 118–137.

Renard Casevitz, France-Marie, T. H. Saignes, and Anne-Christine Taylor. 1988. Al este de los Andes. Lima, Peru: Abya Yala.

Rivera, Claudia. 2015. Arqueología e historia de los valles cruceños: Sociedades locales, interacción y encuentros culturales. *In* Arte rupestre de los valles cruceños. M. Strecker and C. Cárdenas, eds. La Paz: Sociedad de Investigación de Arte Rupestre de Bolivia; Instituto de Capacitación del Oriente.

Rockefeller, Stuart Alexander. 1998. "There Is a Culture Here": Spectacle and the Inculcation of Folklore in Highland Bolivia. Journal of Latin American Anthropology 3(2): 118–149.

———. 2010. Starting from Quirpini: The Travels and Places of a Bolivian People. Bloomington: Indiana University Press.

Rodriguez, Juan Luis. 2016. The National Anthem in Warao: Semiotic Ground and Performative Affordances of Indigenous Language Texts in Venezuela. Journal of Linguistic Anthropology 26(3): 335–351.

Rojas, Cuba, and L. Pablo. 2006. Bolivia: Movimientos sociales, nacionalización y Asamblea Constituyente. Observatorio Social de América Latina:55–64.

Rojas, Leocadio. 1998. Saipina: Aproximación histórica. Santa Cruz, Bolivia. Santa Cruz, Bolivia: Casa la Estrella.

Sahlins, Marshall. 1976. Culture and Practical Reason. Chicago: University of Chicago Press.

———. 1985. Islands of History. Chicago: University of Chicago Press.

Salcedo, Daniela. 2013. Defining Andeanness Away from the Andes: Language Attitudes and Linguistic Ideologies in Lima, Peru. Ph.D. dissertation, Ohio State University.

Sammells, Clare A. 2012. Ancient Calendars and Bolivian Modernity: Tiwanaku's Gateway of the Sun, Arthur Posnansky, and the World Calendar Movement of the 1930s. Journal of Latin American and Caribbean Anthropology 17:299–319.

Sánchez, Liliana. 1996. Word Order, Predication, and Agreement in DPs in Spanish, Southern Quechua and Southern Andean Bilingual Spanish. *In* Grammatical Theory and Romance Languages. K. Zagona, ed. Pp. 209–218. Amsterdam: John Benjamins.

———. 2004. Functional Convergence in the Tense, Evidentiality and Aspectual Systems of Quechua Spanish Bilinguals. Bilingualism: Language and Cognition 7(2): 147–162.

Sánchez de Lozada, Gonzalo. 1994. Ley de Reforma Educativa: Ley 1565 de 7 de julio de 1994. La Paz, Bolivia: La Razón 10.

Sanjinés, Javier. 2004. Mestizaje Upside-Down: Aesthetic Politics in Modern Bolivia. Pittsburgh, PA: University of Pittsburgh Press.

Santos-Granero, Fernando. 2002. Boundaries Are Made to Be Crossed: The Magic and Politics of the Long-Lasting Amazon/Andes Divide. Identities: Global Studies in Culture and Power 9(4): 545–569.

Sassone, Susana María. 2007. Migración, territorio e identidad cultural: Construcción de "lugares bolivianos" en la Ciudad de Buenos Aires. Población de Buenos Aires 4(6): 9–28.

Schevill, Margot Blum, Janet Catherine Berlo, and Edward B. Dwyer. 1996. Textile Traditions of Mesoamerica and the Andes: An Anthology. Austin: University of Texas Press.

Seligmann, Linda J. 1989. To Be in Between: The Cholas as Market Women. Comparative Studies in Society and History 31(4): 694–721.

———. 1993. Between Worlds of Exchange: Ethnicity among Peruvian Market Women. Cultural Anthropology 8(2): 187–213.

Silverblatt, Irene Marsha. 1987. Moon, Sun, and Witches: Gender Ideologies and Class in Inca and Colonial Peru. Princeton, NJ: Princeton University Press.

Silverstein, Michael. 1979. Language Structure and Linguistic Ideology. *In* The Elements: A Parasession on Linguistic Units and Levels. P. R. Clyne, W. F. Hanks, and C. L. Hofbauer, eds. Pp. 193–195. Chicago: Chicago Linguistic Society.

———. 1998. Contemporary Transformations of Local Linguistic Communities. Annual Review of Anthropology 27:401–426.

———. 2003. Indexical Order and the Dialectics of Sociolinguistic Life. Language, and Communication 23:193–229.

Silvey, Rachel. 2005. Borders, Embodiment, and Mobility: Feminist Migration Studies in Geography. *In* A Companion to Feminist Geography, L. Nelson and J. Seager, eds. Pp. 138–149. Oxford: Wiley-Blackwell.

Slack, Jennifer Daryl. 1996. The Theory and Method of Articulation in Cultural Studies. *In* Stuart Hall: Critical Dialogues in Cultural Studies. D. Morley and K. H. Chen, eds. Pp. 112–127. London: Routledge.

Solomon, Thomas. 1994. Coplas de Todos Santos en Cochabamba: Language, Music, and Performance in Bolivian Quechua Song Dueling. Journal of American Folklore 107(425): 378–414.

Spivak, Gayatri Chakravorty. 1988. Can the Subaltern Speak? *In* Marxism and the Interpretation of Culture. C. Nelson and L. Grossberg, eds. Pp. 271–313. Urbana: University of Illinois Press.

Stearman, A. M. L. 1987. Camba y colla: Migración y desarrollo en Santa Cruz, Bolivia. La Paz: Librería Editorial "Juventud."

Stephenson, Marcia. 1997. Faldas y polleras: Las ideologías de la feminidad y la conquista de nuevos espacios públicos en Bolivia (1920–1950). Chasqui: Revista de literatura latinoaméricana. 26(1): 17–33.

———. 1999. Gender and Modernity in Andean Bolivia. Austin: University of Texas Press.

Stepputat, Finn. 2004. Marching for Progress: Rituals of Citizenship, State and Belonging in a High Andes District. Bulletin of Latin American Research 23(2): 244–259.

Sumner, Meghan, and Reiko Kataoka. 2013. Effects of Phonetically-Cued Talker Variation on Semantic Encoding. Journal of the Acoustical Society of America 134(6): EL485–EL91.

Sumner, Meghan, Seung Kyung Kim, Ed King, and Kevin B. McGowan. 2014. The Socially Weighted Encoding of Spoken Words: A Dual-Route Approach to Speech Perception. Frontiers in Psychology 4.

Tapia, Luis. 2009. La coyuntura de la autonomía relativa del Estado. Quito, Ecuador: CLACSO.

Thomason, Sarah G. 2001. Language Contact: An Introduction. Washington, DC: Georgetown University Press.

Thomason, Sarah G., and Terrence Kaufman. 1988. Language Contact, Creolization, and Genetic Linguistics. Berkeley: University of California Press.

Tockman, Jason, and John Cameron. 2014. Indigenous Autonomy and the Contradictions of Plurinationalism in Bolivia. Latin American Politics and Society 56(3): 46–69.

Torero, Alfredo. 1964. Los dialectos quechuas. Anales Científicos de la Universidad Agraria 2(4): 446–478.

Urciuoli, Bonnie. 1995. Language and Borders. Annual Review of Anthropology 24:525–546.

Valdivia, Gabriela. 2010. Agrarian Capitalism and Struggles over Hegemony in the Bolivian Lowlands. Latin American Perspectives 37(4): 67–87.

Valenzuela, Pilar M. 2015. ¿Qué tan "amazónicas" son las lenguas kawapana? Contacto con las lenguas centro-andinas y elementos para un área lingüística intermedia. Lexis 39(1): 5–56.

Vanden, Harry E. 2007. Social Movements, Hegemony, and New Forms of Resistance. Latin American Perspectives 34:17–30.

Van Gijn, Rik. 2014. The Andean Foothills and Adjacent Amazonian Fringe. *In* The Native Languages of South America: Origins, Development, Typology. L. O'Connor and P. Muysken, eds. Pp. 102–125. Cambridge: Cambridge University Press.

Van Vleet, Krista E. 2003. Adolescent Ambiguities and the Negotiation of Belonging in the Andes. Ethnology 42(4): 349–363.

———. 2009. Performing Kinship: Narrative, Gender, and the Intimacies of Power in the Andes. Austin: University of Texas Press.

———. 2010. Narrating Violence and Negotiating Belonging: The Politics of (Self-) Representation in an Andean Tinkuy Story. Journal of Latin American and Caribbean Anthropology 15(1): 195–221.

Voloshinov, Valentin. 1986. Marxism and the Philosophy of Language. Cambridge, MA: Harvard University Press.

Webber, Jeffery R. 2010. Carlos Mesa, Evo Morales, and a Divided Bolivia. Latin American Perspectives 37(3): 51–70.

———. 2016. Evo Morales and the Political Economy of Passive Revolution in Bolivia, 2006–15. Third World Quarterly 37(10): 1855–1876.

Weber, Katinka. 2013. "We Are All Chiquitano": Struggles over Territory and Sovereignty in Lowland Bolivia. Journal of Latin American and Caribbean Anthropology 18(2): 314–336.

Webster, Anthony K. 2009. Explorations in Navajo Poetry and Poetics. Albuquerque: University of New Mexico Press.

Weinreich, Uriel, William A. Labov, and Marvin Herzog. 1968. Empirical Foundations for a Theory of Language Change. *In* Empirical Foundations for a Theory of Language Change. W. P. Lehmann and Y. Malkiel, eds. Pp. 97–188. Austin: University of Texas Press.

Weismantel, Mary. 2001. Cholas and Pishtacos: Stories of Race and Sex in the Andes. Chicago: University of Chicago Press.

Williams, Raymond. 1977. Marxism and Literature. Oxford: Oxford University Press.

Winford, Donald. 2005. Contact-Induced Change: Classification and Processes. Diachronica 22:373–427.

Woolard, Kathryn. 1998. Language Ideology as a Field of Inquiry. *In* Language Ideologies: Practice and Theory. B. Schieffelin, K. Woolard, and P. Kroskrity, eds. Pp. 3–47. New York: Oxford University Press.

Yarnall, Kaitlin, and Marie Price. 2010. Migration, Development and a New Rurality in the Valle Alto, Bolivia. Journal of Latin American Geography 9(1): 107–124.

Zavala, Virginia. 2011. Racialization of the Bilingual Student in Higher Education: A Case from the Peruvian Andes. Linguistics and Education 22(4): 393–405.

Zimman, Lal. 2016. Sociolinguistic Agency and the Gendered Voice: Metalinguistic Negotiations of Vocal Masculinization among Female-to-Male Transgender Speakers. *In* Awareness and Control in Sociolinguistic Research. A. M. Babel, ed. Pp. 253–277. Cambridge: Cambridge University Press.

Zimman, Lal, Jenny Davis, and Joshua Raclaw. 2014. Queer Excursions: Retheorizing Binaries in Language, Gender, and Sexuality. New York: Oxford University Press.

Zorn, Elayne Lesley. 1997. Marketing Diversity: Global Transformations in Cloth and Identity in Highland Peru and Bolivia. Ann Arbor, MI: UMI Research Press.

———. 2004. Weaving a Future: Tourism, Cloth, and Culture on an Andean Island. Iowa City: University of Iowa Press.

INDEX

ABOUT THE AUTHOR

Anna M. Babel is an associate professor of Hispanic Linguistics in the Department of Spanish and Portuguese at Ohio State University. She received her doctorate in linguistics and anthropology in 2010 from the University of Michigan, under the direction of Sarah G. Thomason and Bruce Mannheim. Babel is a sociolinguist and a linguistic anthropologist whose research investigates contact linguistics and Andean Spanish. Her research draws on quantitative and qualitative data from a Quechua-Spanish contact region in central Bolivia gathered from over a decade of fieldwork in Bolivia. She is editor of *Awareness and Control in Sociolinguistic Research* (Cambridge University Press, 2016) and the author of ten journal articles in publications such as *Language and Communication* and *Journal of Sociolinguistics*.